Embodied Computing

Embodied Computing

Wearables, Implantables, Embeddables, Ingestibles

edited by Isabel Pedersen and Andrew Iliadis

The MIT Press
Cambridge, Massachusetts
London, England

This book was set in ITC Stone Serif Std and ITC Stone Sans Std by Toppan Best-set Premedia Limited. Printed and bound in the United States of America.

Library of Congress Cataloging-in-Publication Data

Names: Pedersen, Isabel, editor.

Title: Embodied computing : wearables, implantables, embeddables, ingestibles / Isabel Pedersen and Andrew Iliadis, editors.
Description: Cambridge, Massachusetts : The MIT Press, [2020] | Includes bibliographical references and index.
Identifiers: LCCN 2019025807 | ISBN 9780262538558 (paperback)
Subjects: LCSH: Wearable technology. | Wearable computers. | Artificial intelligence. | Implants, Artificial.
Classification: LCC QA76.592 .E43 2020 | DDC 006.3--dc23
LC record available at https://lccn.loc.gov/2019025807

10   9   8   7   6   5   4   3   2   1

Contents

Acknowledgments

We'd like to thank each of the chapter authors for *Embodied Computing*. They have made a significant contribution and showed unending patience as we finished the book. For that, we are grateful. We'd also like to thank the MIT Press and our editors, Doug Sery and Noah Springer, as well as Elizabeth Agresta, Susan Clark, Bridget Leahy, and the anonymous reviewers who provided rich insights into the collection and the work surrounding it. The book started as a symposium organized by the Decimal Lab at Ontario Tech University. We'd like to thank each of the presenters at that symposium, including Donald Braxton, Gary Genosko, Brian Greenspan, Stuart Murray, Marcel O'Gorman, and Tom Sherman. Nene Brode, Judy Ehrentraut, Kirsten Ellison, Steven Richardson, and Laura Tsang presented in the graduate student conference portion of the event. We thank Olexander Wlasenko and Whitby Station Gallery, who partnered with Decimal Lab to host an exhibit of artwork by Maggie Chan, Izzie Colpitts-Campbell, Kate Hartman, Erin Lewis, Izabella Pruska-Oldenhof, Jessica Thompson, Robert Tu, and Amelia Zhang. We'd also like to thank our schools and departments, Communication and Digital Media Studies in the Faculty of Social Science and Humanities at Ontario Tech University and the Department of Media Studies and Production in the Lew Klein College of Media and Communication at Temple University. Portions from our introduction draw from our article "The Fabric of Digital Life: Uncovering Sociotechnical Tradeoffs in Embodied Computing through Metadata" (June 3, 2018), *Journal of Information, Communication and Ethics in Society* 16, no. 3. On a personal note, we'd like to thank some of our collaborators and mentors for their many conversations, including Dawn Armfield, Sharon Caldwell, Jayden Cooper, Marcel Danesi, Ann Hill Duin, Quinn DuPont, R. Bruce Elder, Jan Fernback, Ihor Junyk, Tracey P. Lauriault, Tony Liao, Matthew Lombard, Sorin Adam Matei, Ashley Rose Mehlenbacher, Tanner Mirrlees, Andrea Slane, Peter Stoett, Peter Turk, and Daniel W. Smith. This research was undertaken, in part, thanks to funding from the Canada Research Chairs program and the Social Sciences and Humanities Research Council of Canada.

Introduction: Embodied Computing

Isabel Pedersen and Andrew Iliadis

In 1961, MIT mathematicians Claude Shannon and Edward Thorp engineered an unusual device that could be placed within a shoe to cheat at roulette. Thorp described the process in a 1998 paper, boldly titled "The Invention of the First Wearable Computer." The goal was to track the roulette ball over periods of time, from the croupier's launch through the stuttering of the moving rotor to the eventual resting pocket location. Thorp and Shannon considered a variety of designs before eventually settling on a computer that had "twelve transistors and was the size of a pack of cigarettes." The wearable worked by inputting data with the operator's big toe via microswitches—but the project was not an enduring success (much to the chagrin of would-be cheaters). Authorities eventually discovered the invention and on May 30, 1985, a law was passed in Nevada that prohibited the use of wearables in casinos. While the "roulette shoe" might be the first recorded instance of a wearable (computational) technology, it is also one of the first cases where a wearable precipitated change in law and policy.

Fast forward to now, and the production of consumer wearable technologies proliferates at an astounding rate. Fitness monitoring devices (Fitbit, for example) are regularly used by many health-conscious people and in some cases even by their pets (the company PetPace has released a collar for monitoring pet health), while the Augmented World Expo and communities like it have expanded interest in body-centered computing around the globe. Currently, there are thousands of wearables available on the market or in development. The Annual CES show in Las Vegas (formerly the Computer Electronics Show) boasts 170,000 attendees and helps circulate wearable tech news about prerelease innovations on social media.

Vandrico Inc.'s Wearable Technology Database contained over 430 devices from 250 companies. Companies such as Google, Snapchat, Huawei, North, and Vuzix have developed smart glasses, and athletes are increasingly training with the aid of smart clothing that records biometrics to help improve performance, an example of what Nafus (2016) describes as biosensing technologies.

Artificial intelligence (AI), now a global industry, has changed computing paradigms in every sector, including those developing the technologies that are worn on and in people's bodies. The drive in these sectors is to make embodied computers intelligent, autonomous, and capable of making decisions, but the sectors also spur popular social movements about the future. Personal computing devices are accruing a much greater range of public expectations than before. Consequently, more immersive embodied technologies are announced, circulated in popular forums, and have started phases of commodification. DARPA has developed brain interface technologies for brain–computer interaction, Google is proposing bionic contact lenses, and epidermal tattoos (skin technologies) are already a consumer product. It is becoming quite clear that the word "wearables" is something of a misnomer because it is used to describe so much more than the act of wearing technology. At the same time, "wearables" usually refers to things like fitness-monitoring devices or wearable cameras. Most people don't tend to think of involuntary tracking technologies as wearables—prisoners' ankle monitoring bracelets or employees wearing tracking devices. Embeddable technologies are not wearable technologies, exactly. "Wearables" doesn't accurately describe things like implants and bionic technology, but that is often the intention. Wearables and embodied computing technologies have also often been tied to utopian dreams of technology-enabled solutions for everything from sickness to security threats, but rarely are such technologies situated within social and cultural frameworks in industry.

This book is a first attempt at thinking through the shifting narratives of what we call *embodied computing* devices—including wearables but also encompassing things such as embeddables, ingestibles, implantables, and other forms of body-centered computing. The chapters in the book address these technologies while focusing on what Suchman (2007) describes as "the irreducibility of lived practice, embodied and enacted" (xii). We argue that embodied computing should be understood as encompassing several domains of human experience, and the diversity of chapters in this book provides evidence of this. With the mass proliferation of AI in embodied computing fields and other advancements in data-driven embodied technologies, we thought that there was a need for more work that explains interactions with devices that envelop the body in, on, and through reontologized environments and datafication. The chapters in this book show that embodied computing devices enact multiple ontologies, and, following Mol (2001), "that ontology is not given in the order of things, but that, instead, ontologies are brought into being, sustained, or allowed to wither away in common, day-to-day, sociomaterial practices" (6). The notion of embodied computing here should include technologies that exist in topographical, visceral, and ambient relationships with the body, to reenvision and revitalize the notion of embodiment for an era of sometimes questionable experimentation and profit.

Starting as a symposium titled *Wear Me: Art, Technology, Body* held at Ontario Tech University in 2015 and organized by Decimal Lab (figure 0.1), our project evolved into this edited collection that includes contributions from practitioners in the field of embodied computing as well as texts from

Figure 0.1
Participants at the *Wear Me: Art, Technology, Body* symposium.

academics doing research on the social, cultural, and historical changes that embodied computing has introduced. This book is also an attempt at thinking through the varied histories of embodied computing, from early experiments with wearables to work conducted at the MIT Media Lab. For example, Steve Mann's definition of a wearable computer, first proposed in 1998, served not only as a technical explanation for the field but also began the dialogue around concepts such as privacy, surveillance, and humanistic and countercultural uses for wearables. As researchers who investigate ethical, cultural, social, and political implications of body-centered computing, we have been interested in reversing the perspective from industry leaders and looking closely at the origins of embodied forms of computation, their various creators, and the underlying motivations that inform their development. Utopian proclamations from Silicon Valley in favor of emerging embodied computing technologies often describe solutions looking for problems, yet there are multiple narratives that are available for understanding technological change. Google develops smart glasses, while at universities researchers attempt to build computerized prosthetics that assist with problems like phantom limb pain. Some narratives originate in Silicon Valley, others at universities, others still with industry promoters scrambling to appear novel or innovative. Technology companies think of progress in terms of their products generating new revenue streams. Most of the time, tech companies build technologies and look for multiple social applications in the quest to collect new data—and ultimately new customers. Platform economics has completely changed the manner through which companies do business and plan for their futures. Universities, on the other hand, will occasionally start from a social problem and then think about a solution. It is with these different types of narratives of technological "progress" in mind that we started to assemble this book.

Just as people make demands on embodied computing technologies those same technologies make demands on people's bodies and the social norms around them. The embodied computing industry and the technologies it produces influence law and policy and, depending on one's level of abstraction, frame narratives about technological progress. Such narratives often change, and multiple narratives can be co-present as embodied computing is developed in a variety of contexts, from the military to the university. Furthermore, ethical issues relating to identity and justice are often not the primary focus in industry discussions about embodied computing, even though such technologies have social and ethical implications that necessarily extend beyond the scope of research and design in the laboratory. New advances in AI will confront bodies through computing devices and infrastructures that are worn, implanted, ingested, and moved among. Embodied computing devices attempt to redefine people as subjects and as data sources in multiple spheres now but also in a future that, if the soothsayers are to be believed, is evolving at rapid speed.

As editors, we collected chapters that explore and examine a range of devices and concepts that concern embodied computing, written by an interdisciplinary group of authors. The range of devices includes popular electronics such as FitBit activity monitors and extends to implanted neural devices that assist with memorization. Many of these devices are often written up as "wearables" designed to be appended to the human body; our book interrogates the boundaries of this category to better account for how these emerging technologies are problematizing processes of embodiment. This introduction and the first two chapters attempt to develop a conceptual frame for the wide array of computational devices that concern human-linked embodiment. Through the concept of embodied computing, the book incorporates many distinct but related technologies—for example, wearables, ingestibles, implantables, embeddables—and resituates understanding of their sociotechnical development.

Histories of Embodied Computing

Embodied computing has a long history of emergence. In the 1990s, it was housed in universities, military hubs, and manufacturing research centers. Meeting at specialized technology conferences to share innovations, these groups produced the first head-mounted eye displays, GPS navigation systems, touchscreens, and biofeedback sensors. Now, many of these technologies fit in today's phones, but in an early internet, presmartphone, pre–Go Pro world, hardware was large, clunky, wired, and extremely awkward. Devices had to be customized in-house or were produced by military supply companies like Xybernaut. There were few standards or platforms to host consumer wearables' movements (specs for the Lizzy—an early wearable computer—were shared freely on the internet). Researchers working on MIThril, another early wearable platform, were not necessarily working toward mass proliferation. The projects were not purely idealistic, but they were sometimes free from any requirement or sustained pressure to commercialize. This later evolved into wearables being associated with maker culture, leading to experimental designs for wearables by nonexperts (Hartman 2014). Projects such as LilyPad foregrounded component technologies such as Arduino that could be easily integrated into e-textiles (Buechley and Eisenberg 2008).

Several well-known and widely published inventors worked in the '90s from established labs where embodied computing technologies were developing. People like Mark Billinghurst of the Human Interface Technology Lab in Christchurch, Adrian David Cheok of the Mixed Reality Lab at the National University of Singapore, Blair MacIntyre of the Augmented Environments Lab at Georgia Tech, Alex Pentland of the MIT Human Dynamics Laboratory, Patti Maes of the MIT Fluid Interfaces Group, Gerhard Tröster of the Wearable Computing Lab at ETH Zurich, Babak Parviz at the University of Michigan, Gudrun Klinker of the Technical University of Munich, Jay Bolter of the School of Literature, Communication and Culture at Georgia Tech, Steve Mann of the EyeTap Lab at the University of Toronto, Hiroshi Ishii's Tangible Media Group, Ben Shneiderman's Human–Computer Interaction Lab, Joseph A. Paradiso of the Things That Think Consortium, and Thad Starner of the Contextual Computing Group at Georgia Tech (Starner was also senior technologist for the Google Glass project) all became key players in developing the embodied computing field and its devices.

Key design concepts also defined the era. The first was about making computers more physically mobile. According to Mann (1998), to be a truly "wearable" computer, users were meant to wear it all the time—a personal device was meant to be private, but mobile. This was a radical shift from desktop computing. Wireless computing only started to emerge at this time, and there were other, more practical concerns to be addressed. If users wore the computer all the time then an energy source was required, but battery packs were large, cumbersome, and had to be strapped to the user's body. Eventually, body energy harvesting for wearable devices was proposed (Starner 1996) but mobility remained the key goal. Another design ideal was for computers that did not require users to look down as they typed. Twiddlers, or single-handed keyers, were developed to be used with eye displays (Mann 2002; Starner 2004) so that users could always look up and walk forward as they typed. This idea led to using heads-up displays to see virtual content, the precursors to products like Google Glass, Snapchat's Spectacles, and Apple's rumored eye display.

Some teams started working on very sophisticated but speculative ideas. A group at MIT worked on affective computing that introduced the idea of allegedly reading emotional feedback on the body (Picard and Healey 1997). The idea was that if users were always wearing a computer, the computer should treat and know users as emotive humans rather than as machines. Media artist Thecla Schiphorst pioneered the idea of somatic, body-based practices as a framework for design (Schiphorst 2011). Artist and inventor Kate Hartman of the Social Body Lab reenvisioned bodies as computational "interfaces for the world"; through her inventions, she introduced the idea of listening to organs inside the body as a communicative channel for personal reflection (Hartman 2011). Today, these ideas are proliferating in the market with research into AI, yet early wearable tech pioneers also worked toward developing AI from a human-centered starting point.

The second major concept was sense augmentation. Patti Maes's MIT group introduced the SixthSense paradigm that advanced gestural interfaces in the style depicted in the film *Minority Report*. Her famous 2009 TED Talk garnered 9 million views, further popularizing the idea for mainstream audiences. Many researchers pioneered eye displays for different reasons. Steve Mann created Wearcomp to stream video to his eye for personal usage. Mann's notion of humanistic intelligence (HI) was meant as political pushback to big corporations and mass-market ideas about how a computer should interact with people. Mann wrote his 2001 manifesto, *Cyborg: Digital Destiny and Human Possibility in the Age of the Wearable Computer* (with Hal Niedzviecki), to establish wearables as countercultural devices. Other researchers and developers used displays for memory augmentation. The Remembrance Agent, an eye display and augmented reality app, contributed to the idea that one could annotate or label real objects with virtual information to help remember things about them, such as the names of people or reminders to water the plants (Schiele et al. 2001). Early embodied computing technology was about combining virtuality with reality and was the site that spawned augmented reality as a field (Azuma 1997; Behringer, Klinker, and Mizell 1999; Feiner 1999; Barfield and Caudell 2001; Milgram and Colquhoun 1999). The drive to get help from computers in mundane aspects of life was underway.

Embodied Computing

Our intention in using the term "embodied computing" is to refer to all types of body-affixed technologies, while building on previous work in the quest to taxonomize various types of body-centered computing (Leigh et al. 2017; Liu et al. 2016). Embodied computing technologies are material, body-centered technologies that can be in, on, or around the body. This includes categories such as wearable, ingestible, implantable, and embeddable—yet, we intend for the term embodied computing to be understood as porous and shifting and not authoritative or restricting. It concentrates on emergent medial relationships as much as it does on the material development of hardware and software. Today, embodied computing ideas (and AI more broadly) are not only pushing the field forward in terms of actual tech advancement; they are also changing how people adopt and adapt to technology in globalized cultures. Embodied computing should be used to help understand the diversity of evolving relationships that these devices engender, represented by augmenting verbs such as playing, restricting, tracking, and so on.

We hope this book will contribute to several fields. As noted above, there exists a categorical problem concerning the catchall designation of wearables and their impact on bodies. What this project does is begin a conversation by proposing to rethink the relationship between bodies and computing technologies, recasting the definition of wearables and related technologies, to examine the nature of embodiment itself. Through that recasting, the project poses questions for understanding relationships to embodied computing.

Building on earlier work in human–computer interaction and more specifically on the affective and informational relationships humans have with their technologies in multiple environments (Dourish 2001; Ekman 2012; Fidel 2012; Irwin 2016; Massumi 2002; Munster 2006; Dourish and Bell 2011; Melancon 2013; Duin et al. 2018), this book also began with the need to problematize previous academic work on body-centric technology. One of us (Isabel) proposed the "continuum of embodiment" as a model to explain how the medium of wearable computers and reality-shifting applications was emerging as a platform of communication, in the book *Ready to Wear: A Rhetoric of Wearable Computers and Reality-shifting Media*. It introduced the idea that mobile computing was setting the grounds for wearable computing, which in turn served as the justification for implantable technology. In a pre–Google Glass world, wearables were invented, designed, built, and proposed as coming phenomena that had to be dealt with as if they were a future waiting to happen. The journalistic claims raged: "Intel wants brain implants in its customer's heads by 2020" (Hsu 2009). This discourse of the seemingly imminent outcomes of progress was powerful. In a post–Google Glass context, wearables not only became mainstream, but the hype solidified into strong market expectations. Elon Musk's Neuralink brain implant company continues the hype and also breeds new markets. *Forbes* hypes near-term financial success with claims such as "Wearable Tech Market to Be Worth $34 Billion By 2020" (Lamkin 2016). Yet, *Forbes* and so many other institutional voices and inventors are still framing wearables as if they exist as an isolated sector, not contingent on dramatic technological turns such as the internet of things, AI, nanotechnology, and quantum computing. Furthermore, there is still room for more work on social, critical, and political aspects of embodied computing relationships.

This book is about computational embodiment. Taken literally, the term embodied computing explores the ways that technology manifests itself on, in, and around an animal body. Yet, embodied computing is also about embodying and the process of incorporating technology in a manner that reaches beyond copresent relationships with media devices. Embodied computing technologies and their makers, under various stages of design and conceptualization, treat humans as data blended entities, and this book begins the task of coming to terms with untangling this predicament. Over the past thirty years, scholars have often used the term "convergence" (Jenkins 2006) to explain the mass digital transformation that has endured. Web 2.0 convergence concentrated on media itself as a central point of departure, but the human body was not well-attended to in those debates— only recently has the body entered convergence debates as an embodied site that produces and receives data via ICTs (Smith 2016). Furthermore, "going online" was once a choice made by individuals to take up the internet to communicate, remember, share, work, and so on. As pointed out by many critical media scholars (Elmer 2003; Andrejevic 2007; Castells 2009), Web 2.0 dynamics proved that participatory culture was a ruse and that individuals are constantly negotiating the internet in ways that are controlling and closed to them. Now, public awareness of digital platforms like Facebook, Amazon, and Google and the incredible influence (and manipulation) that they wield has become mainstream news. Facebook's 2018 scandal over the misuse of its clients' data changes the field with justified skepticism, and embodied computing is also absorbing this mindset (Roose 2018). There is a need to continue thinking about embodied computing devices in these same critical terms.

Metaphoric positioning of digital media converging, crossing, and evolving has led us down an insufficient theoretical path for understanding complex empirical phenomena in the future of embodied computing. The body's tasks, increasingly shaped by technology companies to both incorporate data and be incorporated by it, at every point and in every process, require reenvisioning. Our approach to embodied computing begins to understand profound changes in the composition of bodies by looking at the body from a political economy perspective as a data-blended entity, engaged in numerous relationships at various levels of informational and administrative abstraction. The computational or quantified self (Lupton 2016) is not only instigated through personal choices or actions, it is increasingly revealed to individuals as an imposed process (Neff and Nafus 2015) that affects everyday activities, becoming a concerning condition of some forms of modern life. Desperate to embrace all the solutions that data cultures promise, organizations seem to accept tracking through datafication as given while operating with hope for the future. Taken teleologically, embodied technologies become beacons for this transformation. They provide the opportunity to analyze the ends that are already bound up in the technologies that certain parts of society embrace, or that which is planned for them. Thus, the definition of embodied computing includes all the device parts made and proposed for the organic body. Embodied computing makes privy new aspects of selves exposed to anyone, including the wearers themselves. It leads to the sensation of meeting an exposed self through numerous and novel disclosures. Some disclosures are legitimate, hopeful disclosures that may improve lives, but people are also threatened by outright nefarious outcomes that are questioned often but rarely met in industry with a remedial sense of deliberate attention. This book devotes critical attention to the social predicament that embodied technologies provoke.

We begin with the premise that embodied computing must be observed based on the relationships that are both generated through and challenged by the technology. We are less interested in philosophical debates about omnipresence and do not assert that human consciousness will inevitably blend seamlessly with distributed networks of data. The book is not primarily concerned with debates that focus on extended minds and consciousness, which we think are important, but not the focus here. Rather, this book contains a mosaic, a collection of papers that deal specifically with situated and contextual examples of how various forms of embodied technologies impact life. As sociotechnical systems, embodied computing technologies instigate social, critical, medial, and political relationships that we organize as ambient, topographical, and visceral.

Ambient

As ambient technologies, embodied computing connects and extends the body with its environment or milieu in an act of reciprocal feedback exchange. For example, smart dust microcomputers exist that can be sprinkled everywhere, tracking and recording movements. At NYU-X labs, the Holodeck project is another good example of ambient embodied computing and the thinking behind it. It is planned as a platform, combining different technologies to achieve rich virtual and augmented environments that facilitate both collaborative engagements between people and vocal artificial agents (Burleson and Picard 2007; Gunkel 2016). It will also incorporate remote interaction or various kinds of telepresence (Lombard and Jones 2015) through data streams. The broader goal for ambient technologies is humans augmented in external spaces and places to achieve myriad interrelations with AI technologies (gait and heat detection, facial recognition, and so on) rather than humans working with single-use devices to achieve isolated goals (e.g., getting fit, paying for goods).

Ambient computing is controlled by external actors. Ambient technologies consist of outward-facing contextualized bodies and the environment; they are embodied technologies that exist distally that depend on the body. For instance, facial recognition surveillance systems attempt to contextualize the moving body, in combination with commercial social media platforms (Brundage et al. 2018), allegedly analyzing things like personality characteristics and emotion. Smart cities are another example of ambient technologies that track individual bodies in information spaces (Boyle 2016). Another simple example is Amazon Go's "walk out" purchasing model where consumers take goods off store shelves and simply leave. All the systemic messaging processes for identifying customers, paying for goods, securing transactions, and so on, fall to Amazon's data infrastructure, which communicates with the store's physical environment. Machine-learning and ambient applications will not only track purchases but collect patterns of behaviors that are more like habits (e.g., whether customers are drawn to look at factory farm or organic food). Ambient technologies can monitor the body as an instrument revealing assumed beliefs held by subjects. Broader ideological trends may be attemped to be gleaned through the performance of small everyday acts (Pearson 2019). Another more speculative example is when ride-share services use autonomous vehicles that track how the passenger feels, where the passenger is going, and where they came from—the car becoming an ambient embodied AI technology to be considered as an aspect of a data-blended body.

On a much larger scale, ambient processes bind citizens (for better or worse) to politicized, commercialized, urbanized dataspheres. Backed by three levels of government, Alphabet's urban innovation company Sidewalk Labs has launched a smart-city project in Toronto after searching across North America, Europe, and Australia for a site (Saminather 2018). Despite regular public outcry and citizen-led activist groups, the assumption is that citizens of Toronto will help to revitalize an area of waterfront that includes "autonomous vehicles, a thermal grid that does not use fossil fuels, low-cost modular buildings with flexible uses, and robotic delivery and waste-management systems" (Saminather 2018)—yet researchers have acknowledged that cities are far more than computers and that "urban intelligence is more than information processing" (Mattern 2017). Revitalizing an urban space is no longer an act of beautification but entails turning citizens into blended entities that both draw from and contribute to third-party clouds provided by companies, through the mundane data exhaust that urban dwellers produce. Here, the notions of cloud and exhaust are not exclusive of embodied computing but should be understood rather as a form of ambient embodied computing environments. All of this creates new sets of problems for bodies in terms of administrative control over them. As Shaw and Graham (2017) note, what will happen when people's geographic information is controlled by powerful internet organizations?

Topographical

As topographical technologies, embodied computing exists on the surface of the body and transforms its layer into a technological surface for interaction. These are the most typical forms of embodied computing. Wrist-based wearables, fitness and health-based trackers are the most common, monitoring the body for biofeedback data that can be measured and compared with previous activity. This kind of personal data self-tracking (Neff and Nafus 2015) has also been manufactured into shoes (Nike), sports shirts (Hexoskin, OMSignal), and pendant-style jewelry. Electronic textiles and soft computation also fall in this category. Google's Project Jacquard enables garments to respond to haptic feedback, for example, using conductive threads and fabrics. Topographical technologies also include skin-based tech such as epidermal electronics (Kim et al. 2011) adhered to the skin that can not only read movements or even brainwaves but also stimulate brain activity. They are becoming the funnel between third-party companies' AI and the participant's body, moving data to and from the body. Such haptic technologies produce haptic subjects, embodied in a "particular relationship between touch and processes of scientific-technical knowledge production" (Parisi 2018). The eyes are also a technosocial topos undergoing transformation with the proliferation of eye displays. Virtual reality (VR) and augmented reality (AR) headsets provide either full immersion in a virtual space with VR, or a 3D virtual overlay on the real world with AR. Gestural interaction (moving virtual objects around with the hands) adds hand movements to both VR and AR to begin to simulate the body's natural movements in a computing space. Topographical technologies could potentially augment all worn garments, whereby clothing acts as a secondary skin functioning to extend the computational or quantified self (Parkes, Kumpf, and Ishii 2009).

Different from ambient and visceral embodied computing, topographical technologies have generated much recent academic study in nontechnical and nonhealth spheres. A decade of commercial wearable computing in its rich variations has informed wearable communication as a unique field in Communication and Media Studies. Wearing media in addition to tracking biofeedback or location is considered a communicative act (Mann and Niedzviecki 2001; Pedersen 2005; Pedersen 2013; Ryan 2014; Rettberg 2014; Gouge and Jones 2016; Jack 2016; Duin et al. 2018; Armfield et al. 2018; Tham et al. 2018). Duin et al. (2016) write, "we now live in an age of wearables, and composition pedagogy must further evolve our notions and understanding of teaching writing" (Duin, Moses, McGrath, and Tham 2016). Genres, heuristics, and composition strategies for wearable communication have matured, making topographical computing the most mainstream of all three embodied categories.

Visceral

As visceral technologies, embodied computing devices resonate internally, interacting with the body's core. These might be neurotech, implantables, ingestibles, and other forms of internal technologies. Visceral technology might also power wearable robotics. RFID (Radio-Frequency Identification) chips have been embraced by biohackers and consumers, a signal of the advancement of internal tech. The Neural Engineering System Design (NESD) program at DARPA's Brain Initiative is currently designing a brain implant the size of a centimeter to bridge the electronic–organic divide and help augment memory. Neuralink and Kernel brain implant companies seek to merge the brain with AI in a bid to attach customers to a neural datasphere, goading society with the fear that ignoring implanted AI will result in impoverished human intellect (Recode 2016).

Ingestible technology that involves swallowing computing sensors or robotic devices that function as digital pills is yet another example. What will it mean when such devices are regulated through governmental agencies and companies obtain intimate data about people's insides? The push to use ingestibles by insurance companies for tracking medications will inevitably affect insurance rates and partnerships between internet companies and health providers will introduce complex regulatory problems. Along with ingestibles, we offer these general categories to serve as a heuristic for thinking about embodied computing in terms of its relationship to human–machine communication (Guzman 2018) and all the rich ways that these devices produce information about bodies.

Data-Blended Bodies of Embodied Computing

Is it no longer sufficient to think of the body as a discrete, singular entity with distinct boundaries? Rather, should bodies be thought of in terms of levels, both corporeal and abstract, as data-blended entities that are susceptible to outside manipulation, surveillance, and control? In the past, bodies were assumed to be converging with technological advancements (Jenkins 2006; Haraway 1991), but should people consider them, in the face of large internet companies and governmental control, as data-blended bodies, forcibly merged with extended ambient environments as wearable or implantable sensors feed back into external receptors and the internet? As embodied technologies are connected to the internet, the human body becomes another point or landmark in a sociotechnical process. The telos or end goal of smart technologies is to have every object connected to the internet, and it is not naïve to think of the human body in these terms in anticipation of how we might develop forms of resistance. The Internet of People (IoP) is a topic discussed in several passages in this book. Teleological convergences have already headed in the direction of converging the body with forms of ambient media and technology—but taken a step further, the body may be seen not only as layered material convergence but also as data blended with embodied devices. Pacemakers, RFID tags, epidermal electronics, and other forms of embodied computing are already bridging the gap between the human and the technological, as are examples like bionic contact lenses (Pedersen and Ellison 2015; Pedersen and Ellison 2016). The body as connected to the internet of things is compromised by external forces that act on the body while the body acts. In this respect, human-produced data is blended with technologically derived data in a reciprocal exchange. Blended data sources, admixtures of tools, technologies, and networks, create multiple levels for understanding embodied computing. The blended body is one beyond convergence where reality shifting (Pedersen 2013) intermingles with affective computing practices (Picard 1997) and augmented reality (Azuma 1997).

This book addresses human bodies, but its main concern is with data-blended bodies where things like brain–computer interaction, exoskeletons, ingestible smart pills, and other forms of blended technology exist. While much of the book concentrates on humans, it does not ignore non-human agents (e.g., robots, digital assistants). Nanotechnologies, devices that will run in the bloodstream, and other embodied computing devices represent a need for a renewed approach to conducting social scientific research on media and communication that suits not only mechanical but also chemical, biochemical, biomedical, and other nonconscious processes. In this respect, emerging fields such as human–machine communication (Guzman 2018) may supplement narratives in fields such as science and technology studies on the differences between technological determinism (Dafoe 2015) and social constructivism (Bijker, Hughes, and Pinch 1987), providing a nuanced way to think about data assemblages and the affordability of embodied computing platforms and infrastructures. There is a need to address embodied computing devices as assemblages bound up in data that spread across human and technological realms, from biochemistry to algorithms.

The work of embodied computing increasingly infiltrates daily life, yet data processes remain in many ways opaque. Information exchange about data subjects goes on without providing the data subjects the opportunity to grasp the exchange, follow it, or really understand it—much less control it. Algorithms make decisions about people based on their data profiles. People negotiate with myriad hybrid agencies as embodied devices intrude onto and under the skin to allegedly read feelings, reactions, anxieties, delights, and fears (Pedersen 2013). Digital data profiles are generated by embodied computing. Ethical questions arise from the opacity of storing these data and how they will be used through data assemblages, or structures of power for control. As Hutchinson and Novotny (2018) observe, there is a need for "a critical digital literacy of wearables" as well as ingestibles, embeddables, and implantables. Going further, how can embodied computing devices be used to promote diversity, as Daugherty, Wilson and Chowdhury (2018) rightly ask of the artificial intelligence industry more broadly? The limited task we set ourselves when editing this book was to try to begin to understand how the bodily integration of technology, or what Hayles terms technogenesis (2012), is occurring in embodied computing in domains like policy, government, standards, socializing, religion, privacy, and other areas.

Data Subjects and Data Harms

The blended bodies of embodied computing also bring with them data harms relating to data subjects and the datafication (Lycett 2013; van Dijck 2014; Baack 2015; Strauß 2015; Iliadis and Russo 2016; Schüll 2016) of personal experience. Data harms and data violence (Hoffman 2018) are the real and projected future circumstances where data may be used to undermine human subjectivity and forcibly control potentials under the aegis of security and order. The quantified self and self-tracking movements have hinted at some of the concerns that come with bodies that are constantly emitting information and producing data for storage and forecasting (Neff and Nafus 2015; Nafus 2016; Lupton 2016). Ethical considerations, such as those surrounding embodied computing and surveillance, dataveillance, überveillance, and sousveillance (Abbas, Michael, and Michael 2014) must be vocalized given the increase in data capture techniques and their power over sociotechnical arrangements overlooking data subjects. What sorts of ethical frameworks around physiological data collection and analysis need to be considered before and during the design of embodied computing devices? There is a need for democratic methods to counter data exploitation (McKelvey 2014; Slane 2018) due to an industry-wide tendency to emphasize the value of embodied computing data analytics at the expense of user privacy and protections. The agency of the user is reduced when embodied computing devices do not allow users to be a transparent part of the data collection and analysis.

The data generated by embodied computing devices have the potential to alter relationships and social structures within multiple environments. As people move beyond the continuum of wearables, embodied computing and data-blended bodies produce various levels of abstraction, meaning, and framing that can be utilized for a variety of ends at multiple moments in time. Adopting a level of abstraction determines what the data or information can be about (Floridi 2011), and careful attention should be paid to cases where data may be repurposed or manipulated by jumping between levels of abstraction. Data-mining and communication systems are intended to "talk" to each other and eventually produce new information and knowledge when previously disconnected data silos are integrated. Often users of embodied computing devices will have no foreknowledge of the types of practices to which their data will be applied. User identification should take many items into consideration, including design, safety, record keeping, and the rights of data subjects. The sharing of data between companies and institutions must be regulated in some way—information sharing between institutions is the result of too much data and the need to integrate heterogeneous data, potentially leading to new forms of data harms when one person's individual data becomes mixed and added into alternative datasets unknown to the user.

Subjects and citizens should not be forced to engage with data-harvesting embodied computing devices, yet the practice is appearing everywhere, from prisons to the workplace. Any time there is a wide implementation of embodied computing across industries or institutions there must also be checks and balances that gauge the validity of chosen levels of data extraction. Feedback loops that gather information must be explained and users should understand the information that is being extracted from them. There must be some way of balancing data extraction with data literacy and providing users with information about their data exposure when it comes to emerging forms of embodied computing. As patients are encouraged to track biofeedback data for healthcare practitioners in what could be quite urgent situations, they need to know the risks. Sensitive groups like children are increasingly exposed to embodied technologies in schools and at home, further complicating the issue of consent. At what age do children earn the right to consent to data-harvesting practices and, further, how long will their data be stored and retained for future use? Such questions are asked in many fields, yet the field of embodied computing is lagging in this regard.

Lastly, integrating multiple heterogeneous datasets that were collected under different ethical guidelines through embodied computing is a huge issue that does not receive enough attention. For example, when tracking fitness levels, are our locations also being logged without consent? Certain types of physiological data can produce too much information, which runs the risk of excess data—what to do with extra data and how is it stored or destroyed? There are various frameworks that can be used to address these issues, including frameworks that pay careful attention to stakeholders in decision-making processes and invitations to stakeholders for taking part in such processes. Frameworks that emphasize the importance of making an accessible view of what researchers and institutions are doing should be valued, though not oversimplified (they should be situated and transparent). Data structures that communicate to provide broader context should be available, as should the ability for users to track their data over time. In general, the black box of data-harvesting practices must be pried open if embodied computing technologies are to be ethically nurtured and politically sensitive.

Social Value Systems

Embodied technologies must also be contextualized within specific social value systems. While it exists, there is not enough literature on the different narratives, ethical frameworks, value systems, and ideologies that inform work on embodied computing technologies—and many of these are overlapping, conflicting, or contradictoary, much in the same way as Stark and Hoffmann (2019) show in the domain of data ethics and data metaphors. Such competing ethical and political value systems shape and dictate the social direction of technology. Work on technological innovation and diffusion has approached this topic but our intention with this collection is to elaborate on the different varieties of value systems, elaborate on how they are reflected in situated practices, and to show how they lead to new forms of embodied computing depending on value positioning. What are the differences in design ethics and justice (Costanza-Chock 2018; Keyes 2018) that can be usefully applied to embodied computing research? Our intention is to look at some of the predesign values that inform the development of embodied technologies and anticipate future subjects. Some of the chapters in this collection focus on the institutions behind embodied computing and their motives, including regulatory agencies and universities. What institutions produce embodied computing devices, and what values do they hold? Institutions such as Carnegie Mellon and the University of California, Berkeley, produce embodied computing technologies, as do Google, Apple, Huawei, and DARPA. Each institution frames its work according to specific value systems, and some feature ethics more prominently than others. Where does funding for embodied computing come from? What are the complex agencies, policies, institutions, thoughts, and philosophies that inform embodied computing? Our book only begins to shed light on these different narratives and establish an integration between different groups. For example, professors in the humanities must learn to work with individuals in the technology sector. This book is a contribution to building that dialogue.

The research made available through large technology conferences may be geared to technical novelty first and a socioethical goal as a secondary consideration. Technology companies appear to create ethics committees as an afterthought, as evidenced by Google's failed ethics board (Piper 2019). Novel technologies need to prove that engineering or computing advancements in the field have been achieved to garner funding and justify large research hubs, often at the expense of social, cultural, ethical, or individual needs. Sometimes this hinders a researcher's ability to develop technology toward loftier, human-centric ends. The point we are making is that the way original research in STEM has been legitimized into the academy has not always simultaneously advanced a relevant ethics. Recently, however, some associations have evolved mandates to counter this trend by widening the goals for annual events and conferences and empowering presenters who privilege ethical goals. The International Conference on Tangible, Embedded, and Embodied Interaction (TEI), the International Symposium on Wearable Computers (ISWC), the Augmented Human Conference (AH), the International Symposium on Mixed and Augmented Reality (ISMAR), and the Conference on Human Factors in Computing Systems (CHI) are some examples.

Why This Book?

Our primary motivations for this collection are threefold. First, we noticed that the language and discourse surrounding wearables and other varieties of body-centered computing technologies have become limited and sectorized, obscuring the breadth of what is happening as this media emerges. We needed to reconsider the word "wearable" and its associations with a variety of alternative technologies connected to the body, including embeddables (things like prosthetics), implantables (microchips implanted under the skin), and ingestibles (such as emerging varieties of smart pills). We looked for chapters that might more accurately reflect the shifting ecologies and emerging states of body-centred technologies. We decided to use "embodied computing" for a couple of reasons. There is a precedent, particularly in theoretical work on the body, to affix the word "embodied" to additional fields or areas of inquiry. Embodied cognition or the extended-mind thesis (Clark and Chalmers 1998) and embodied interaction (Dourish 2001) stand out as two examples that showcase the importance of embodied forms of thinking and activity. Furthermore, in cultural studies forums, critical embodiment involves understanding how subjects occupy sites of power in public spheres through bodily engagement (Brophy and Hladki 2014). With embodied computing, we chose a general term that can encompass multiple forms of body-centered computing as rapid advancements in technology increase. Embodied computing also points to media infrastructures that body-centered technologies increasingly require.

A secondary aim was to provide some literature and storified context for the rapidly evolving state of embodied technologies. As early as 2012, wearables such as Google Glass (announced on April 4, 2012) caused a media sensation and elicited (in some cases) violent reactions from the public.

Glass was mostly a marketing campaign to crowdsource reasons for using wearables. It was meant to spark interest in these devices to feed Google's search engine regime, that is, more clicking, searching, and consuming. Through the Google Explorer program, 8,000 winners of the Twitter #ifihadglass campaign proposed both mainstream and wild ideas for the eye display in return for the privilege to purchase it. While Glass flopped as a consumer device, Google established wearables as a mainstream phenomenon that its competitors embraced. The backlash was ultimately highly productive. We felt it was prime time for a collection that focused on embodied computing technologies, old and new, one that described historical and emerging contexts. In 2012, we started this project online. The cultural analytics database Fabric of Digital Life (FABRIC) is a collection of over 3,000 artifacts that track the evolution of embodied computing from inception to production. Interested readers can view the archive at http://www .fabricofdigitallife.com (Pedersen and Baarbé 2013; Pedersen and DuPont 2017; Iliadis and Pedersen 2018; Duin, Armfield, and Pedersen 2019).

Our third aim was to build on the valuable perspectives offered by theoretical and philosophical frameworks that inform embodied computing. Such literature continues to offer invaluable perspectives on the archeology, genealogy, history, and philosophy of body-centered technologies. Building on historical work on embodied computing, we wanted to refine and add a layer of complexity to the conceptual grounding and frameworks. We wanted to collect a group of papers that evoked a strong sense of the diversity and multiplicity of embodied computing technologies. The papers collected here come from engineers, theorists, artists, and users, and they examine embodied technologies from a variety of contexts, including collaboration, civil engagement, co-authorship, friendship, hegemony, nostalgia, play, surveillance, symbiosis, amelioration, parasitism, imprisonment, and many others—some concentrating on the past, others speculating over the future. The purpose of including such a diverse group was to broaden the field of embodied computing research and its dimensions.

The Chapters in This Book

We hope we have staged a conversation that assembles an unlikely but necessary cast of scholars. The collection is wide-ranging but rightly so. It attempts to corral a disparate and far-reaching set of technological developments and practices through an equally disparate set of academic disciplines. The scholarship represented here include Media Studies, but also Information Studies, Communication, Science and Technology Studies, and adjacent disciplines. Each is complementary and reinforcing of one another. In all, the manuscript identifies a problem with current conceptual frames of wearable devices; it offers a response in the form of a more inclusive and inventive frame (embodied computing); it offers many trial runs of concepts through the form of an extra-disciplinary conversation across its several chapters and sites. The conversation is well positioned to contribute to the conceptual terrain of these pervasive technologies.

In chapter 1, Andrew Iliadis introduces companies and products in the ingestible computing industry, outlines some of their functions and affordances, and tracks how the US Federal Communications Commission is working to build a policy around ingestibles and other forms of embodied computing. Ingestibles represent a growing market, yet there is relatively little work on the policy implications of ingestible computing and their associated benefits and, more importantly, risks. In chapter 2, Isabel Pedersen examines embodied computing and the rise of body area networks. If society adopts them, body area networks will funnel data from bodily devices and implants to intermediaries and then on to the internet. Embodied computing, AI, and the internet of things will undergo radical proliferation because these networks will create a stable link between visceral, topographical, and ambient information flows. The chapter looks at justifications for body area networks, their cultural origins, and predictions about them.

In chapter 3, Deborah Lupton addresses the sociocultural dimensions of wearable devices: small, lightweight, topographical technologies that can be readily placed on human bodies as they move around in time and space. While wearable devices have not always been and need not be digital (examples are spectacles, pedometers, and prosthetic limbs), this chapter focuses on the new range of wearables with embedded sensors that generate digital data that have emerged over the past decade, in concert with mobile smart devices and Wi-Fi technologies. In chapter 4, Kevin Warwick provides a look into cyborg experiments and how implant and electrode technologies can be "employed to create biological brains for robots, to enable human enhancement, and to diminish the effects of certain neural illnesses." The key is linking a biological brain directly with a computer, and to this end, Warwick examines experimental scientific studies, including biohacking and neurohacking, before outlining some of their ethical considerations. In this chapter, a range of embodied technologies is considered.

In chapter 5, Katina Michael, M. G. Michael, Christine Perakslis, and Roba Abbas provide an analysis of the internet of things and people, emphasizing the end user as the final frontier. Their chapter probes the concept of the internet of things in the context of ambient embodied computing and includes human subjects in the frameworks. Embodied devices that are connected to the internet are increasingly implanted, embedded, and ingested by human users who "form an integral part of end-to-end network architecture." They envision the user as the "last mile" in global networked technologies, provide examples of biohacking cases, and shed light on the many individuals who now have implanted and embedded technologies that are no longer associated only with health. In chapter 6, Marcel O'Gorman looks at several projects from the Critical Media Lab that "pay special attention to the collision of technical prosthetics with both digital and religious ritual." Informational technologies are discussed as creating affordances for serious religious play. He explores delicate areas where wearables are asked to mediate behavior, perform in technocultural rituals, and help avoid digital temptations.

In chapter 7, Gary Genosko discusses the interesting case study of the failed attempt at creating a toe mouse for the computer. Genosko argues that "the interface of the most human yet base part of the human body and wearable computing confounds the low with the high." He offers a look at Douglas Engelbart's late-1960s proposal for a knee-controlled proto-mouse, along with other examples of foot-operated technological interfaces. In chapter 8, Suneel Jethani traces the evolution of electronic monitoring technology in domestic environments as a form of embodied computing. He considers the affordances of electronic monitoring technology, proposes a methodological approach to studying wearable technology based on the incorporation of intrusion, and anticipates how these devices might evolve.

In chapter 9, Elizabeth Wissinger leads the discussion of fashion tech, surveying many important writers working on the cultural implications of style in a field that had ignored aesthetics for decades. She argues that fashionable wearables seek to harness and meter human energy for profit in return for social capital and the aura of being "cool." Engaging in what she terms creepy levels of data transactions, wearers trade data for the convenience and access to forums that make them feel as though they are part of an elite membership. In the tenth and final chapter, Maggie Orth ends our collection with a sublime critique of technosupremicism and technologies that seek to read minds. On the future of brain implants, she provokes people to face remarks made by Elon Musk in order to consider the extreme outcomes they could instigate. Her chapter takes a no-holds-barred approach to challenge assumptions about implantables because they will ultimately challenge selfhood.

We knew when editing this book that it will, like many volumes before it, eventually become outdated due to rapid advances in technology. Some parts will be futuristic for many years whereas others will appear far and distant. What is meant by "bodies" in the book will vary widely. We see this variance as a feature and not a bug of the collection. The book addresses scholars in several fields, and we hope some of these audiences (largely overlapping, but still distinct) will benefit from the book's approach to computational embodiment.

References

Abbas, Roba, Katina Michael, and M. G. Michael. 2014. Using a Social-Ethical Framework to Evaluate Location-Based Services in an Internet of Things World. *International Review of Information Ethics* 22: 42–73.

Andrejevic, Mark. 2007. *iSpy: Surveillance and Power in the Interactive Era*. Lawrence: University Press of Kansas.

Armfield, Dawn W., Ann Hill Duin, and Isabel Pedersen. 2018. Experiencing Content: Heuristics for Human-Centered Design for Augmented Reality. Paper presented at the 2018 IEEE International Professional Communication Conference (ProComm), Toronto, Ontario, Canada, July 22–25. https://doi.org/10.1109/ProComm.2018.00057.

Azuma, Ronald. 1997. A Survey of Augmented Reality. *Presence: Teleoperators and Virtual Environments* 6 (4): 355–385.

Baack, Stefan. 2015. Datafication and Empowerment: How the Open Data Movement Re-articulates Notions of Democracy, Participation, and Journalism. *Big Data & Society* 2 (2): 1–11. https://doi.org/10.1177/2053951715594634.

Barfield, Woodrow, and Thomas Caudell. 2001. *Fundamentals of Wearable Computers and Augmented Reality*. Mahwah, NJ: Lawrence Erlbaum Associates.

Behringer, Reinhold, Gudrun Klinker, and David Mizell. 1999. International Workshop on Augmented Reality 1998: Overview and Summary. In *Augmented Reality: Placing Artificial Objects in Real Scenes. Proceedings of IWAR '98*, edited by Reinhold Behringer, David Mizell, and Gudrun Klinker, xi–xx. Natick, MA: A. K. Peters.

Bijker, Wiebe E., Thomas P. Hughes, and Trevor Pinch. 1987. *The Social Construction of Technological Systems: New Directions in the Sociology and History of Technology*. Cambridge, MA: MIT Press.

Boyle, Casey. 2016. Pervasive Citizenship through #SenseCommons. *Journal Rhetoric Society Quarterly* 46 (3): 269–283.

Brophy, Sarah, and Janice Hladki. 2014. *Embodied Politics in Visual Autobiography*. Toronto: University of Toronto Press.

Brundage, Miles, Shahar Avin, Jack Clark, Helen Toner, Peter Eckersley, Ben Garfinkel, Allan Dafoe, Paul Scharre, Thomas Zeitzoff, Bobby Filar, Hyrum Anderson, Heather Roff, Gregory C. Allen, Jacob Steinhardt, Carrick Flynn, Seán Ó hÉigeartaigh, Simon Beard, Haydn Belfield, Sebastian Farquhar, Clare Lyle, Rebecca Crootof, Owain Evans, Michael Page, Joanna Bryson, Roman Yampolskiy, and Dario Amode. 2018. The Malicious Use of Artificial Intelligence: Forecasting, Prevention, and Mitigation. Report, submitted February 20. https://arxiv.org/pdf/1802.07228.

Buechley, Leah, and Michael Eisenberg. 2008. The LilyPad Arduino: Toward Wearable Engineering for Everyone. *IEEE Pervasive Computing* 7 (2): 12–15.

Burleson, Win, and Rosalind Picard. 2007. Affective Learning Companions. *Educational Technology* 47 (1): 28–32.

Castells, Manuel. 2009. *Communication Power*. Oxford: Oxford University Press.

Clark, Andy, and David J. Chalmers. 1998. The Extended Mind. *Analysis* 58 (1): 7–19.

Costanza-Chock, Sasha. 2018. Design Justice, A.I., and Escape From the Matrix of Domination. *Journal of Design and Science*. https://doi.org/10.21428/96c8d426.

Dafoe, Allan. 2015. On Technological Determinism: A Typology, Scope Conditions, and a Mechanism. *Science, Technology, & Human Values* 40 (6): 1047–1076.

Daugherty, Paul R., H. James Wilson, and Rumman Chowdhury. 2018. Using Artificial Intelligence to Promote Diversity. *MIT Sloan Management Review*, November 21. https://sloanreview.mit.edu/article/using-artificial-intelligence-to-promote-diversity/.

Dourish, Paul. 2001. *Where the Action Is: The Foundations of Embodied Interaction*. Cambridge, MA: MIT Press.

Dourish, Paul, and Genevieve Bell. 2011. *Divining a Digital Future: Mess and Mythology in Ubiquitous Computing*. Cambridge, MA: MIT Press.

Duin, Ann Hill, Joe Moses, Megan McGrath, and Jason Tham. 2016. Wearable Computing, Wearable Composing: New Dimensions in Composition Pedagogy. *Computers and Composition Online*. http://cconlinejournal.org/wearable/.

Duin, Ann Hill, Diane Willow, Julianna Abel, Aaron Doering, Lucy Dunne, and Maki Isaka. 2018. Exploring the Future of Wearables and Embodied Computing: A Report on Interdisciplinary Collaboration. Paper presented at the 2018 IEEE International Professional Communication Conference (ProComm), Toronto, Ontario, Canada, July 22–25. https://doi.org/10.1109/ProComm.2018.00018.

Duin, Ann Hill, Dawn Armfield, and Isabel Pedersen. 2019. Human-Centered Content Design in Augmented Reality. *Context Is Everything: Content Strategy in Technical Communication*, edited by Guiseppe Getto, Jack Labriola, and Sheryl Ruszkiewicz, 89–116. New York: Routledge.

Ekman, Ulrik. 2012. *Throughout: Art and Culture Emerging with Ubiquitous Computing*. Cambridge, MA: MIT Press.

Elmer, Greg. 2003. *Profiling Machines: Mapping the Personal Information Economy*. Cambridge, MA: MIT Press.

Feiner, Steven. 1999. The Importance of Being Mobile: Some Social Consequences of Wearable Augmented Reality Systems. In *International Workshop on Augmented Reality*, 145–148. San Francisco: IEEE.

Fidel, Raya. 2012. *Human Information Interaction: An Ecological Approach to Information Behavior*. Cambridge, MA: MIT Press.

Floridi, Luciano. 2011. *The Philosophy of Information*. Oxford: Oxford University Press.

Gouge, Catherine, and John Jones. 2016. Wearables, Wearing, and the Rhetorics That Attend to Them. *Rhetoric Society Quarterly* 46 (3): 199–206. https://doi.org/10.1080/02773945.2016.1171689.

Gunkel, David J. 2016. Computational Interpersonal Communication: Communication Studies and Spoken Dialogue Systems. *communication +1* 5 (1): 1–20, article 7. https://doi.org/10.7275/R5VH5KSQ.

Guzman, Andrea. 2018. Introduction: "What Is Human–Machine Communication, Anyway?" In *Human–Machine Communication: Rethinking Communication, Technology, and Ourselves*, edited by Andrea L. Guzman, 1–28. New York: Peter Lang.

Haraway, Donna J. 1991. *Simians, Cyborgs, and Women: The Reinvention of Nature*. New York: Routledge.

Hartman, Kate. 2011. The Art of Wearable Communication. Filmed March 3, 2011, in Long Beach, CA. TED video, 8:59 https://www.ted.com/talks/kate_hartman_the_art_of_wearable_communication/.

Hartman, Kate. 2014. *Make: Wearable Electronics: Design, Prototype, and Wear Your Own Interactive Garments.* San Francisco: Maker Media.

Hayles, N. Katherine. 2012. *How We Think: Digital Media and Contemporary Technogenesis.* Chicago: University of Chicago.

Hoffman, Anna Lauren. 2018. Data Violence and How Bad Engineering Choices Can Damage Society. *Medium*, April 30. https://medium.com/s/story/data-violence-and-how-bad-engineering-choices-can-damage-society-39e44150e1d4.

Hsu, Jeremy. 2009. Intel Wants Brain Implants in Its Customers' Heads by 2020. *Popular Science*, November 20. http://www.popsci.com/technology/article/2009-11/intel-wants-brain-implants-consumers-heads-2020.

Hutchinson, Les, and Maria Novotny. 2018. Teaching a Critical Digital Literacy of Wearables: A Feminist Surveillance as Care Pedagogy. *Computers and Composition* 50 (December): 105–120. https://doi.org/10.1016/j.compcom.2018.07.006.

Iliadis, Andrew, and Federica Russo. 2016. Critical Data Studies: An Introduction. *Big Data & Society* 3 (2): 1–7.

Iliadis, Andrew, and Isabel Pedersen. 2018. The Fabric of Digital Life: Uncovering Sociotechnical Tradeoffs in Embodied Computing through Metadata. *Journal of Information, Communication and Ethics in Society* 16 (3): 1–18. https://doi.org/10.1108/JICES-03-2018-0022.

Irwin, Stacey O'Neal. 2016. *Digital Media: Human–Technology Connection.* Lanham, MD: Rowman & Littlefield.

Jack, Jordynn. 2016. Leviathan and the Breast Pump: Toward an Embodied Rhetoric of Wearable Technology. *Rhetoric Society Quarterly* 46 (3): 207–221. https://doi.org/10.1080/02773945.2016.1171691.

Jenkins, Henry. 2006. *Convergence Culture: Where Old and New Media Collide.* New York: New York University Press.

Keyes, Os. 2018. The Misgendering Machines: Trans/HCI Implications of Automatic Gender Recognition. *Proceedings of the ACM Conference on Human–Computer Interaction—Computer-Supported Co-operative Work*, edited by Karrie Karahalios, Andrés Monroy-Hernández, Airi Lampinen, and Geraldine Fitzpatrick, vol. 2. New York: 1–22, article 88.

Kim, Dae-Hyeong, Nanshu Lu, Rui Ma, Yun-Soung Kim, Rak-Hwan Kim, Shuodao Wang, Jian Wu, Sang Min Won, Hu Tao, Ahmad Islam, Ki Jun Yu, Tae-il Kim, Raeed Chowdhury, Ming Ying, Lizhi Xu, Ming Li, Hyun-Joong Chung, Hohyun Keum,

Martin McCormick, Ping Liu, Yong-Wei Zhang, Fiorenzo G. Omenetto, Yonggang Huang, Todd Coleman, and John A. Rogers. 2011. Epidermal Electronics. *Science* 333 (6044), 838–843. https://doi.org/10.1126/science.1206157.

Lamkin, Paul. 2016. Wearable Tech Market to Be Worth $34 Billion by 2020. *Forbes*, February 17. http://www.forbes.com/sites/paullamkin/2016/02/17/wearable-tech-market-to-be-worth-34-billion-by-2020.

Leigh, S., H. Sareen, H.-L. Kao, X. Liu, and P. Maes. 2017. Body-borne Computers as Extensions of Self. *Computers* 6 (1): 12. https://doi.org/10.3390/computers6010012.

Liu, Xin, Katia Vega, Pattie Maes, and Joe A. Paradiso. 2016. Wearability Factors for Skin Interfaces. Paper presented at the 7th Augmented Human International Conference (AH '16), Geneva, Switzerland, February 25–27.

Lombard, Matthew, and Matthew T. Jones. 2015. Defining Presence. In *Immersed in Media: Telepresence Theory, Measurement and Technology*, edited by Matthew Lombard, Frank Biocca, Jonathan Freeman, Wijnand IJsselsteijn, and Rachel J. Schaevitz, 13–34. London: Springer.

Lupton, Deborah. 2016. *Quantified Self*. Cambridge: Polity.

Lycett, Mark. 2013. "Datafication": Making Sense of (Big) Data in a Complex World. *European Journal of Information Systems* 22 (4): 381–386.

MacIntyre, Blair, Marco Lohse, Jay Bolter, and Moreno Emmanuel. 2001. Ghosts in the Machine: Integrating 2D Actors into a 3D AR System. In *The Second International Symposium on Mixed Reality*, Yokohama, Japan: 73–80.

Mann, Steve. 1998. Wearable Computing as Means for Personal Empowerment. Keynote address given at the First International Conference on Wearable Computing (ICWC-98), Fairfax, VA, USA, May 12–13.

Mann, Steve. 2002. *Intelligent Image Processing*. New York: IEEE.

Mann, Steve, and Hal Niedzviecki. 2001. *Cyborg: Digital Destiny and Human Possibility in the Age of the Wearable Computer*. Toronto: Doubleday Canada.

Massumi, Brian. 2002. *Parables for the Virtual: Movement, Affect, Sensation*. Durham, NC: Duke University Press.

Mattern, Shannon. 2017. A City Is Not a Computer. *Places Journal*, February. https://doi.org/10.22269/170207/.

McKelvey, Fenwick. 2014. Algorithmic Media Need Democratic Methods: Why Publics Matter. *Canadian Journal of Communication* 39 (4): 597–614.

Meloncon, L. 2013. Toward a Theory of Technological Embodiment. In *Rhetorical Accessability: At the Intersection of Technical Communication and Disability*, edited by Lisa Meloncon, 67–81. New York: Routledge.

Milgram, Paul, and Herman Colquhoun. 1999. A Taxonomy of Real and Virtual World Display Integration. In *Mixed Reality: Merging Real and Virtual Worlds*, edited by Yuichi Ohta and Hideyuki Tamura, 5–30. Tokyo: Ohmsha.

Mol, Annemarie. 2002. *The Body Multiple: Ontology in Medical Practice*. Durham, NC: Duke University Press.

Munster, Anna. 2006. *Materializing New Media: Embodiment in Information Aesthetics*. Hanover, NH: Dartmouth University Press.

Nafus, Dawn, ed. 2016. *Quantified: Biosensing Technologies in Everyday Life*. Cambridge, MA: MIT Press.

Neff, Gina, and Dawn Nafus. 2015. *Self-Tracking*. Cambridge, MA: MIT Press.

Parisi, David. 2018. *Archaeologies of Touch: Interfacing with Haptics from Electricity to Computing*. Minnesota: University of Minnesota Press.

Parkes, Amanda J., Adam Kumpf, and Hiroshi Ishii. 2009. Piezing: A garment Harvesting Energy from the Natural Motion of the Human Body. In *TEI 2009—Proceedings of the 3rd International Conference on Tangible and Embedded Interaction*, edited by Nicholas Villar, Shahram Izadi, Mike Fraser, and Steve Benford, 23–24. New York: ACM. https://doi.org/10.1145/1517664.1517674.

Pearson, Bryan. 2019. The Soup Has a Familiar Face: How Artificial Intelligence Is Changing Kroger, Walgreens and Others. *Forbes*, January 28. https://www.forbes.com/sites/bryanpearson/2019/01/28/the-soup-has-a-familiar-face-how-artificial-intelligence-is-changing-kroger-walgreens-and-others.

Pedersen, Isabel. 2005. A Semiotics of Human Actions for Wearable Augmented Reality Interfaces. *Semiotica* 2005 (155) 183–200. https://doi.org/10.1515/semi.2005.2005.155.1-4.183.

Pedersen, Isabel. 2013. *Ready to Wear: A Rhetoric of Wearable Computers and Reality-shifting Media*. Anderson, SC: Parlor Press.

Pedersen, Isabel, and Jeremiah Baarbé. 2013. Archiving the "Fabric of Digital Life." Paper presented at the IEEE International Symposium on Mixed and Augmented Reality—Arts, Media, & Humanities, Adelaide, SA, Australia, October 1–4. https://doi.org/10.1109/ISMAR-AMH.2013.6671260.

Pedersen, Isabel, and Quinn DuPont. 2017. Tracking the Telepathic Sublime as a Phenomenon in a Digital Humanities Archive. *Digital Humanities Quarterly* 11 (4). http://www.digitalhumanities.org/dhq/vol/11/4/000344/000344.html.

Pedersen, Isabel, and Kirsten Ellison. 2015. Startling Starts: Smart Contact Lenses and Technogenesis. *M/C Journal of Media and Culture* 18 (5). http://journal.media-culture.org.au/index.php/mcjournal/article/view/1018/.

Pedersen, Isabel, and Kirsten Ellison. 2016. Hiding in Plain Sight: The Rhetoric of Bionic Contact Lenses in Mainstream Discourses. *International Journal of Cultural Studies* 20 (6): 669–683. https://doi.org/10.1177/1367877915625234.

Picard, Rosalind. 1997. *Affective Computing*. Cambridge, MA: MIT Press.

Picard, Rosalind, and Jennifer Healey. 1997. Affective Wearables. *Personal Technologies* 1 (4): 231–240. https://doi.org/10.1007/BF01682026.

Piper, Kelsey. 2019. Exclusive: Google Cancels AI Ethics Board in Response to Outcry, April 4. https://www.vox.com/future-perfect/2019/4/4/18295933/google-cancels-ai -ethics-board.

Recode. 2016. We Are Already Cyborgs | Elon Musk | Code Conference 2016. YouTube video, 5:12. https://www.youtube.com/watch?v=ZrGPuUQsDjo.

Rettberg, Jill Walker. 2014. *Seeing Ourselves through Technology: How We Use Selfies, Blogs and Wearable Devices to See and Shape Ourselves*. Basingstoke, UK: Palgrave Macmillan.

Roose, Kevin. 2018. What It's Like Watching Mark Zuckerberg Get Grilled by Congress. *New York Times*, April 15. https://www.nytimes.com/2018/04/15/insider/ facebook-congress-roose.html.

Ryan, Susan Elizabeth. 2014. *Garments of Paradise: Wearable Discourse in the Digital Age*. Cambridge, MA: MIT Press.

Saminather, Nichola. 2017. Alphabet Unit to Start Toronto Smart-City Tech Pilot in Summer, Build in 2020. *Reuters*, April 9. https://ca.reuters.com/article/topNews/ idCAKBN1HG2WS-OCATP.

Schiele, Bernt, Thad Starner, Brad Rhodes, Brian Clarkson, and Alex Pentland. 2001. Situation Aware Computing With Wearable Computers. In *Fundamentals of Wearable Computers and Augmented Reality*, edited by Woodrow Barfield and Thomas Caudell, 511–537. Mahwah, NJ: Lawrence Erlbaum Associates.

Schiphorst, Thecla. 2011. Self-Evidence: Applying Somatic Connoisseurship to Experience Design. Paper presented at the 2011 CHI Conference on Human Factors in Computing Systems (CHI '11), New York, NY, USA, May 7–12. https://doi .org/10.1145/1979742.1979640.

Schüll, Natasha Dow. 2016. Data for Life: Wearable Technology and the Design of Self-Care. *BioSocieties* 11: 317–333. https://doi.org/10.1057/biosoc.2015.47.

Shaw, Joe, and Mark Graham. 2017. An Informational Right to the City? Code, Content, Control, and the Urbanization of Information. *Antipode* 49 (4): 907–927. https://doi.org/10.1111/anti.12312.

Slane, Andrea. 2018. Search Engines and the Right to Be Forgotten: Squaring the Remedy with Canadian Values on Personal Information Flow. *Osgoode Hall Law Journal* 55 (2): 349–397. https://doi.org/10.2139/ssrn.3028072.

Smith, Gavin J. D. 2016. Surveillance, Data and Embodiment: On the Work of Being Watched. *Body & Society* 22 (2): 108–139. https://doi.org/10.1177%2F1357034X15623622.

Stark, Luke, and Anna Lauren Hoffmann. 2019. Data Is the New What? Popular Metaphors and Professional Ethics in Emerging Data Culture. *Journal of Cultural Analytics*, May 2. https://doi.org/10.22148/16.036.

Starner, Thad. 1996. Human-powered Wearable Computing. *IBM Systems Journal* 35 (3–4): 618–629.

Starner, Thad. 2004. Keyboards Redux: Fast Mobile Text Entry. *IEEE Pervasive Computing* 3 (3): 97–101. https://doi.org/10.1109/MPRV.2004.1321035.

Strauß, Stefan. 2015. Datafication and the Seductive Power of Uncertainty—A Critical Exploration of Big Data Enthusiasm. *Information* 6 (4): 836–847. https://doi.org/10.3390/info6040836.

Suchman, Lucy. 2007. *Human–Machine Reconfigurations Plans and Situated Actions*, 2nd ed. Cambridge: Cambridge University Press.

Tham, Jason, Megan McGrath, Ann Hill Duin, and Joseph Moses. 2018. Guest Editors' Introduction: Immersive Technologies and Writing Pedagogy. *Computers and Composition* 50 (December): 1–7. https://doi.org/10.1016/j.compcom.2018.08.001.

van Dijck, José. 2014. Datafication, Dataism and Dataveillance: Big Data between Scientific Paradigm and Ideology. *Surveillance & Society* 12 (2): 197–208. https://doi.org/10.24908/ss.v12i2.4776.

1 Computer Guts and Swallowed Sensors: Ingestibles Made Palatable in an Era of Embodied Computing

Andrew Iliadis

Introducing Ingestibles

Picture the following three scenarios. You have an elderly uncle named Buck. Given his advanced age, on rare occasions, Uncle Buck forgets to take his prescribed dosages of phenytoin and azathioprine, both lifesaving medications. Stephanie, your best friend's niece, has spent the last two weeks in pain and requires risky surgery to dislodge a foreign object that has become stuck somewhere in her gastrointestinal tract. Once a week, you worry about an increased heartrate, shortness of breath, and begin to wonder whether you should slow down your run. A company, Visceral Data, begins producing smart pills to assist in each of the above three cases. Currently, numerous partners and organizations in academia, government, and the private sector are in fact building ingestible computational technologies that would feature prominently in each of the above scenarios, including the policy frameworks that govern them.[1] As former Alphabet executive chair Eric Schmidt once stated, "You will—voluntarily, I might add—take a pill, which you think of as a pill but is in fact a microscopic robot, which will monitor your systems" and share information about what is happening in your body (Bilton 2013).

This chapter discusses ingestible computing, or what are sometimes called "ingestibles"—that is, embodied computing technologies that enter the mouth and, in most cases, eventually travel through (and out of) a user's body. Estimates predict the global smart pills market size to be worth roughly $3 billion by 2025 (Grand View 2017). Though the technology may seem new, speculative fictional portrayals of ingestible technology began half a century ago with films like the 1966 sci-fi classic *Fantastic Voyage* and then later with films like the 1987 sci-fi comedy *Innerspace* (technically the object is injected but the general idea is the same) and the 2011 nootropic thriller *Limitless*. Today, several dozen companies and research teams are producing ingestible computational technologies and products that are already hitting the market, yet there is relatively little social scientific research on these emerging developments. In this chapter, I untangle some of the conceptual and policy implications of ingestibles and their relation to embodied, specifically *visceral*, computing (computing happening inside the body) and discuss some of the emerging people, places, and practices in the ingestibles market, before ending with a few of the developing political and ethical issues that are at stake in ingestible computing for their users and manufacturers.

While ingestibles may be the least established form of embodied computing, companies like Proteus Digital Health—which began research and development before 2008 and is one of the most visible ingestibles manufacturers on the market—continue to design and deliver products that include ingestible sensors, small wearable sensor patches, and applications on mobile devices that are connected to provider portals.[2] One can easily imagine some obvious user resistance to these forms of ingestibles—people have trouble visualizing and accepting that they would *swallow* a sensor or a computer. Yet, if the technofuturists and companies like Proteus Digital Health are correct, ingestibles will become palatable to users in the same way wearable technologies have. They will be commonplace as patients adopt ingestibles as part of their long-term health strategies at the behest of insurance companies, as users begin to track biodata over time to regulate their bodies, and as unique applications develop, such as using ingestibles for things like gaming and security. As such, it is necessary to consider the sociotechnical affordances and constraints of ingestible technology, along with the trade-offs that users make when interacting with them. Central to these concerns will be our visceral relationship to our biodata, who controls it, and who can make actionable and legal decisions based on it (Stark 2018). We can start by addressing how media and communications researchers have theorized computing and embodiment, and then contextualize the ways in which media and communication policy in the United States is currently handling new technological developments in ingestible computing. I highlight several areas of emerging ingestible media centered on visceral data, smart pills, and microbots, and I end by considering the social implications of these technologies, including potential ethical concerns.

Three Theoretical Precursors: Embodied Interaction, Ubiquitous Computing, Biomedia

Theorizing embodied forms of computation has a long history in literature on communication and media technologies. Long ago, the cyberneticist Norbert Wiener proclaimed, "information is information, not matter or energy" (1965, 132). There was a tendency in Wiener's early information theory to think of information as being distinct from the material world—bodies and relationships could ultimately be reduced to information systems. Of course, information and energy are a couple in the mutual composition of materiality, but thinkers such as Wiener privileged the notion of foregrounding cybernetic and informational processes to organize and understand reality from an information systems perspective. Hayles (1999) provided a famous corrective to Wiener's account by instead asking, "When and where did information get constructed as a disembodied medium?" (50). Hayles asks us to "recall the embodied processes that resist" the "separation between information and materiality" (20). Information here should be understood as embodied in material forms, and there is a certain degree to which it might acceptable to think of our data as being literally a *part* of ourselves. How could those data be generated if not for their visceral connection to the existence of our own material bodies? The body has a fundamental role to play in the production and manipulation of information, and today ethics researchers interested in developing frameworks for understanding embodiment and data ownership are returning to contextualizing the body's privileged relationship to the data that it generates. Stark (2018) rightly identifies the importance of understanding visceral data through "a wider focus on the emotional, affective, and visceral aspects of human experience" (42). Stark goes further and notes the critically important social and political implications of a viscerally embodied form of computing, writing that:

> To make data more visceral is to grapple with the injustices and inequalities persisting in many of the lives mediated by digital technologies. The concept of viscerality, of gut feelings, is not a conceptually neutral one, but is instead tied intimately to the imbrication of intersections between race, class, gender and sexuality within hierarchies of knowledge and power (44).

Particularly in the context of health services, one might ask why it is that we should give up sensitive visceral data about our bodies to large companies who might then manipulate users through various mechanisms like insurance incentives and enforcement of noncompliance disciplinary measures.

Before confronting here the explicitly political issues that Stark (2018) raises, it is important to note how researchers have previously identified the undeniably social dimension to our interactions with embodied information and computation. Using a combination of Heideggerian philosophy that privileges a bodily, situated being-in-the-world with diversified forms of material computing, Dourish (2004) famously highlights the notion of embodiment and interaction in social computing. Dourish's philosophical approach foregrounds embodied interaction over abstract reasoning to "understand the contributions and opportunities emerging from dynamic new forms of technological practice" (ix). Embodied interaction describes a new way of interacting with computer systems that is sensitive to the environment where interaction takes place. The main thesis that Dourish presents in his book is that embodied interaction can provide a common basis for understanding tangible and social computing, and that we should understand computation in terms of phenomenological presence and action. Going even further down the corporeal road, Dourish and Bell (2011) provide a rich ethnographic and historical account of the emergence of the ubiquitous computing industry, including its many key actors and products. They situate ubiquitous computing (ubicomp) as uniquely situated, adjacent to alternative areas of technical computing, since ubicomp is as much an idea as it is a technical product—similar to how Big Data, cloud computing, and the internet of things function today. Ubicomp "encompasses a wide range of disparate technological areas brought together by a common vision of computational resources deployed in real-time, real-world environments" (61). By emphasizing that "the domain of technology and that of everyday experience cannot be separated from each other; they are mutually constitutive" (73), Dourish and Bell show how computing permeates the social life and environments of bodies-in-action and that cognition is wrapped up in our everyday interactions with the corporeal world in "embodied practice" (101). Such frameworks are useful for thinking about our embodied interactions with newer, visceral forms of ubiquitous computing like ingestibles because they highlight the embodied nature of these technologies.

Perhaps most importantly, data and their biopolitical relevance to actionable decisions over bodies play a crucial role in our conceptualizations of bodies as viscerally entangled in computational and biological embodiment. Looking past a phenomenological situating of bodies as embodied *interfaces* with the world, as well as past ubiquitous computing *environments*, the types of biodata generated by embodied computing technologies like wearables, implantables, embeddables, and ingestibles collapse these two notions of embodiment into what Thacker has termed "biomedia" (2004). Biomedia, according to Thacker, are the product of bioinformatics technologies enhancing biological materiality. Thacker notes that that the body situates itself between the phenomenological concept of embodiment and technoscientific frameworks, and it is here where he proposes thinking of the body-as-media (10). Today one might push this notion even further, as Cheney-Lippold (2017) has, by seeing ourselves reflected in and potentially determined by the data structures and algorithms that process biological information about us. Drawing on Foucault's notion of biopolitics and Deleuze's concept of modularity, Cheney-Lippold situates the body as a corporeal entity managed by institutions that remain at a distance, governing our embodied selves through datafication. And in the domain of ingestible visceral data, such relationships might represent the most immanent (and imminent) threat to an agential bodily autonomy against disciplinary external institutions.

Embodied Visceral Computing, Bodily Negotiations, Data Ontologies

Building on and extending theoretical work on embodied interaction, ubiquitous computing, and biomedia, empirical and theoretical work on new and emerging forms of wearables, ingestibles, implantables, and embeddables complicate our relationships to perception and action as necessary and sufficient conditions for comprehending the effects of tangible and social computing. Here, the notion of embodied computing that I associate with such technologies should be understood as a double articulation where computing is at once embodied *through* computational materiality and, more importantly, passively embodied *in* the user's enhanced body, rather than as an embodiment of how we come to conceptualize biomateriality, or the user's external interactional interfacing with computers. The viscerally immanent, corporeally interactive environment where embodying takes place is in this case not the exterior world but rather the enhanced activity of the user's body—the user does not necessarily *interact* with the environment but *becomes* the environment. Meaningful engagement with the world defines embodied interaction—but what happens when internal activity produces meaning for understanding bodily capabilities, rather than external activity between user and tool in their environment? If embodied interaction and ubiquitous computing are about the intentional manipulation of external artifacts, and biomedia provide a clearer imaging of what happens inside the human body, the concept of embodied computing signals what happens when computational artifacts are manipulating us from the inside, computationally enhancing our bodies, while they share visceral information about ourselves with external (sometimes institutionally disciplinary) entities.

Embodied interaction stresses intentionality, as far as the computer products we use typically require representations. Of course, it is not a black and white distinction—but how can we think about ingestible technology, where the user does not necessarily interact with the produced representations based on the internally visceral processes that are taking place? Here I am thinking of practices like data collection, robotic surgery, automated security authentication, and so on. If embodied interaction is about how we intentionally act on and through technology (Dourish 2004, 154), then embodied computing might be how computing acts on and through us, producing new power asymmetries with external regulators and administrators who have privileged access to data generated by viscerally embodied computing devices like ingestibles. Where embodied interaction amplifies our external activities, embedded in a set of social practices, embodied computing sees devices extending our enhanced bodily activities and practices alongside new relationships of governmentality based on access to privileged visceral information.

Following Mol's (2002) important anthropological work on the ontology of the body in medical practice, I understand embodied computing as the site where negotiations about the human body take place and where data and governmental frameworks deploy new ontologies of bodies-in-the-making. My intention in drawing attention to bodily negotiations about data and the ontologies they introduce is to circumvent received knowledge of technologies like wearables (from companies and corporations) as technologies where the user maintains control (as in fitness monitoring), and to highlight ways in which governing frameworks associated with embodied computing devices like ingestibles cast users' bodies in specific data contexts. Embodied computing aligns here with biopolitics and theoretical traditions that do not separate the social body from captive technological or political apparatuses. This approach also draws on Haraway's (1991) conceptualization of organisms as hybrid, intertwined with technology. Haraway notes that the concepts of nature and experience are not innocent or self-evident aspects of culture and embodiment, and embodied computing highlights this distinction. More specifically, Lupton (2016) theorizes the ontologies of personal digital data through embodied computing technologies like ingestibles. Drawing on the work of Haraway and Mol, Lupton (2016) theorizes what happens when we literally eat data and become digital data-human assemblages, writing that "the human subject may be conceptualised as both data-ingesting and data-emitting in an endless cycle of generating data, bringing the data into the self, generating yet more data" (4). Ingestibles and embodied computing devices are engaged in bodily negotiations and their data ontologies are the new frontiers where such negotiations will take place.

Reality Shifts in Governmentality, Privacy, Policy

New bodily ontologies are being constructed by corporations that lean on governments to facilitate policy shifts, instantiating revolutions in institutional conceptualizations of the body. Pedersen (2013) has described embodied computing in terms of reality shifting along a continuum of embodiment, and movements in policy orientations about ingestibles show how such changes occur. Today, governments and nongovernmental organizations are debating the policy implications of these shifts. The US Food and Drug Administration (FDA) has product classifications for an ingestible event marker, which they describe as a system "composed of an ingestible microsensor, a data recorder in the form of a skin patch, and software," and an ingestible telemetric gastrointestinal capsule imaging system "used for visualization" (FDA 2018a, 2018b). In 2001, the FDA approved ingestibles for assisting with gastrointestinal visualization and listed several risks, including biocompatibility, electrical and mechanical safety, radiofrequency radiated power, and electromagnetic compatibility, including interference, functional reliability, and misinterpretation (FDA 2018c). Yet, while the FDA lists many safety controls on ingestible cameras, privacy and user data does not appear on the guidance document. One may chalk this up to less concern about private data in 2001, yet today the datafication of health is a primary issue in embodied computing (Ruckenstein and Schüll 2017). Government attention is purposefully redirected away from such concerns to make room for boosting the innovations and efficiencies promised by technologies like ingestibles to make them more palatable to the consumer market.

The FDA recently approved the first ingestible in 2017. The product was Abilify MyCite, a pill with a sensor that digitally tracks whether patients have ingested their medication (FDA 2018d). In the FDA's press release, Mitchell Mathis, director of the Division of Psychiatry Products in the FDA's Center for Drug Evaluation and Research, states that "being able to track ingestion of medications prescribed for mental illness may be useful for some patients." Although this may be true, the press release about the Abilify MyCite approval did not mention privacy or users' data, and the product website contains limited information about data retention.[3] Abilify MyCite's parent company is Proteus, in partnership with Otsuka Pharmaceutical Co. Ltd. (Proteus 2018). In the company's own press release, Proteus's President and Chief Executive Officer Andrew Thompson suggested that "the time is right for the category of Digital Medicines to be available. [...] Consumers already manage important tasks like banking, shopping, and communicating with friends and family by using their smart phones, as they go about their daily lives." The language interestingly frames ingestibles next to activities like shopping, even though they transmit sensitive biodata. But such framing is in the interest of Proteus, which would prefer to be viewed as providing choice and freedom rather than as collecting vast troves of valuable private information. There is no obvious indication of what happens to users' health data, or how access to such data may affect insurance premiums, coverage, privacy, or retention in the future.

Among several other mandates—including the wildly unpopular Restoring Internet Freedom initiative, which sought to repeal Obama-era net neutrality regulations—the US Federal Communications Commission (FCC) has put forward a task force to advance health care technologies and create interest about them, including ingestibles. Titled Connect2HealthFCC, the proposal explores "the intersection of broadband, advanced technology and health" (FCC 2016a). Among the projects that lay under the purview of Connect2HealthFCC is a mandate to boost health care technology and knowledge in the form of ingestibles, wearables, and embeddables (FCC 2016b). The FCC innocuously frames Connect2HealthFCC in terms of convenience and efficiency, pointing to embodied computing devices as enhancing routine tests, appointments, and results waiting periods. They describe internet-enhanced technologies like wearables and radio-frequency identification (RFID) chips as offering the potential of "more convenient, ultimately less-costly—and less-invasive—solutions," pointing to examples like smart clothing and smart tattoos.

Speaking specifically to ingestibles, the FCC describes the new technology as "digital tools that we actually 'eat'" and include examples such as smart pills that use RFID to monitor physiological reactions to medicine. They invoke smart pills that might track blood or dosage levels and describe tiny pill cameras used during surgeries or checkups. The FCC also describes wearables and embeddables, but implantables are curiously absent. In any event, documents like this one show that governing bodies like the FCC are paying attention to ingestibles and are currently laying down policy frameworks for how ingestibles are regulated and conceptualized by government. Connect2HealthFCC focuses almost exclusively on the efficiency improvements and innovation benefits of ingestibles, without providing much content about their potential harms and negative consequences in terms of users' data.

Lacking content on the historical development and potential ethical implications of these technologies, there is a need to understand the historical emergence of ingestibles and their sociotechnical status and ethical frameworks. How are current inventors and industry leaders framing and using ingestibles? Where the FDA lacks information about ingestibles and privacy, as a communications regulatory body, the FCC should conceivably pick up some of that slack. More generally, there is a need to understand the people, products, and practices in the ingestibles industry, and to tease out ethical concerns that might affect potential consumers and the communication of their data. Articles in the popular press have only started this task, yet they fall behind when mischaracterizing ingestibles as wearables (Jervis 2016), and so there is a need to track the emergence of ingestible tech and other forms of embodied computing to understand this emerging field, its promises, and tradeoffs for customers. Our FABRIC (Fabric of Digital Life) database (Iliadis and Pedersen 2018), alluded to in this book's introduction and throughout these chapters, is one such approach and contains information about a wide variety of embodied computing products, including information about ingestibles (http://www.fabricofdigitallife.com). Turning to material gathered in FABRIC, below I outline some of the primary contexts in which ingestibles are being developed and used on the market. Some are FDA/FCC approved, while others remain in the prototyping stage—though all are being championed by new leaders in industry. The list is my own take on what Edwards (2018) refers to as the interactive implications of "ontological classification" in the domain of human–machine communication—what I imagine as a list of types of ingestibles and their affordances and constraints. Here, I understand human–machine communication as "the creation of meaning among humans and machines" (Guzman 2018, 17), focusing specifically on ingestibles' capacity to alter our current understanding of our bodies and the meaningful effects that visceral forms of embodied computing have on them, particularly when they are connected at a distance to disciplinary institutions (insurance, education, etc.) that govern our lives.

Inside Out: Ingestibles as Visualization-Enhancing Technologies

One of the primary and earliest aims of ingestibles was to act as literal cameras inside the human body. Currently, there are three main companies involved in the production of ingestible cameras in the form of smart pills approved by the FDA. Given Imaging is an Israeli medical technology company that manufactures and markets the PillCam SB 3, while Olympus America Inc., based in Pennsylvania, produces the EndoCapsule. The Intromedic Company out of Korea produce the MicroCam, and there is a fourth company based out of China called Jianshan Science and Technology Group Co. Ltd. that develops a product called the OMOM capsule, but this last product has not been approved by the FDA (Van de Bruaene, De Looze, and Hindryckx 2015). PillCam SB 3 is the most well known among the wearable cameras and is used for detecting illnesses like Crohn's disease.

Technologies like the ones listed above will generate vast amounts of visual data about our guts. It is reasonable to question what the production of such internal visualizations will mean for our future interactions, much in the same way that facial recognition technologies are currently introducing unique social problems related to stereotyping, racism, and prejudice. Facial recognition is illegitimately being used for dubious purposes including "determining" individuals' race, sexuality, and gender for purposes of control. How might future algorithmic recognition technologies frame and contextualize an authority's perceptions of our bodies once access to vast amounts of internal images and imaging technologies are made available? For example, might such phenomena as internal stereotyping of bodies occur, creating new biases and problematic epistemologies? Could individuals be forced to use ingestibles as visualization-enhancing technologies by authorities like the police or health insurers? What would it mean for police to request access to an image of inside your guts? Would a warrant be required? Such questions should be asked by critical technology scholars in advance of ingestibles' widespread use on the market.

Visceral Data: Ingestibles as Data-Enhancing Technologies

Privacy is becoming a huge concern in ingestible computing, specifically around user data and monitoring (Bilton 2013). HQ Inc.'s CorTemp (Ingestible Core Body Temperature Sensor) transmits biodata as it travels through the digestive tract of the user (HQ Inc. 2018). Proteus's digital pill system tracks patients' health with an ingestible sensor made with magnesium and copper that interacts with stomach acid, a sensor patch, and a smartphone application. The pill notifies physicians when patients have taken their medicine and can track dosage accuracy. Further, researchers at MIT found that they could record the acoustic wave of the gastrointestinal tract and measure heart and respiratory rates (Traverso et al. 2015). There are also pseudo-ingestibles like the "pill on a string" developed by researchers at the University of Cambridge, which could help doctors detect esophageal cancer by providing data on a regular basis (Ross-Innes et al. 2015). Even smart bottles such as those produced by AdhereTech produce data about our bodies—they emit colors when it is time to take a pill and signal if you have missed a dose, tracking the event; Vitality's GlowCap also offers such a service (Silverman 2017). Embodied computing devices may also include visceral data-enabling technologies that promote sensations, including "data that we see, hear, feel, breathe and even ingest" (Stark 2014).

It would be useful to consider the future forms of visceral data generated by ingestibles and to unpack the ways in which those data may be operationalized against the best interests of the users to whom those data belong. What would it mean if a private healthcare company had permanent access to your internal biodata on an everyday basis? What types of new power and regulatory frameworks would be enforced that disadvantage individuals who may not understand or comply with directions related to ingestibles? There would be potential privacy problems related to the collection of metadata about users' geolocation, as well as the potential to increase insurance premiums if noncompliance is discovered. The main point is that, much in the same way that we care about our privacy in environments like those provided by social media sites and platforms, similarly we should be attentive to the privacy implications of mass-distributed biodata produced by ingestibles. Currently, the FTC and FCC are not addressing these areas, so it will be up to critical technology scholars to put pressure on the industry to consider issues of harm and justice in the context of visceral data generated by ingestibles as data-enhancing technologies.

Nootropics: Ingestibles as Intelligence-Enhancing Technologies

Nootropics are cognitive enhancing smart drugs that are supposed to improve intelligence and memory, even including things like creativity and motivation. While nootropics are not embodied computing devices per se, they are sometimes included in the category of ingestibles. HVMN, previously known as Nootrobox, is an American company that manufactures and sells nootropics products.[4] There are many nootropics on the market, including Aniracetam, Oxiracetam, Noopept Phenibut, Vinpocetine, Huperzine-A, 5-HTP GABA, Alpha GPC, among others. There are few long-term studies of nootropics and more research must be conducted to determine the exact effects (if any) of these drugs. Some nootropics are prescription only and are developed by big pharmaceutical companies (Modafinal being a popular example, used to increase alertness). Nootropics are often grouped into natural and synthetic varieties, and the FDA has approved a limited few nootropics for nonmedical purposes.

Depending on the legitimacy of nootropics, which can only be established after more long-term studies, it will be useful to consider what the use of nootropics would mean in terms of advantaging certain users while disadvantaging others. There are obvious fairness problems involved when someone who can afford highly expensive nootropics uses them to perform better (perhaps gaining them admission to college after a successful test or interview) while those who cannot afford nootropics remain at a disadvantage. How would such technologies be regulated and what best practices would be put in place by authorities who must ensure fairness? Would nootropics be banned in certain intellectual pursuits in the same way that performance-enhancing drugs like steroids are in sports?

Microbots: Ingestibles as Surgery-Enhancing Technologies

Ingestibles can also take the form of tiny, sometimes molecular, robots that are used for performing surgery inside your body. Researchers at MIT, the University of Sheffield, and the Tokyo Institute of Technology have recently shown that a tiny origami robot can unfold itself inside the human body—once the user swallows it in pill form—and can be manipulated by an external magnetic field to move inside the body and potentially remove foreign objects from stomach lining, such as a button battery, or to patch a wound (Hardesty 2016). Researchers in Germany have created a robot that resembles a tiny piece of rubber that can move, run, jump, crawl, and swim, and can be used to perform noninvasive surgery on patients (Gorman 2018). Such microbots can also be used to deliver drugs into a patient's system, sometimes in slow-release stages, in order to accurately track prescription dosage—tests have already been conducted on mice and have been shown to "have cured bacterial infections in the stomachs of mice, using bubbles to power the transport of antibiotics" (Revell 2017). Such devices may be able to even swim in your veins or bloodstream (Crane 2017).

The introduction of autonomous foreign artificial agents inside of our human bodies might be the most saliently problematic aspect of ingestibles. Today, we worry about internet of things–connected devices and the potential ability of hackers to gain access to these technologies for nefarious ends. Our internet-connected cars, fridges, home security systems, even city grids are open to exploitation on the network. What would happen if similar problems occur around internet-connected devices in our bodies? As Pedersen describes in this book, what will happen when ingesibles effectively contribute to producing the body as a platform—just another node connected on the internet of things? There is already evidence that pacemakers can be hacked, and such problems would only be exacerbated in a context where even greater amounts of autonomous foreign artificial agents were inserted into our bodies. Potential problems are not limited to a directed attack. Accidents happen regularly, and there is higher degree at which life-threatening accidents may occur if such ingestible technologies are working inside us.

Other Uses for Ingestibles

There are many other unique areas where ingestibles can be used, and their applications are almost limitless. For example, researchers have developed an ingestible for games where users swallow a digital sensor to play. The researchers designed a game called Guts Game to investigate ingestible game design and "ultimately help designers to create a wider range of future play experiences" (Li et al. 2017, 1). Ingestibles will also someday be produced at home. Google has patented the 3D printing of ingestible shells for medicine (Google 2017) and Intel has also patented ingestible tech (Intel 2016). Ingestibles have also been shown to assist with things like security and tasks such as storing passwords inside our bodies (Bilton 2013)—a natural extension of biosecurity. Perhaps more innocuously, ingestibles can also track gas development inside the body to let users know when it might be time to visit the bathroom (Mole 2018).

Innovators in the technology industry clearly spend time thinking about researching and developing ingestibles in a wide variety of cases and contexts, often at the expense of thinking about potential harms. It is incumbent on critical technology researchers to similarly engage in speculative design practices to stay apace with these inventions, and to think about the various sociotechnical affordances, constraints, and trade-offs that would occur once technologies like ingestibles are widely adopted, such as the types of tracking that might be imposed (Neff and Nafus 2015). As shown earlier in this chapter, federal regulating bodies and industry are mostly interested in assisting the development of the market for embodied computing devices, along with their efficiencies, than in the privacy of users' data produced through visceral computing technologies such as ingestibles.

Conclusion: Let's Attend to the Distastefulness of Ingestibles

While there are seemingly limitless applications of ingestible technologies, there is also the potential for ingestibles to produce distasteful harms and negative effects that are related not only to health and to medical safety. Many developers of ingestibles will argue that not using ingestibles can result in health care problems once ingestibles are in widespread use in the market. Ingestibles can be used for things like tracking your medicine intake, reminding you to take drugs, repairing your guts, and tracking data about your body over time. This will reduce visits to the doctor and, in some cases, potentially save people's lives. All of this is true, yet few ingestibles developers pay any considerable attention to privacy issues regarding user health data, or the ways in which ingestibles may be used to coerce users by insurers. For example, through a content meta-analysis, Mittelstadt and Floridi (2016) analyzed five major ethical themes that have emerged from the literature on biomedical Big Data, including informed consent, privacy, ownership, epistemology, and the Big Data divide. Products like ingestibles may create future problems if customers do not provide adequate consent. Customers may be nudged or forced to use ingestibles and give up valuable data about themselves that can later be sold, traded, or used against their wishes, often in ways that are unimaginable by them when they sign up to use the technology. User privacy is at stake when ingestibles are used to save data in the form of images, sounds, and biodata about things like heart rate, body temperature, and movement. Such data can be used against people, for example, when insurance providers require users to successfully track themselves to receive lower insurance premiums. Such problems are also associated with ownership. What happens when individuals cannot afford ingestibles or when they do not have the means to track themselves? Who owns the data when successful tracking does occur, or when it occurs through rented or free technologies?

Ingestibles act as new forms of surveillance and stand to monitor users in unknown ways (Schlaefli 2016). The *New York Times* wonders if the first digital pill will create a biomedical Big Brother (Belluck 2017). There are new epistemologies of the body that will be created by ingestibles and their various uses in the market, and these will change conceptions of the body and what it means to interact with it. Otsuka and Proteus state that their Abilify MyCite system "records medication ingestion and communicates it to the patient and healthcare provider" and that "it can collect data on activity level, as well as self-reported rest and mood which, with patient consent, can be shared with the healthcare provider and selected members of the family and care team"—yet there is little information about what will happen with this data (Proteus 2018). Brandom (2015) states that patients' "best protections are medical privacy laws like HIPAA, which prevent medical data from being shared with anyone outside the hospital system." Such protections, Brandom states, prevent employers or authorities from using products like those developed by Proteus to track you, yet they do not "keep data out of the hands of healthcare providers"; ingestibles can be used to enforce compliance, or insurers can increase co-pays if there is evidence of noncompliance. Cloud-connected medical devices save lives, but also raise questions about privacy, security, and oversight (Alexander 2018).

As we move into a new era of embodied computing devices, ingestibles are one of the least studied forms of visceral computing. Much talk and research has focused on the innovative and efficient outcomes of ingestibles, but more time should be spent, particularly by media and communication researchers, and critical technology scholars, on investigating the distastefulness of ingestibles, and how ingestibles will affect users in the future. Embodied computing is here, and we should be proactive to the problems generated by ingestibles, not reactive. Only when ingestibles are thoroughly regulated should they become palatable to users.

Notes

1. See the FABRIC archive for various examples: https://www.fabricofdigitallife .com/.

2. Proteus website: https://www.proteus.com/.

3. See https://www.abilifymycite.com/.

4. See https://hvmn.com/.

References

Alexander, Neta. 2018. My Pacemaker Is Tracking Me From Inside My Body. *Atlantic*, January 27. https://www.theatlantic.com/technology/archive/2018/01/my -pacemaker-is-tracking-me-from-inside-my-body/551681/.

Belluck, Pam. 2017. First Digital Pill Approved to Worries About Biomedical "Big Brother." *New York Times*, November 13. https://www.nytimes.com/2017/11/13/health/digital-pill-fda.html.

Bilton, Nick. 2013. Disruptions: Medicine That Monitors You. *New York Times*, June 23. https://bits.blogs.nytimes.com/2013/06/23/disruptions-medicine-that-monitors-you/.

Brandom, Russell. 2015. The Frightening Promise of Self-Tracking Pills. *Verge*, October 7. https://www.theverge.com/2015/10/7/9466121/proteus-digital-pill-tracking-privacy-quantified-self.

Cheney-Lippold, John. 2017. *We Are Data: Algorithms and the Making of Our Digital Selves*. New York: New York University Press.

Crane, Leah. 2017. Tiny Robots Swim the Front Crawl through Your Veins. *New Scientist*, July 24. https://www.newscientist.com/article/2141595-tiny-robots-swim-the-front-crawl-through-your-veins/.

Dourish, Paul. 2004. *Where the Action Is: The Foundations of Embodied Interaction*. Cambridge, MA: MIT Press.

Dourish, Paul, and Genevieve Bell. 2011. *Divining a Digital Future: Mess and Mythology in Ubiquitous Computing*. Cambridge, MA: MIT Press.

Edwards, Autumn. 2018. Animals, Humans, and Machines: Interactive Implications of Ontological Classification. In *Human-Machine Communication: Rethinking Communication, Technology, and Ourselves*, edited by Andrea L. Guzman, 29–49. New York: Peter Lang.

FCC. 2016a. Connect2HealthFCC. https://www.fcc.gov/about-fcc/fcc-initiatives/connect2healthfcc.

FCC. 2016b. Ingestibles, Wearables and Embeddables. https://www.fcc.gov/general/ingestibles-wearables-and-embeddables.

FDA. 2018a. Ingestible Event Marker. https://www.accessdata.fda.gov/scripts/cdrh/cfdocs/cfPCD/classification.cfm?ID=973.

FDA. 2018b. System, Imaging, Esophageal, Wireless, Capsule. https://www.accessdata.fda.gov/scripts/cdrh/cfdocs/cfPCD/classification.cfm?ID=NSI.

FDA. 2018c. Class II Special Controls Guidance Document: Ingestible Telemetric Gastrointestinal Capsule Imaging System; Final Guidance for Industry and FDA. https://www.fda.gov/MedicalDevices/ucm073393.htm.

FDA. 2018d. FDA Approves Pill with Sensor That Digitally Tracks If Patients Have Ingested Their Medication. https://www.fda.gov/NewsEvents/Newsroom/PressAnnouncements/ucm584933.htm.

Google. 2017. 3D Printing of Digestible Shells for Medicaments. http://www.google
.tm/patents/US20160120808.

Gorman, James. 2018. This Tiny Robot Walks, Crawls, Jumps and Swims. But It Is Not
Alive. *New York Times*, January 24. https://www.nytimes.com/2018/01/24/science/
tiny-robot-medical.html.

Grand View Research. 2017. Smart Pills Market Size Worth $3.0 Billion By 2025;
CAGR: 15.5%. https://www.grandviewresearch.com/press-release/global-smart-pills
-market.

Guzman, Andrea. 2018. Introduction: "What Is Human–Machine Communication,
Anyway?" In *Human–Machine Communication: Rethinking Communication, Technology, and Ourselves*, edited by Andrea L. Guzman, 1–28. New York: Peter Lang.

Hardesty, Larry. 2016. Ingestible Origami Robot. *MIT News*, May 12. http://news
.mit.edu/2016/ingestible-origami-robot-0512.

Haraway, Donna J. 1991. *Simians, Cyborgs, and Women: The Reinvention of Nature*.
New York: Routledge.

Hayles, N. Katherine. 1999. *How We Became Posthuman: Virtual Bodies in Cybernetics,
Literature, and Informatics*. Chicago: University of Chicago Press.

HQ Inc. 2018. CorTemp Sensor. http://www.hqinc.net/cortemp-sensor-2/.

Iliadis, Andrew, and Isabel Pedersen. 2018. The Fabric of Digital Life: Uncovering
Sociotechnical Tradeoffs in Embodied Computing through Metadata. *Journal of
Information, Communication and Ethics in Society* 16 (3): 1–18. https://doi.org/
10.1108/JICES-03-2018-0022.

Intel. 2016. Technologies for Managing Device Functions of an Ingestible Computing
Device. https://patentscope.wipo.int/search/en/detail.jsf?docId=WO2016105739.

Jervis, Shivvy. 2016. The Future Will Eat Itself: Digesting the Next Generation
of Wearable Tech. *Guardian*, January 13. https://www.theguardian.com/media
-network/2016/jan/13/future-eat-digesting-next-generation-wearable-tech.

Li, Zhuying, Florian Mueller, Felix Brandmueller, and Stefan Greuter. 2017. Ingestible Games—Swallowing a Digital Sensor to Play a Game. Poster presented at the
ACM SIGCHI Annual Symposium on Computer–Human Interaction in Play (CHI
PLAY '17), October 15–18, Amsterdam, The Netherlands. https://doi.org/10.1145/
3130859.3131312.

Lupton, Deborah. 2016. Digital Companion Species and Eating Data: Implications
for Theorising Digital Data–Human Assemblages. *Big Data & Society* 3 (1): 1–5.
https://doi.org/10.1177/2053951715619947.

Mittelstadt, Brent Daniel, and Luciano Floridi. 2016. *Science and Engineering Ethics*
22 (2): 303–341. https://doi.org/10.1007/s11948-015-9652-2.

Mol, Annemarie. 2002. *The Body Multiple: Ontology in Medical Practice*. Durham, NC: Duke University Press.

Mole, Beth. 2018. With Ingestible Pill, You Can Track Fart Development in Real Time on Your Phone. *Ars Technica*, September 1. https://arstechnica.com/science/2018/01/with-ingestible-pill-you-can-track-fart-development-in-real-time-on-your-phone/.

Neff, Gina, and Dawn Nafus. 2015. *Self-Tracking*. Cambridge, MA: MIT Press.

Pedersen, Isabel. 2013. *Ready to Wear: A Rhetoric of Wearable Computers and Reality-shifting Media*. Anderson, SC: Parlor Press.

Proteus. 2018. Otsuka and Proteus Announce the First U.S. FDA Approval of a Digital Medicine System: Abilify MyCite (Aripiprazole Tablets with Sensor). https://www.proteus.com/press-releases/otsuka-and-proteus-announce-the-first-us-fda-approval-of-a-digital-medicine-system-abilify-mycite/.

Revell, Timothy. 2017. Tiny Robots Crawl through Mouse's Stomach to Heal Ulcers. *New Scientist*, August 16. https://www.newscientist.com/article/2144050-tiny-robots-crawl-through-mouses-stomach-to-heal-ulcers/.

Ross-Innes, Caryn S., Jennifer Becq, Andrew Warren, R. Keira Cheetham, Helen Northen, Maria O'Donovan, Shalini Malhotra, Massimiliano di Pietro, Sergii Ivakhno, Miao He, Jamie M. J. Weaver, Andy G. Lynch, Zoya Kingsbury, Mark Ross, Sean Humphray, David Bentley, and Rebecca C. Fitzgerald. 2015. Whole-Genome Sequencing Provides New Insights into the Clonal Architecture of Barrett's Esophagus and Esophageal Adenocarcinoma. *Nature Genetics* 47 (9): 1038–1046. https://doi.org/10.1038/ng.3357.

Ruckenstein, Minna, and Natasha Dow Schüll. 2017. The Datafication of Health. *Annual Review of Anthropology*, 46 (1): 261–278. https://doi.org/10.1146/annurev-anthro-102116-041244.

Schlaefli, Samuel. 2016. The Microdoctors in Our Bodies. Eidgenössische Technische Hochschule Zürich. https://www.ethz.ch/en/news-and-events/eth-news/news/2016/09/the-micro-doctors-in-our-bodies.html.

Silverman, Lauren. 2017. "Smart" Pill Bottles Aren't Always Enough to Help the Medicine Go Down. *NPR All Things Considered*, August 22. https://www.npr.org/sections/health-shots/2017/08/22/538153337/smart-pill-bottles-arent-enough-to-help-the-medicine-go-down.

Stark, Luke. 2014. Come On Feel the Data (and Smell It). *Atlantic*, May 19. Available at: https://www.theatlantic.com/technology/archive/2014/05/data-visceralization/370899/.

Stark, Luke. 2018. Visceral Data. In *Affect and Social Media: Emotion, Mediation, Anxiety and Contagion*, edited by Tony D. Sampson, Stephen Maddison, and Darren Ellis, 42–51. London: Rowman & Littlefield.

Thacker, Eugene. 2004. *Biomedia*. Minneapolis: University of Minnesota Press.

Traverso, G., G. Ciccarelli, S. Schwartz, T. Hughes, T. Boettcher, R. Barman, R. Langer, and A. Swiston. 2015. Physiologic Status Monitoring via the Gastrointestinal Tract. *PLOS ONE*, 10 (11): e0141666. https://doi.org/10.1371/journal.pone.0141666.

Van de Bruaene, Cedric, Danny De Looze, and Pieter Hindryckx. 2015. Small Bowel Capsule Endoscopy: Where Are We after Almost 15 Years of Use? *World Journal of Gastrointestinal Endoscopy*, 7 (1): 13–36. https://doi.org/10.4253/wjge.v7.i1.13.

Wiener, Norbert. 1965. *Cybernetics, or Control and Communication in the Animal and Machine*. Cambridge, MA: MIT Press.

2 Will the Body Become a Platform? Body Networks, Datafied Bodies, and AI Futures

Isabel Pedersen

Introduction

In September 2017, news emerged that a computer virus had been created to target all Bluetooth networks. Dubbed "BlueBorne," the attack vector would allow "attackers to take control of devices ... and spread malware laterally to adjacent devices" (Armis 2017). BlueBorne spread across Bluetooth devices—smartphones, watches, tablets, speakers, fitness trackers, and even smart cars—searching for weak spots in these personal networks. At one point, it was reported that it could affect 8.2 billion units, the entire range of Bluetooth-enabled devices (Armis 2017). Google, Apple, and Microsoft dealt with the risk, and some immediately issued security patches to stop it in its tracks. But the BlueBorne event was noteworthy beyond the technical fix. Most people were completely unaware of the threat and potential disaster, and even more so, how it could harm them personally. Designed to be nearly invisible, the virus was developed to be infectious as it moved through the air, device to device over Wi-Fi with agility.

BlueBorne might have been even more dangerous if current proposals for new technologies called body area networks (BANs) had been in operation. BANs, or *body networks* (the term I will adopt for this chapter), are wireless network technologies designed for embodied devices. In this chapter, I discuss what happens when our bodies become platforms during the next computing revolution. Once networks are on and inside the body, collecting data from within, what would happen if body networks were attacked? Who would control these devices (and, by extension, ourselves)? What would happen to the people who rely on them? The BlueBorne event hints at a future of embodied computing, when immediate threats to our bodies will be hidden, and when data about human thoughts, emotions, vital signs, and movements can be uploaded and monitored. Connected to the internet, bodily information would be available to algorithms and actors who might be anonymous to us. One can imagine the positive possibilities with constant bodily monitoring ("auto-monitoring") for disease, for anxiety, for security. Yet, the negative possibilities are equally concerning (Catherwood, Finlay, and McLaughlin 2015; Jiang, Tan, and Liu 2018). The BlueBorne story notes obvious risks, but it also evokes the potential for profound societal change. As Shoshana Zuboff (2019) writes in *The Age of Surveillance Capitalism*, "automated machine processes not only know our behavior but also shape our behavior at scale" (7). I am suggesting we are on the brink of another significant turn that will shape our digital futures.

In earlier work, I contributed the term "continuum of embodiment" as a critical framework to explore the ideological justifications for technology hardware platforms that are increasingly embodied (Pedersen 2013). Framing the phenomenon as a continuum enabled me to write about how public, academic, journalistic, fictional, and commercialized discourses valorize prerelease personal technology on a continuum linking mobile to wearable to implantable innovations as a seemingly necessary, imminent, and determined future (Pedersen 2008, 2013). I made the argument that this is a ruse that contributes to a constant mediatization of lifestyle. Through popular public discourses or even through spectacles of wealth, marketers celebrate how mobile technology evolves to become wearable, a process that would then lay the groundwork (and expectations) for implantable technology as one exigent next step, with little or no consideration for how people will be dehumanized by it. Likewise, many scholars are now researching the biased, harmful social implications of artificial intelligence and algorithmic decision making, emphasizing that "computational methods are not inherently neutral and objective" (Whittaker 2018, 24). Embodied computing has advanced tremendously due to both euphoria over future tech imaginaries, on the one hand, and seemingly neutral science and technology descriptions that go unchallenged, on the other (Pedersen and Dupont 2017). It also develops against a backdrop of widespread biotechnical advancement, economic upheaval, social disruption, and mass automation through AI, under the hyped conditions that some refer to as the Fourth Industrial Revolution (*Economist* 2016).

In a sense, this book is about how the body is imposed upon to become a platform across a series of technologies that are increasingly interdependent. This chapter's focal point is the concept of body networks, and it brings critical attention to the mounting expectations that personal computing is going to achieve much more direct, bodily integration with automated processes. I look at body networks as a prerelease, preadoption computing paradigm to ask questions about how they will impact us in reontologized future environments. Early standards are being agreed upon and conventionalized (again in neutral, objective terms), and social science and humanities critiques are not included in the dialogue, to our detriment.

Critical Data Contexts

If topographical (*on* the body), visceral (*in* the body), and ambient (*around* the body) computing are to combine to function as an embodied ecosystem, body networks are the innovation that will bring about the change. Technologists are beginning to create systems to absorb bodily processes into more developed architectures that could eventually evolve to host mature platforms. The political economies of platforms have been exposed as sites for the purpose of driving profit for intermediaries at the expense of users and workers (Gillespie 2010; Gillespie 2018). The concept of platformatization is also relevant because it foregrounds the idea of programmability and the "material-technical perspective" that informs the business model behind platforms (Helmond 2015). I am concerned with how these networks will also make people's data vulnerable in myriad ways by treating the body as a platform and making bodily data further monetized. Following Fiore-Gartland and Neff (2016), I examine infrastructure-focused policy attempts to platformize the body "to examine the role that power plays in the discursive process of framing new technologies," including biosensing (101).

How will the platformized body create new sources of datafication? Mosco (2017) aptly calls the quantified self, the "commodified self" when talking about embedded body sensors on the rise in postinternet society (16). The related notion of "datafication" draws much attention from critical data studies circles (van Dijck 2014; Iliadis and Russo 2016; Lupton 2016; see Lupton's chapter in this collection). Hildebrandt (2014) defines "datafication" as "the process of translating the flux of life into discrete, machine-readable data points" (38). The "flux of life" imagery is apt for body networks that are designed for continuous or *flowing* data capture. If biosensors will be able to mine data from inside, they will further perpetuate how "the body functions dialectically as both a producer and recipient of data" (Smith 2016, 110). In this vein, Smith calls upon scholars to concentrate more work on what he terms the "embodiment–datafication–affective nexus" (Smith 2016, 114). Likewise, Nafus (2016) draws attention to instances where "social choices about biosensors are being made" (xii). The adoption of cloud applications for bodies, formalized as the idea of an Internet of People (IoP) or *human intranet*, is one such area of concern. As Moin et al. write, "A Human Intranet should seamlessly integrate an ever-increasing number of sensors, actuation, computation, storage, communication, and energy nodes located on, in, or around the human body, and acting in symbiosis with the functions provided by the body itself" (2017). In this model, the body takes on the labor of sensing, computing, energizing, storing (data), transmitting, and hosting a network, with a seemingly infinite capacity for expansion. It connotes the "ever-increasing" instrumentalization of humans through bodily functions.

Human–Machine Relationships

In 1967, Marshall McLuhan made a provocative comment in a famous interview: "Technologies are highly identifiable objects made by our own bodies." His scholarship helped launch the rich heritage of writing that treats bodies as media. In 1997, Frank Biocca tellingly asked, "Are media progressively embodying the user?" (3). Lombard and Ditton (1997) wrote about how embodied technologies such as virtual reality produce the feeling of nonmediated presence. They named that bodily feeling of simply *being there*, of feeling wholly present in virtual experiences (Lombard and Ditton 1997).

Embodiment, human–machine relationships and affective computing are broad areas that many have explored for a long time, contributing to a rich theoretical dialogue on interrelated topics (Picard 1997; Picard 2000; Hayles 1999; Hayles 2012; Hayles 2017; Clark and Chalmers 1998; Dourish 2001; Massumi 2002; Danesi 2008, Blackman 2012; Karppi 2018). Germane to this chapter are the concepts of *adoption* and *adaptation*. In a projected future, body networks will connect and report on such things as human thoughts, memories, and feelings, along with organ functionality, biochemistry, and brainwaves. Bodies will participate in cooperative relationships with other human and nonhuman actors and digital infrastructures. In simplified terms, these networks could make bodies adapt, respond, and communicate in combinations that are only now being discussed in the emerging field of human–machine communication (Guzman 2018). Body networks will hyperaccelerate embodied computing adoption, which in turn, instigates adaptation. Hayles (2012) posits that "contemporary technogenesis, like evolution in general, is not about progress ... [it] is about adaptation, the fit between organisms and their environments, recognizing that both sides of the engagement (human and technologies) are undergoing coordinated transformations" (81). In later work, Hayles (2017) contributes a redefinition of human cognition and digital interaction into three layers: "consciousness and unconsciousness," "nonconscious cognition," and "material processes" (69–76). The notion of "cognitive assemblages" recognizes how complex systems between "human and nonhuman cognizers" enlist both material and decision-making forces (269). Likewise, writing about implantable brain chips, Fitz and Reiner claim, "we have entered a transitional era in which we are commingling our cognitive space with technology" (2016, S9). Describing a variation of ambient computing, they speculate over a future cultural trajectory whereby device "comingling" will define identity.

Body Networks Defined

Wireless Body Area Networks (WBANs) or Body Area Networks (BANs) are body networks; They connect wireless sensors that can be sewn into clothing, placed directly on the skin, or implanted into the body. Body networks involve Human Body Communication (HBC) or intrabody communication that uses the body itself as the channel, rather than air for transfer. Currently in the prototyping stages, body networks will enable powerful convergences among technologies by providing a single unified solution for connectivity. They are meant to be safer (e.g., less radiation, lower power emission), faster (e.g., higher data rate with higher bandwidth), and much more data secure (Astrin, Li, and Kohno 2009). Topographical and visceral body networks would connect with each other for controlled data flows, able to translate life signs into data points.

The demand for them is a response to calls from many sectors for more sophisticated and safer kinds of connectivity for personal data capture, essentially something better than Bluetooth.

An example of a body network configuration for medical monitoring appears in figure 2.1. The first layer depicts a human data provider wearing topographical biosensor devices (e.g., EEG sensors). It also depicts a body network connecting all of the devices together. In theory, it could string together countless wearable and implantable sensors, some at the nanoscale. The second layer depicts handheld mobile devices for user manipulation or for transfer through a central processing unit to the third layer. In layer two, users might get a glimpse of their data, visualized for them through interfaces as it streams to the next layer. Layer three involves data analytics and "black box" data interpretation on external servers that filter, analyze, and make decisions based on data collected from the human subject. In the fourth layer, collected data are dispersed to multiple potential external actors that have remote access, including third-party platforms, in this case, health care providers. Information resides on a "medical

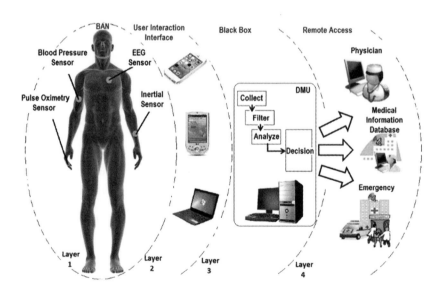

Figure 2.1
One example of an architecture of an eHealthcare system using a body network, or "BAN". (Ghamari et al. 2016) Creative Commons Attribution (CC-BY) license (http://creativecommons.org/licenses/by/4.0/).

information database" in this example, but it could go to government, corporate, academic, military, or numerous other types of data users.

There are countless visual depictions of body networks like this one on the internet; images usually focus on a solo body providing data, decontextualized from any social situation. The datasphere imagined for them is usually tied to health, sports, or entertainment, where people will enjoy some kind improved experience due to heightened connectivity. Further, these design schemata represent neutral relationships among technologies, people, governments, and corporations, as if the body is part of the platform. They do not reveal or portray power relationships, for instance, or the kinds of social bias increasingly "baked" into AI (Layer 3) during filtering, analyzing, and deciding by machines. They do not account for the way platforms are "sociotechnical assemblages" often used for profit by stakeholders (Gillespie 2018, 19). Body network architectures incorporate human subjects and vitalized bodies as mechanisms in larger dataspheres.

History

In an ongoing body networks case study, I collected more than 1,300 articles from the Association for Computing Machinery (ACM) digital library that reference body networks. The earliest mention, from 2001, explains: "These networks are also called Body Area Networks or Personal Area Networks. Unlike the mobile technologies mentioned above, they are not based on a fixed network infrastructure (e.g., base stations). The possibility of building up such networks in a spontaneous and fast way gave them the name ad hoc networks" (Eberspaecher, Bettstetter, and Vjogel 2001). Many of the current papers are from the annual International Conference on Body Area Networks ("BodyNets"), which self-describes its aim "to provide a world-leading and unique opportunity for bringing together researchers and practitioners from diverse disciplines to plan, analyze, design, build, deploy and experiment with/on Body Area Networks (BANs)." Academic papers usually emphasize urgent or legitimate needs such as saving lives, curing illness, and securing information; however, ideas creep into design cycles that go unchallenged, without a contextualized vision for future outcomes in myriad social spheres. They take future technology convergence as a given to justify a current stage of development. One paper opens with this sentiment, "In recent years, the Internet of Things

(IoT), cloud computing, and wireless body area networks (WBANs) have converged and become popular due to their potential to improve quality of life" (Ramu 2018). One might argue that they have *not* converged yet, but futuristic speculative events appear justified as a neutral given.

The wireless Bluetooth standard was invented in 1994 by Jaap Haartsen of Ericsson. Bluetooth advanced device connectivity dramatically; nearly all personal wireless devices today use Bluetooth (Ericsson 2012). However, Bluetooth has been deemed insufficient for the needs of body networks. The road to agreeing to any new international engineering standard is long. The governing organization is the Institute of Electrical and Electronics Engineers (IEEE). Its Internet networking standards committee, the "802," deliberates and eventually votes on the standards that govern protocols for networking of all kinds. The key focus for the 802.15.6 BAN standard is "for a short-range, low power, and highly reliable wireless communication for use in close proximity to, or inside, a human body" (Astrin, Li, and Kohno 2009). The BAN or body network standard forms part of the Personal Area Network standards PAN IEEE 802.15, which defined the original Bluetooth. But the intent now is to create networks for controlled, safe data flows to and from the body. Another concern is device interoperability, with the goal to ensure that a wide range of devices can connect to each other. Because biometrics are now used for authentication, for example, in place of passwords, personal data conveyed over a body network will need to incorporate much more robust encryption. 5G, or *fifth-generation*, network technology promises much higher and more efficient capacities to send data; body networks will become intergrated in the global movement for 5G networks to advance ehealth, smart cars, and connected homes.

Arthur "Art" Astrin, one of the pioneering architects of Wi-Fi, led the IEEE 802.15.6 task group that finally approved the standard, which was published in 2013 after a five-year consultation process (Computer History Museum 2016). In many ways, this event serves as a benchmark historical moment; many corporate representatives were concerned with data vulnerability, but also clearly wanted to further intensify data mining using sensing devices. Interestingly, Astrin gained his expertise by working for Apple, IBM, Siemens, ROLM, Memorex, and Citicorp. He was a key figure in the global mobile turn; some even say Astrin "birthed Wi-Fi" (Computer History Museum 2016).

In the year before his death, Astrin was interviewed by the *Computer History Museum* and he described the slow-moving process to pass the standard, discussing his personal goals for body networks (Computer History Museum 2016). He served as the IEEE chair at the start and explained that he was influenced by Ray Kurzweil's 2006 *The Singularity Is Near*, which Astrin says predicted "little robots going around in the body" (Computer History Museum 2016). Kurzweil's predictions fuel innovation in many sectors; they act as transhuman beacons that people race toward (Satell 2016). Astrin's role as standardizer brought an important ethos to the idea. Naming specific diseases that might be alleviated by these networks, Astrin's goal was to better the health and longevity of human subjects. However, he mentions the fact that large multinationals were also at the table with him, altering choices at the early stages for this standard. Tellingly, he points out that cyberthreats are a key concern—for example, that denial of service attacks could cause fatalities.

The Lure of Body Networks

The discourse analysis and narratives surrounding Astrin's work led me to frame three conceptual themes for why body networks are proposed as a desirable mediated future. These include approaching body networks as technologies for seamless computing, the dominance of data profiles, and the ruse of human–cloud infrastructures.

Seamlessness

Seamless interaction has developed into a value-based governing logic. It reveals itself through calls to make computing "friendly" or unified with other tasks, but it also appears through transgressions, when computing is fractured. Nick Bilton of *Vanity Fair* writes about social media's fractured activities:

> One of the problems is that these platforms act, in many ways, like drugs. Facebook, and every other social-media outlet, knows that all too well. Your phone vibrates a dozen times an hour with alerts about likes and comments and retweets and faves. The combined effect is one of just trying to suck you back in, so their numbers look better for their next quarterly earnings report. ... And then, there's the biggest reason why people are abandoning the platforms: the promise of connection has turned out to be a reality of division (Bilton 2017).

Bilton discusses the trend of abandoning social media. He points to the physical disruption social media provoke, goading people to participate despite the fractured or impoverished experiences they cause. Through his distaste, he also simultaneously reveals value-based expectations for personal computing, that it should involve efficient, continuous interactions. Seamlessness is also used to promote much more invasive technologies. Mikael Wiberg discusses the idea of using the body as interface: "No longer are peripherals a necessity for interacting with computers when gestures, our bodies, our eyes, our skin, our position, or even our fingertips can do the job for us" (Wiberg 2013). The drive for seamless, constant connection makes the assumption that the body will be the interface.

Skin-based computing is one hyped future-proposed, sensing technology that works along these lines (Rogers, Someya, and Huang 2010; Kim et al. 2011; Ma 2011; Boyle 2011). *Digital skin* is also known as "epidermal electronics" (Kim et al. 2011), "electronic skin" (Ma 2011), "smart skin," or "digital tattoos" (Boyle 2011). It resembles the temporary stick-on tattoos that children adhere to their bodies. But they are ultrathin, flexible devices intended to sense brain, heart, and skeletal activity and that promise to revolutionize medical biofeedback. Described by one team as having "superior flexibility and a mobility," another team notes their "sensing skin" breakthrough as "[having] key characteristics of artificial skin designed to sense touch or temperature" (Marks 2013). Yet, using human skin as the site for a computer interface is still very much in development. Preceding the adoption of skin interfaces are wearables that are normalizing the idea.

One current wearable, Hexoskin, is described as "a smart device that connects to a compatible high-tech intelligent garment with integrated sensors that captures body metrics including heart rate, breathing rate, and acceleration" (AZoSensors 2019). The Hexoskin intelligent shirt uses "skin" metaphorically. These are wearable interfaces and hardware that aspire to be more like skin by design. They entail covering the torso or a significant portion of the body. They seek to mine the body through topographical contact. However, the idea sometimes fractures the promise of seamlessness. Many applications still require users to log on to web dashboards and work with their data (see figure 2.2). The imagery of using "dashboards" for monitoring the body always strikes me as discordant; the user suddenly meets her own body the way a pilot meets a plane, a panel of instruments

Figure 2.2
Screenshot of the Hexoskin online dashboard demonstrating sleep metrics, © Isabel Pedersen

and controls in front of her to manipulate, making the body seem a disconnected vehicle.

With the coming era of body networks, the proposition is to progress seamlessness one more step, whereby the body *is* the channel (Astrin, Li, and Kohno 2009). The idea is to make bodily monitoring (like that of skin tech) and data transfer more active and direct.

Earlier in the chapter, I touched on emotion monitoring. Once a body network for brain–computer interaction (BCI) can be established, interactivity will evolve in dramatic ways. Cognitive experiences will not only be used for digital telepathy (i.e., moving computer interfaces with the brain), they could be stored by third parties, or they could be used in predictive models to draw conclusions about thoughts and feelings (Nick, Berman, and Barnehama 2015). Smith (2016) expresses the risk of the body as "a walking sensor platform":

> In a similar vein, but with different motivations in mind, Irma van der Ploeg points to how our implication in such processes of networked surveillance is initiating a new bodily ontology and politics, where bodies exist in a "symbiont" relationship with the digital data they produce. She notes how the notion of autonomy, of being able to freely decide an identity and trajectory, is increasingly contingent on the data profile one accrues and/or is assigned. (109)

Smith is not necessarily referring to cognitive sensors, but the premise applies. The concern is with data profiling and the kinds of surveillance that instigate a "'symbiont' relationship with the digital data they produce" (109). In keeping with this view, I think that body networks have been proposed as constituting symbiosis, but they also run the risk of parasitism through bodily data profiling. Seamless interaction with cognitive processes, if networked, would risk parasitic relationships where humans (i.e., thoughts, ideas, memories, lies, etc.) are the source for data, rather than positioning humans as the benefactor of seamless services.

Writing about the technocultural adoption of the internet of things, Nicholas Fitz and Peter Reiner also weigh in on the risk of achieving seamless interaction by assigning "intelligent objects" cognitive predictive tasks:

> As the Internet of Things gains momentum, we will find ourselves interacting with "intelligent" objects that predict our preferences and make decisions on our behalf. Ideally, delegation of these tasks to our devices would allow us to expend more energy pursuing challenging activities such as improving willpower and analytical thinking. ... But that is not how the human–technology connection is playing out. Instead, the same devices that extend some cognitive abilities degrade others (Fitz and Reimer 2016, S9).

Using predictive analytics to delegate tasks to achieve a seamless lifestyle might end up degrading human capacities. We need to ask if automated and networked biosurveillance initiatives are instigating a new bodily politic that we did not expect.

Discussed earlier, remote patient monitoring for disease control is a concept under discussion as technologies are imagined, designed, and developed (Vegesna et al. 2017; Hernandez 2014; DeAngelis 2015). The belief is that emerging technologies, network culture, and human and nonhuman processes of datafication will revolutionize healthcare and everyday life by directly sensing the body's core through passive monitoring (Hernandez

2014). To meet such a speculative scenario, brain, heart, skin, skeletal, and other topographical and visceral sensors would need to track biometric data continuously through biomedical telemetry. The bio-surveilled body would be datafied in numerous ways. Furthermore, connectivity would be of paramount concern because data would be sent to remote servers to be interpreted. Safer, more robust personal data infrastructures and body networks would be required to connect and transfer all the data. In this ambient and utopian scenario, algorithmic decisions would interpret "life signs" directly from inside the body. If one extrapolates from obvious and already proposed medical goals, then military, entertainment, and lifestyle will be inculcated with the same momentum for interconnectivity.

Bodywise, Data Profiles, and Surveillance

In this section, I point to another justification that is related to seamlessness, an ideology I call *bodywise*. Bodywise focuses on passive, continuous, tracking and quantifying of bodily functions, combined with the value system that assumes automated feedback is superior to human-interpreted information or human feelings. Bodywise is related to *dataism*, the belief in "objective quantification and potential tracking of all kinds of human behavior and sociality through online media technologies" (Van Djick 2014). However, bodywise takes the assumption a step further, whereby human intervention is seen as inept. Body networks are often justified as a more sophisticated means to collect biofeedback:

> As data sources of the BAN system, body sensors are used for collecting the vital signals of a user or patient. Based on these body signals, an accurate diagnosis can be obtained to give the patient correct and timely treatments. Traditionally, measurements via body sensors involve human intervention by medical staff. With the continuous advances in circuit design, signal processing, and Micro Electro-Mechanical Systems (MEMS), body sensory data can be collected in a non-invasive fashion. (Chen et al. 2011, 176)

In the proposed body network, human intervention is diminished as traditional in favor of a modern automated system. The rhetoric argues that directly collecting bodily data will be a better diagnosis paradigm. While monitoring patients with devices on the body has long been accepted as more illuminating, correct, and timely, this description mistrusts human doctors ("medical staff"). The patient is subordinate and objectified, while automated processes, coordinated by the BAN, have agency. Bodywise justifications maintain that body monitoring can and should be done by a network that yokes together a system of sensors, data to be transferred for analysis, and software for algorithmic decision making, rather than human medical professionals.

The more embodied technology becomes internalized, the more body-wise rhetoric will underpin justifications. For instance, ingestible technology is a new frontier under much development in the sphere of visceral computing, but one that is also meeting the public in popular science forums. The idea of swallowing a computer device (see Iliadis's chapter in this collection), allowing it to either act on or surveil the body from within, then to leave the body, is a tantalizing notion. The "chip in a pill," "digital drugs," or ingestible tech paradigm is unique because its effects are fleeting and invisible (Nikita 2014, 2). Ingestibles are often designed as antennas that require the omnidirectional ability to transmit signals as they float through the body (Kiourti and Nikita 2014, 210). They are intended to visualize, monitor, and diagnose internal processes such as blood pressure, PH balance, core body temperature (Nikita 2014), and ultimately report to an external receiver. One example is MicroCam, a tiny surveillance camera that uses "the body as a communication medium" (Nikita 2014, 18). In subtle bodywise terms, the intent is to constitute the body as data ready for transfer to external agents and corporate platforms.

Bodywise rhetoric also operates through the quantified self movement, which is proposed as a way to know the self by tracking one's own bodily processes, largely with personal wearable devices. However, others frame self-tracking in alternative terms: "A counter-argument to the empowering view of (self-)surveillance, however, is that emerging forms of self-tracking (e.g., in mHealth or other measurement apps) in combination with participation as a design principle could be seen as a facade or illusion of self-control, where actually users are being tracked and traced in the background" (Galič, Timan, and Koops 2017, 30). Infiltrating our lives through myriad devices, data processes create a paradoxical relationship with the self. Like a one-way mirror, information exchange goes on without our ability to fully grasp, follow, or understand it, much less determine it. In cyber-capitalism, algorithms make decisions for us, and computers filter what we read and what we buy (or consider buying), map our whereabouts, remember faces of people we know, and often inform our next move. For us, this leads to estrangement rather than cohesion because data processes are operating covertly. Paradoxically, quantified health/self applications report some information back to us with seemingly overt precision and clarity. In a sense, we are coming to terms with a new self—a datafied body—that negotiates itself differently with selective information.

I align the notion of bodywise with previous ideas concerning self-tracking. Paula Gardner and Barbara Jenkins note the reductionist nature of displayed biometric data when working with mobile devices (Gardner and Jenkins 2016). In a point made by Nora Young concerning the self-tracking movement, ambient awareness becomes an overt system of signs: "In our new digital lives, though, ambient awareness is achieved precisely by making explicit statements about how we are feeling and what we are doing. The digital realm required replacing that which is embodied and physical with that which is literal, specific, and disembodied" (Young 2012, 62). Things we used to simply feel or do are assigned meaning requiring us to *know* them, essentially disembodying them. Data produce a conflicting semiotic of self-awareness; signs are both covert and overt.

Smith (2016) proposes a useful vocabulary on data profiling involving surveillance, speaking of the "embodiment–surveillance nexus" and "the way in which the body functions dialectically as both a producer and recipient of data" in a form of "disembodied exhaust" and "embodied exhaustion" (110). By referring to data in this way, Smith pinpoints how our twinned roles as consumer and producer yoke the surveilled body into service. When advancing the notion of the embodiment–surveillance nexus, he also discusses sensor devices "in terms of their developing mass surveillance dragnets and a profusion of data flows" (115). Because body networks are proposed so that sensory data can be collected automatically from internally implanted sensors, they will be a core conduit for further bodily surveillance. But unlike Smith, I do not see a "bordered" body anymore. When a person ingests the surveillance device into her organs, the border disappears.

The implications will range into how people constitute selves and identity. Gillespie (2014) writes of data algorithms in a manner relevant to embodiment: "A sociological analysis must not conceive of algorithms as abstract, technical achievements, but must unpack the warm human and institutional choices that lie behind these cold mechanisms" (169). Gillespie goes on to write of the dual relationship we have with data providers: "digital providers are not just providing information to users, they are also providing users to their algorithms. And algorithms are made and remade in every instance of their use because every click, every query, changes the tool incrementally" (173). Both quotes are key. With cognitive computing, every thought or feeling will also "change the tool incrementally." With cognitive analyses made possible with brain-computer interaction and algorithms being written to interpret emotional interactions, embodied data will amount to a storing of self that is far more intrusive than anything seen before. Data profiling of our digital selves will expand to include deciphering of emotions by digitizing affect (Montero and Suhonen 2014; Jaques, Chen, and Picard 2015; Pedersen and DuPont 2017). Emotional profiling could be reductive and lead to decisions made for us by autonomous machines through artificial intelligence (AI) protocols. In the next section, I examine the concept of the *personal cloud* more closely.

Cloud Computing and Embodiment

Body networks emerge amid a culture that generally accepts cloud computing as a given. Historically, the concept of a personal cloud can be traced to several sources. One emerged from an Apple spin-off company called General Magic in the early 1990s. *Wired* writer Stephen Levy quotes developers Bill Atkinson and Andy Hertzfeld on the cloud concept in 1994, when personal digital assistants (PDAs) were first spawned:

> We have a dream of improving the lives of many millions of people by means of small, intimate life support systems that people carry with them everywhere. These systems will help people to organize their lives, to communicate with other people, and to access information of all kinds. They will be simple to use, and come in a wide range of models to fit every budget, need, and taste. They will change the way people live and communicate. (Levy 1994)

The dream of carrying "small, intimate life support systems" was an early primary goal. The desire to inhabit one's own computing cloud, inspired the development of early personal digital assistants. The idea of "access[ing] information of all kinds" is pivotal as it worked against the idea that devices should be geared to single task spheres such as work, fitness, or entertainment. A conceptual life support system was to sustain all needs. Over the twenty years that followed, cloud computing became popular.

In 2013, I attended the ACM Special Interest Group on Computer–Human Interaction (SIGCHI) conference in Paris.[1] The trend at that time was the confident belief that cloud computing could be combined with wearable computer devices to create a set of networking cloud applications that would surround an individual and mine her data—a personal or human cloud. And the trend was celebrated as a perfect business opportunity, one that Big Data would bring when human activities, opinions, bodily sensations, and thoughts could be digitized, data mined, and aggregated in profound ways to create a focused, personal, profit-generating data cloud. Conversation could breeze over the technicalities, which reduced and obfuscated questions about the algorithms that would need to be deployed to create this augmentation.

For example, in 2013, Rackspace released *The Human Cloud*. One paragraph framed the larger goal:

> With adoption becoming mainstream, wearable technology will form an integral part of the 'Internet of Things'—a growing network of devices—from wearable tech and smartphones to road traffic sensors—that connect to the internet to share data in real time. "The rich data created by wearable tech will drive the rise of the 'human cloud' of personal data," said Chris Brauer, co-director of CAST at Goldsmiths, University of London. "... with health insurance firms encouraging members to use wearable fitness devices to earn rewards for maintaining a healthier lifestyle. It is likely that the public sector will look to capitalise on the wearable technology trend with a view to boosting telehealth and smart city programs." (Rackspace 2013, 8)

This speculative model for a personal human cloud locates an imaginary subject as an ideal center, amid a network geared to surround her. Wearables, internet of things, and telehealth would eventually feed smart cities. Human wearers would be empowered to become healthy, but also goaded to work to create this cloud infrastructure, with a view to helping companies capitalize on it. Inculcated by institutions that would co-host it— "health insurance firms," "healthcare institutions," "third parties"—the human cloud would bind people to a transformed, utopian, commodity-driven, urban lifestyle.

A Wi-Fi network does not exist to funnel this kind of data from humans to third parties. Consequently, this passage serves marketing goals to help leverage innovation that marketers want; for example, "a growing network of devices—from wearable tech and smartphones to road traffic sensors" (Rackspace 2013). Interestingly, even in 2013, researchers had begun to deal with the rise (and ruse) of cloud computing and its trajectories.

At the same Paris 2013 SIGCHI conference, Bruno Latour delivered the closing keynote lecture to an audience of three thousand. The room was filled with HCI designers, developers, and engineering professors— individuals employed in creating embodied computing, such as wearables, smartphone apps, and personalized cloud computing platforms. Despite his academic fame in social science disciplines, Latour is not recognized in computer science to any great degree. One of Latour's many books, *Science in Action: How to Follow Scientists and Engineers through Society* (1987) has more than 23,000 citations in social sciences publications. Yet, the digital library of the world's largest educational and scientific computing society, ACM, only cites him nineteen times in total. At this conference, his was the voice of an outsider bringing social theory to computer scientists to explain a "conundrum" (ACM 2013). Latour went on to discuss the "oligopticon," a reverse panopticon as a form of governance assembled by the microstructures of computer surveillance and individual bodies acting as relational networks. An oligopticon involves governance consisting "of a set of partial vantage points from fixed positions with limited view sheds" (Galič, Timan, and Koops 2017). Latour's speech, aimed at a technical audience (many working in cloud computing), sought to reveal a fallacy in the notion of personal cloud. A computing cloud is simply an ideology that operates to promote more data collection for profit-generating entities, "collecting devices," socioeconomic practices, and networked surveillance infrastructure (ACM 2013). When discussed as business speculation, the cloud concentrates on the number of units that will be sold or the money that will be made, without much consideration for social, political, or economic implications for everyday citizens. Interpreted as speculation, however, personalized cloud applications stand to transform multiple spheres of life.

Increasingly, people are writing about digital citizenship in light of what Obar terms "the fallacy of data privacy self-management, or the misconception that digital citizens can be self-governing in a digital universe defined by Big Data" (2015, 2). He explains, "Even if we had the faculties and the system for data privacy self-management, the digital citizen has little time for data governance" (13). If we consider body networks along these lines, concepts such as privacy, safety, and data self-management change in fundamental ways, and we need to think about that at this stage, while we are standardizing technology. A body network that funnels personal data (cognitive and physiological) directly to data clouds needs considerable discussion; however, I point out that the desire to have "small, intimate life support systems that people carry with them everywhere" (Levy 1994) persists as such a captivating offer that it will likely overshadow people's hesitancy.

Conclusion

This chapter asked if the body will become a platform. I have explored body networks as a coming phenomenon promoted by technologists that needs critical attention at this stage. I have argued that they will be the glue to connect bodies and brains with the cloud through myriad embodied computing devices in the future. As society expects computing to be increasingly seamless, the idea of a networked body working autonomously through data assemblages seems less futuristic than before. A tandem concept is a value system that places more authenticity on machines reading and analyzing the body. Bodywise rhetoric serves as the rational underpinning for body networks. Finally, the neo-liberal broad acceptance of cloud computing makes body networks seem inevitable, the continuum of embodiment will meet the lofty goals proposed decades ago.

One thing this chapter has not discussed to any great extent is the impact of big tech companies and the sway they hold over technology adoption and adaptation. A quick catalogue of key people makes the point. Brain implants have been glorified by Elon Musk (see Orth's chapter in this collection) through the announcement of his new company, Neuralink, "for the uploading and downloading of thoughts to a computer" (Johnson 2017). In a video introduction to the early phase of his research, Musk explains the implants he calls "neural threads" and emphasizes their tiny size (CNET 2019). The video discusses the wireless connectivity that will be required to run the implanted tech to send data to a wearable called "the link" to be controlled through an "iPhone app" (CNET 2019), a setup that is essentially a body network. The video justifies the implant through a doctor-thyself rhetoric by encouraging people to be self-sufficient in configuring their own implants, rejecting "exotic programmers" in doctors' offices (CNET 2019). His other endeavor, the nonprofit OpenAI, originally claimed to be "building safe Artificial General Intelligence (AGI), and ensuring it leads to a good outcome for humans" (OpenAI 2017). OpenAI has since transformed into a for-profit company run by Sam Altman with significant investment from Microsoft (Metz 2019). The frenzy around AI is rapidly changing expectations of what computers can and will do. Digital life can be stored, counted, curated, shared, reexperienced, and reimagined as data on AI-fueled platforms. Even earlier, Sergey Brin was the front man for the announcement of Google Glass in 2012, which launched the wearable turn. Apple's Tim Cook regularly hosts spectacles at his developers' conferences and makes announcements that Apple Watch will make life better (CNBC 2017). The spectacle of Silicon Valley wealth obfuscates, challenges, and makes an already hailed public assume a positive outcome long before the reality of a development is even possible to chart.

Another topic that plays a role is cultural impetus. The popularity and commercial successes of wireless communication have also evolved expectations about how people understand human communication and the sharing of personal experiences. Vincent Mosco places the onus of this kind of innovation on the commercialized cloud, writing that "mastery of the Cloud is one of the primary reasons why Amazon, Google, Microsoft, Apple, and Facebook are the most valuable companies in the world" (2017, 20). Wireless devices have become much less clunky. Big headphones are no longer plugged into giant cell phones to augment listening. Apple's iPod/iPhone ecosystem changed all that awkwardness over the past decade. Apple sets cultural expectations for how wearable tech ought to look and act through its leading minimalist design philosophy (Wissinger 2017, 2; see Wissinger's chapter in this collection). Yet, ten years earlier than the first iPod release, Steve Mann defined wearables in several criteria including that a wearable should be "unrestrictive to the user: ambulatory, mobile, roving, 'you can do other things while using it,' e.g., you can type while jogging, etc." (Mann 1998). We are only now beginning to understand unrestrictive as a value for wearable interactivity.

Popular press is glorifying automation, algorithmic decision making, and deep learning by machines, despite critical questions over the opacity and ambiguity that surround these processes (Wachter, Mittelstadt, and Floridi 2017). Dourish (2016) points out that the concept of an algorithm has come to stand for much broader social issues than the scope of the original definition, noting the conflation of "algorithm" with "digital automation." Any discussion of network connectivity and future augmentation for humans is implicated in this rhetorical friction. Embodied computing is deeply contextualized in a moment absorbed in machine-centricity (e.g., machine automation, machine learning, AI decision making) that appears impervious to challenge. Another related, popular-culture factor is the collaboration between the military-industrial complex and American culture industries that glorify technology in films and videogames (Mirrlees 2016). Transhuman military ideologies promote fictional embodied computing devices across a wide range of film franchises, making them seem exciting and destined for real-world emergence.

Current hype touts a future that will transform the internet into an immersive landscape, a glossy new reality, where iPads will be chucked aside for full-body pointing, swiping, and scrolling of virtual components that will fill our physical spaces. Yet, the undercurrent is a place where we will passively offer data to invisible networks we host, where malicious actors threaten attacks, where our facial expressions, heartbeats, thoughts, feelings, memories, sensations, movements and ambitions will be exchanged across data spheres far beyond our total control.

Note

1. https://chi2013.acm.org/.

References

ACM. 2013. CHI 2013 Closing Plenary: Bruno Latour—From Aggregation to Navigation. Video, 56:48, March 5. https://youtu.be/VDr2qBVIQjI.

Armis. 2017. The Attack Vector "BlueBorne" Exposes Almost Every Connected Device. https://www.armis.com/blueborne/.

Astrin, Arthur, Huan-Bang Li, and Ryuji Kohno. 2009. Standardization for Body Area Networks. *IEICE Transactions on Communications* E92.B (2): 366–372. https://doi.org/10.1587/transcom.E92.B.366.

AZoSensors. 2019. Hexoskin. July 17. https://www.azosensors.com/suppliers.aspx?SupplierID=3795.

Bilton, Nick. 2017. The End of the Social Era Can't Come Soon Enough. *Vanity Fair*, November 23. https://www.vanityfair.com/news/2017/11/the-end-of-the-social-era-twitter-facebook-snapchat.

Biocca, Frank. 1997. The Cyborg's Dilemma: Progressive Embodiment in Virtual Environments. *Journal of Computer-Mediated Communication* 3 (2): 1–11. https://doi.org/10.1111/j.1083-6101.1997.tb00070.x.

Blackman, Lisa. 2012. *Immaterial Bodies: Affect, Embodiment, Mediation*. London: Sage.

Boyle, Rebecca. 2011. "Epidermal Electronics" Paste Peelable Circuitry on Your Skin, Just Like a Temporary Tattoo. *Popular Science*, August 12. https://www.popsci.com/science/article/2011-08/epidermal-electronics-paste-peelable-circuitry-your-skin-just-temporary-tattoo/.

Catherwood, P. A., D. D. Finlay, and J. A. D. McLaughlin. 2015. Subcutaneous Body Area Networks: A SWOT Analysis. Paper presented at the 2015 IEEE International Symposium on Technology in Society (ISTAS), Dublin, Ireland, November 11–12. https://doi.org/10.1109/ISTAS.2015.7439414.

Chen, Min, Sergio Gonzalez, Athanasios Vasilakos, Huasong Cao, and Victor C. Leung. 2011. Body Area Networks: A Survey. *Mobile Networks and Applications* 16 (2): 171–193. https://doi.org/10.1007/s11036-010-0260-8.

Clark, Andy, and David Chalmers. 1998. The Extended Mind. *Analysis* 58 (1): 7–19. https://doi.org/10.1093/analys/58.1.7.

CNBC. 2018. Tim Cook: Apple Watch No. 1 in the World. Video, 2:01, September 12. http://www.cnbc.com/video/2018/09/12/tim-cook-apple-watch-no-1-in-the-world.html.

CNET. 2019. Watch Elon Musk's Neuralink Presentation. Video, 18:28, July 17. https://youtu.be/lA77zsJ31nA.

Computer History Museum. 2016. Oral History of Arthur "Art" Astrin. Interview by Rich Redelfs and Marc Weber. Video, 2:51:32, April 12. https://youtu.be/Tj5NNxVwNwQ.

Danesi, Marcel. 2008. The Medium Is the Sign: Was McLuhan a Semiotician? *MediaTropes* 1:113–126. https://mediatropes.com/index.php/Mediatropes/article/view/1764.

DeAngelis, Stephen F. 2015. Patient Monitoring, Big Data, And the Future of Healthcare. *Wired*, August 6. http://www.wired.com/insights/2014/08/patient-monitoring-big-data-future-healthcare/.

Dourish, Paul. 2001. *Where the Action Is: The Foundations of Embodied Interaction*. Cambridge, MA: MIT Press.

Dourish, Paul. 2016. Algorithms and Their Others: Algorithmic Culture in Context. *Big Data & Society* 3 (2): 1–11. https://doi.org/10.1177%2F2053951716665128.

Eberspaecher, Joerg, Christian Bettstetter, and Hans-Jhorg Vhogel. 2001. *GSM: Switching, Services and Protocols*. 2nd ed. New York: John Wiley & Sons.

Ercisson. 2012. Bluetooth Inventor Nominated for Top European Honor. June 12. https://www.ericsson.com/en/news/2012/6/bluetooth-inventor-nominated-for-top-european-honor.

Fiore-Gartland, Brittany, and Gina Neff. 2016. Disruption and the Political Economy of Biosensor Data. In *Quantified: Biosensing Technologies in Everyday Life*, edited by Dawn Nafus, 101–122. Cambridge, MA: MIT Press.

Fitz, Nicholas S., and Peter B. Reiner. 2016. Perspective: Time to Expand the Mind. *Nature* 531 (S9). https://doi.org/10.1038/531S9a.

Galič, Maša, Tjerk Timan, and Bert-Jaap Koops. 2017. Bentham, Deleuze and Beyond: An Overview of Surveillance Theories from the Panopticon to Participation. *Philosophy & Technology* 30 (1): 9–37. https://doi.org/10.1007/s13347-016-0219-1.

Gardner, Paula, and Barbara Jenkins. 2016. Bodily Intra-actions with Biometric Devices. *Body & Society*, 22 (1): 3–30. https://doi.org/10.1177%2F1357034X15604030.

Ghamari, Mohammad, Balazs Janko, S. R. Sherratt, William Harwin, Robert Piechockic, and Cinna Soltanpur. 2016. A Survey on Wireless Body Area Networks for eHealthcare Systems in Residential Environments. *Sensors* 16 (6): 831. https://doi.org/10.3390/s16060831.

Gillespie, Tarleton. 2010. The Politics of "Platforms." *New Media and Society* 12 (3): 347–364. https://doi.org/10.1177%2F1461444809342738.

Gillespie, Tarleton. 2014. The Relevance of Algorithms. In *Media Technologies: Essays on Communication, Materiality, and Society*, edited by Tarleton Gillespie, Pablo J. Boczkowski, and Kirsten Foot, 167–194. Cambridge, MA: MIT Press.

Gillespie, Tarleton. 2018. *Custodians of the Internet: Platforms, Content Moderation, and the Hidden Decisions that Shape Social Media*. New Haven, CT: Yale University Press.

Guzman, Andrea L. 2018. Introduction: "What Is Human–Machine Communication, Anyway?" In *Human–Machine Communication: Rethinking Communication, Technology, and Ourselves*, edited by Andrea L. Guzman. New York: Peter Lang.

Hayles, N. Katherine. 1999. *How We Became Posthuman: Virtual Bodies in Cybernetics, Literature, and Informatics*. Chicago: University of Chicago Press.

Hayles, N. Katherine. 2012. *How We Think: Digital Media and Contemporary Technogenesis*. Chicago: University of Chicago.

Hayles, N. Katherine. 2017. *Unthought: The Power of the Cognitive Nonconscious*. Chicago: University of Chicago Press.

Helmond, Anne. 2015. The Platformization of the Web: Making Web Data Platform Ready. *Social Media + Society* 1 (2): 1–11. https://doi.org/10.1177/2056305115603080.

Hernandez, Daniella. 2014. Big Data Healthcare: The Pros and Cons of Remote Patient Monitoring. *MedCityNews*, March 10. https://medcitynews.com/2014/03/big-data-healthcare-pros-cons-remote-patient-monitoring/.

Hildebrant, Mireille. 2014. Location Data, Purpose Binding, and Contextual Integrity. In *Protection of Information and the Right to Privacy—A New Equilibrium?*, edited by Luciano Floridi. New York: Springer.

Iliadis, Andrew, and Federica Russo. 2016. Critical Data Studies: An Introduction. *Big Data & Society* 3 (2): 1–7. https://doi.org/10.1177%2F2053951716674238.

Jaques, Natasha, Weixuan Chen, and Rosalind W. Picard. 2015. SmileTracker: Automatically and Unobtrusively Recording Smiles and Their Context. Paper presented at the 33rd Annual ACM Conference on Human Factors in Computing Systems (CHI 2015), Seoul, Republic of Korea, April 18–23. https://doi.org/10.1145/2702613.2732708.

Jiang, Wenbin, Jin Tan, and William Liu. 2018. An Internal Node Reprogrammable Security Scheme Based on IEEE 802.15.6 in Wireless Body Area Networks. Paper presented at the 2nd International Conference on Telecommunications and Communication Engineering (ICTCE 2018), Beijing, China, November 28–30. https://doi.org/10.1145/3291842.3291862.

Johnson, Madeleine. 2017. What is Neuralink, Elon Musk's Brand New Company? Nasdaq, March 28. http://www.nasdaq.com/article/what-is-neuralink-elon-musks-brand-new-company-cm766902.

Karppi, Tero. 2018. *Disconnect: Facebook's Affective Bonds*. Minneapolis: University of Minnesota Press.

Kim, Dae-Hyeong, Nanshu Lu, Rui Ma, Yun-Soung Kim, Rak-Hwan Kim, Shuodao Wang, Jian Wu, Sang Min Won, Hu Tao, Ahmad Islam, Ki Jun Yu, Tae-il Kim, Raeed Chowdhury, Ming Ying, Lizhi Xu, Ming Li, Hyun-Joong Chung, Hohyun Keum, Martin McCormick, Ping Liu, Yong-Wei Zhang, Fiorenzo G. Omenetto, Yonggang Huang, Todd Coleman, and John A. Rogers. 2011. Epidermal Electronics. *Science* 333 (6044), 838–843. https://doi.org/10.1126/science.1206157.

Kiourti, Asimina, and Konstantina S. Nikita. 2014. Antennas and RF Communication. In *Handbook of Biomedical Telemetry*, edited by Konstantina S. Nikita, 209–251. Piscataway, NJ: IEEE Press.

Levy, Steven. 1994. Bill and Andy's Excellent Adventure II. *Wired*, April. https://www.wired.com/1994/04/general-magic/.

Lombard, Matthew, and Theresa Ditton. 1997. At the Heart of It All: The Concept of Presence. *Journal of Computer-Mediated Communication* 3 (2): JCMC321. https://doi.org/10.1111/j.1083-6101.1997.tb00072.x.

Lupton, Deborah. 2016. The Diverse Domains of Quantified Selves: Self-Tracking Modes and Dataveillance. *Economy and Society* 45 (1): 101–122. https://doi.org/10.1080/03085147.2016.1143726.

Ma, Zhenqiang. 2011. An Electronic Second Skin. *Science* 333 (6044): 830–831. https://doi.org/10.1126/science.1209094.

Mann, Steve. 1998. Wearable Computing As Means for Personal Empowerment. Keynote address presented at the International Conference on Wearable Computing, Fairfax, VA, USA, May 12–13. http://wearcam.org/icwckeynote.html.

Marks, Paul. 2013. Feather-light Sensors Are as Comfy as a Second Skin. *New Scientist*, July 24. https://www.newscientist.com/article/dn23932-feather-light-sensors-are-as-comfy-as-a-second-skin/.

Massumi, Brian. 2002. *Parables for the Virtual: Movement, Affect, Sensation*. Durham, NC: Duke University Press.

McLuhan, Marshall. 1967. The Hot and Cold Interview with Gerald Emanuel Stearn. In *McLuhan: Hot & Cool, A Critical Symposium*, edited by Gerald Emanuel Stearn. New York: Dial Press.

Metz, Cade. 2019. With $1 Billion from Microsoft, an A.I. Lab Wants to Mimic the Brain. *New York Times*, July 22. https://www.nytimes.com/2019/07/22/technology/open-ai-microsoft.html.

Mirrlees, Tanner. 2016. *Hearts and Mines: The US Empire's Culture Industry*. Vancouver: University of British Columbia Press.

Moin, Ali, Pierluigi Nuzzo, Alberto L. Sangiovanni-Vincentelli, and Jan M. Rabaey. 2017. Optimized Design of a Human Intranet Network. Paper presented at the 54th Annual Design Automation Conference 2017 (DAC '17), Austin, TX, USA, June 18–22. https://doi.org/10.1145/3061639.3062296.

Montero, Calkin Suero, and Jarkko Suhonen. 2014. Emotion analysis meets learning analytics: online learner profiling beyond numerical data. Paper presented at the 14th Koli Calling International Conference on Computing Education Research, Koli, Finland, November 20–23. https://doi.org/10.1145/2674683.2674699.

Mosco, Vincent. 2017. *Becoming Digital: Toward a Post-Internet Society*. Bingley, UK: Emerald.

Nafus, Dawn. 2016. Introduction. In *Quantified: Biosensing Technologies in Everyday Life*, edited by Dawn Nafus, ix–xxxi. Cambridge, MA: MIT Press.

Nick, Teresa A., Laura M. Berman, and Arye Z. Barnehama. 2015. Personalized Neuroscience: User Modeling of Cognitive Function and Brain Activity in the Cloud. Paper presented at the 10th EAI International Conference on Body Area Networks

(BodyNets '15), Sydney, NSW, Australia, September 28–30. https://doi.org/10.4108/eai.28-9-2015.2261443.

Nikita, Konstantina S., ed. 2014. *Handbook of Biomedical Telemetry*. Piscataway, NJ: IEEE Press.

Obar, Jonathan. 2015. Big Data and the Phantom Public: Walter Lippmann and the Fallacy of Data Privacy Self-Management. *Big Data & Society* (July–December): 1–16. https://doi.org/10.1177%2F2053951715608876.

OpenAI. 2017. *Join Open AI*. https://openai.com/jobs/.

Pedersen, Isabel. 2008. MyLifeBits, Augmented Memory, and a Rhetoric of Need. *Continuum: Journal of Media and Cultural Studies* 22 (3): 375–384. https://doi.org/10.1080/10304310801919429.

Pedersen, Isabel. 2013. *Ready to Wear: A Rhetoric of Wearable Computers and Reality-Shifting Media* Anderson, SC: Parlor Press.

Pedersen, Isabel, and Quinn DuPont. 2017. Tracking the Telepathic Sublime as a Phenomenon in a Digital Humanities Archive. *Digital Humanities Quarterly* 11 (4). http://www.digitalhumanities.org/dhq/vol/11/4/000344/000344.html.

Picard, R. W. 2000. Synthetic Emotion. *IEEE Computer Graphics and Applications* 20 (1): 52–53. https://doi.org/10.1109/38.814561.

Picard, Rosalind W. 1997. *Affective Computing*. Cambridge, MA: MIT Press.

Rackspace. 2013. The Human Cloud: Wearable Technology from Novelty to Productivity—A Social Study into the Impact of Wearable Technology. https://web.archive.org/web/20131125205847/http://www.rackspace.co.uk/sites/default/files/whitepapers/The_Human_Cloud_-_June_2013.pdf.

Ramu, Gandikota. 2018. A Secure Cloud Framework to Share EHRs Using Modified CP-ABE and the Attribute Bloom Filter. *Education and Information Technologies* 23 (5): 2213–2233. https://doi.org/10.1007/s10639-018-9713-7.

Rogers, John A., Takao Someya, Yonggang Huang. 2010. Materials and Mechanics for Stretchable Electronics. *Science* 327 (5973): 1603–1607. https://doi.org/10.1126/science.1182383.

Satell, Greg. 2016. 3 Reasons to Believe the Singularity Is Near. *Forbes*, June 3. https://www.forbes.com/sites/gregsatell/2016/06/03/3-reasons-to-believe-the-singularity-is-near/.

Smith, Gavin. 2016. Surveillance, Data and Embodiment: On the Work of Being Watched. *Body & Society* 22 (2): 108–139. https://doi.org/10.1177%2F1357034X15623622.

Economist. 2016. G Force. Review of *The Rise and Fall of American Growth: The US Standard of Living Since the Civil War*, by Robert Gordon. https://www.economist .com/books-and-arts/2016/01/07/g-force.

van Dijck, José. 2014. Datafication, Dataism and Dataveillance: Big Data between Scientific Paradigm and Ideology. *Surveillance & Society* 12 (2): 197–208. https:// doi.org/10.24908/ss.v12i2.4776.

Vegesna, Ashok, Melody Tran, Michele Angelaccio, and Steve Arcona. 2017. Remote Patient Monitoring via Non-invasive Digital Technologies: A Systematic Review. *Telemedicine Journal and e-Health* 23 (1): 3–17. https://doi.org/10.1089/tmj.2016.0051.

Wachter, Sandra, Brent Mittelstadt, and Luciano Floridi. 2017. Why a Right to Explanation of Automated Decision-Making Does Not Exist in the General Data Protection Regulation. *International Data Privacy Law* 7 (2): 76–99. https://doi.org/ 10.1093/idpl/ipx005.

Whittaker, Meredith, Kate Crawford, Roel Dobbe, Genevieve Fried, Elizabeth Kaziunas, Varoon Mathur, Sarah Myers West, Rashida Richardson, Jason Schultz, and Oscar Schwartz. 2018. *AI Now Report 2018*. New York: AI Now Institute. https:// ainowinstitute.org/AI_Now_2018_Report.pdf.

Wiberg, Mikael. 2013. An interFACE or to INTERface? On Joineries of Interactables. *Interactions* (blog), March 13. https://interactions.acm.org/blog/view/an -interface-or-to-interface-on-joineries-of-interactables.

Wissinger, Elizabeth. 2017. Wearable Tech, Bodies, and Gender. *Sociology Compass* 11 (11): e12514, 1–14. https://doi.org/10.1111/soc4.12514.

Young, Nora. 2012. *The Virtual Self: How Our Digital Lives Are Altering the World Around Us*. Toronto: McClelland and Stewart.

Zuboff, Shoshana. 2019. *The Age of Surveillance Capitalism*. New York: PublicAffairs.

3   Wearable Devices: Sociotechnical Imaginaries and Agential Capacities

Deborah Lupton

Introduction

In this chapter, I address the sociocultural dimensions of wearable devices: small, lightweight technologies that can be readily placed on human bodies as they move around in time and space. While wearable devices have not always been and need not be digital (examples are spectacles, pedometers, and prosthetic limbs), I focus here on the new range of wearables with embedded sensors that generate digital data that have emerged over the past decade, in concert with mobile smart devices and Wi-Fi technologies. These new digital wearable devices include bands that are worn on the wrist, leg, ankle, around the chest or forehead, smart rings, smartwatches, pendants, devices that can be clipped onto clothing or worn on helmets, smart clothing and footwear, headsets and smart glasses, headphones, ear buds and other ear wear, and medical devices such as hearing aids, smart contact lenses, and electronic skin patches. Some wearables offer digital displays so that wearers can view the data they collect. Many communicate wirelessly with apps on other smart devices, such as smartphones, tablet computers, and laptops.

Most wearables are marketed for voluntary use by individuals to engage in self-monitoring for health, wellbeing, sport, and fitness purposes. These devices monitor biometrics such as steps taken, energy expended, route traveled, body temperature, sleep patterns, body mass and composition, heart rate, stress levels, perspiration, and sexual activity. Some wearables have been designed for patients to use as part of at-home monitoring of chronic conditions such as high blood pressure, and for rehabilitation. Wearables are also used for console game playing, to take photographs or make videos, make payments, to monitor or protect workers, to communicate with others, to train elite sportspeople, listen to music, as part of fashion design, or for artistic endeavors. Some wearables can perform a multitude of functions. Smartwatches like Apple Watch, for example, act as self-tracking devices, but also work with smartphones to communicate notifications, messages, and alerts, and they can also be used to make transactions and payments and to play music.

Wearables are gradually moving into the workplace, educational institutions, and homes. Emergency service workers, members of the armed forces, or police officers may now wear digital devices to assist their work, including body-worn cameras in the case of police and devices to monitor heat and other environmental conditions for firefighters. Fitness-tracking bands are increasingly incorporated into workplace wellness programs. Devices such as smart eyewear are used in medical training. Different devices, including badges with radio frequency identification (RFID) chips, are used in some workplaces to monitor employees' movements as part of tracking how well they are performing. Some schools also require students to wear RFID badges. A range of wearable devices specifically tailored for children are available, including wristbands with GPS tracking so that their parents can be assured of their location, and others that encourage them to exercise. There is even an array of wearable devices for infants for use from birth onward, such ankle bands, socks, or onesies embedded with sensors that measure their movements and other biometrics such as heart rate, oxygen levels, and body temperature. At the other end of the age spectrum, elderly people are often encouraged to wear digital devices as part of "ageing in place" initiatives.

Many claims have been made for the potential of wearables in recent times—some of which are detailed later in this chapter. Media coverage, industry blogs and events, art and design exhibitions, and other public discussions have contributed to sociotechnical imaginaries about wearables. In this chapter, I adopt a feminist new materialism perspective to examine how the promises and affordances of wearable devices are articulated in sociotechnical imaginaries and are animated or closed off via agential capacities. I discuss the ways in which wearables come to matter in people's lives; or alternatively, fail to engage users and realize their agential capacities. This approach is underpinned by the understanding that when wearables come together with humans and other nonhuman actors, they generate dynamic human–nonhuman assemblages that create specific agential capacities that are distributed between the humans and nonhumans involved. From this perspective, agency is viewed as a relational force: a vitality that is continually generated with and through these assemblages.

The feminist new materialism perspective draws on a range of scholarship, including Merleau-Ponty, Spinoza, Deleuze and Guattari, and Latour. In this work, emphasis is placed on the entanglements of humans and nonhumans in what is considered to be a more-than-human world. The poststructuralist emphasis on language, discourse, and symbolic representation is enhanced by a turn toward the material: human embodied practices and interactions with objects, space, and place. Feminist new materialism, as espoused in the scholarship of Donna Haraway (2008, 2015, 2016), Karen Barad (2007, 2003), Jane Bennett (2010, 2004) and Rosi Braidotti (2013, 2002), emphasizes the micropolitics of embodied encounters of humans with nonhumans, and the ways in which all agents work together to generate agential capacities that impel and shape human action. From this perspective, humans are inextricably intertwined in the physical as well as symbolic contexts in which they live. Their bodies extend beyond the fleshly envelope into the environment, and the environment likewise colonizes their bodies. As such, humans are always inevitably "blended bodies" (a term employed by Pedersen and Iliadis in the introduction to this volume) as they gather with other humans and with nonhumans.

These scholars suggest analysing the micropolitics of these relationships between humans and nonhumans, involving identifying and tracing the agential capacities, affects, and vitalities that give meaning and power to them at the level of everyday mundane practices. This kind of analysis also involves looking at how actors affect each other, taking up the concept of affect as a vital force that has the power to act on other actors and assemblages. Bennett (2004, 348) uses the term "thing-power" to encapsulate these lively forces and agential capacities that are generated when humans are entangled with nonhumans.

None of the above scholars devotes much, if any, attention to digital devices or personal data materializations. However, there are clear implications of concepts such as thing-power, affective forces, and agential capacities for theorizing human experiences with wearables. When applied to the assemblages of flesh-device-data generated by wearable technologies, a feminist new materialist perspective can draw attention to the potentialities, challenges, and limitations offered by wearables as humans learn to live with and through them (Lupton 2019). From this position, wearable devices are conceptualised as objects that possess, generate, and distribute sensory and affective capacities. They can enhance features of embodiment; but also ignore or sideline other bodily capacities. The data generated by these devices can also be conceptualised as agential and lively, constantly changing and mutating as humans move through time and space with their devices (Lupton 2017).

Adopting this approach, I interpret the term "embodied computing" as involving all those devices with which humans come together in assemblages as they move through their daily lives. As more spatial environments become embedded with digital monitoring devices, people do not need to be wearing or carrying digital technologies to be part of these assemblages. Humans are part of embodied computing simply by being colocated in space with digital sensors. They may be encountering these technologies simultaneously with carrying other devices on their bodies, so that a multitude of technologies are gathering with humans. Many of these technologies are collecting and emitting digitized information that in turn contribute to human–data assemblages. They may be communicating with each other as part of the so-called internet of things, exchanging data about and making inferences and decisions for humans. The constantly changing and heterogeneous nature of these enactments, encounters, and assemblages are highlighted by feminist new materialism theory (Lupton 2018b, 2019, 2018a).

In what follows, some of these key features of wearable assemblages are examined. I begin with outlining the sociotechnical imaginaries that are frequently employed in public forums to give meaning to wearable devices. I go on to review research that has investigated the lived experiences of using wearables, identifying the agential capacities and affects that are central to these experiences. The discussion then moves to the lively data generated by these devices, and how people make sense of their personal information. The concluding section summarizes the major arguments developed in the chapter and outlines directions for further research.

Wearable Devices and Sociotechnical Imaginaries

Sociotechnical imaginaries are described by Jasanoff (2015, 4) as "collectively held, institutionally stabilized, and publicly performed visions of desirable futures, animated by shared understandings of forms of social life and social order attainable through, and supportive of, advances in science and technology." There are many sociotechnical imaginaries about wearables that are articulated in the popular media and industry outlets. Developers' websites and in app stores and other promotional material draw on and reproduce concepts of the ideal-type user to target their markets. They frequently articulate futurist and speculative promissory narratives, in which wearables are portrayed as offering novel possibilities (Encheva and Pedersen 2014; Pedersen 2013; Wilmott, Fraser, and Lammes 2017). Boosterish techno-utopian claims center on the opportunities for users to learn more about themselves and their bodies, be better motivated to make major behavioural changes, to solve problems (such as how to become fitter or more productive or better control their moods), generate insights into aspects of their lives and bodies that otherwise would be hidden or invisible, and in some cases, to find support and interactions with other device users (Fotopoulou and O'Riordan 2017, Berg 2017, Schüll 2016, Lupton 2016b, Wilmott, Fraser, and Lammes 2017). The playful capacities of some wearables are also often emphasized. These devices are frequently promoted as being fun and intriguing, helping to ludify elements of everyday life that might otherwise be experienced as tedious or hard work (Fotopoulou and O'Riordan 2017; Wilmott, Fraser, and Lammes 2017).

A strong pedagogical element is frequently incorporated into the design and promotion of wearables. They are portrayed by their developers and other promotors as conduits by which personal data are generated that users can then employ to make changes in their habits, improve their health and fitness levels, prevent or manage disease, alleviate anxieties or keep as a record of their lives. Thus, for example, when I reviewed various wearable technology developers' websites at the time of writing (2018), I noted that on the Fitbit website, the developers contended that using their devices "motivates you to reach your health and fitness goals" and can "help you exercise, eat, sleep & live better." On their website, the makers of the OURA smart ring for monitoring sleep claimed that using the ring "helps you understand how your lifestyle choices affect your sleep

& performance." The Jawbone UP team's website presented their fitness band and app as allowing people to "take charge" of their lives by building "better habits." Apple went so far as to claim that its Watch promotes "freedom" for its users, not only helping them to monitor their physical activities and receive a "nudge when you need it" to move more, but also to "stay in touch" with contacts and listen to motivating music. A tagline for the GoPro action camera on its website was "Wear it. Mount it. Love it," to "capture life in a whole new way." The developers of the Owlet Smart Sock to measure infants' heart rate and oxygen levels used the selling points that these socks provide parents "a better way to know" about their babies' well-being than their embodied observations, and therefore reassurance.

As these promotions suggest, wearables are directed at monitoring, recording, and enhancing human life itself. Underpinning all these claims and promises are the mobility and ease of use, the "always on" affordances and opportunities to optimize and improve the user's life that wearables offer. They suggest that the affordances of wearables can seduce users into sustained engagements with them, working with users to generate a set of agential capacities that "empower" users to make sustained changes in their habits and to experience life more fully and with greater confidence.

Many potential uses for and developments in wearables have been proposed by tech entrepreneurs. Gadi Amit, a designer who developed the Fitbit fitness tracker range, speculated in an interview conducted in 2014 that within a decade, most people would be wearing up to ten digital devices for monitoring their bodies and that could predict, for example, whether a heart attack, anxiety, or depression were imminent. He envisaged that these devices would become increasingly unobtrusive and incorporated into human bodies—more like implants than wearables. For Amit, the ultimate promissory narrative is that wearables can allow users to be more, rather than less, human by fulfilling their potential: "The ideal is that we will have more fulfilled emotional human life, where technology is just an assistant and allows us to be more personable, more human, giving us an ability to explore and enjoy life at ease" (quoted in Ryan 2014).

Artists and designers have also experimented with wearables as a means of stimulating reflection on the nature of human embodiment. For example, the "Eloquent Robes" interactive installation (Núñez-Pacheco and Loke 2014) featured fabric robes with an insert for a digital heart-rate monitor. When worn, the robe monitored the wearer's heart rate and sent data to a projector, which in turn projected colored lights onto the white robe in real time. Observers—and the wearer of the robe—could then see these lights as materializations of the wearer's heart rate. Participants were invited to compare their own heart-rate data materializations with other participants, as part of a reflective exercise about biofeedback and rendering previously invisible and private dimensions of the body into aesthetic visual displays.

The capacities of wearables to act as communicative devices to facilitate human relationships have also been explored. Designers who worked for the *New York Times* Labs experimented with prototypes of wearable devices that they dubbed "social wearables/augmentation." One example is Blush, an object worn like a broach that is designed "to highlight the moments when your online interests and offline behaviors overlap." Blush listens to conversations with and around the wearer, and lights up when the conversation refers to topics that the user has listed in an app developed by the same team, Curriculum. The idea of Blush is that it engages with the world around it, including the online interests of the wearer, as listed in the Curriculum app. When it reveals the online topics that interest the wearer when she or he is conversing face-to-face with others, it is bringing these interests into the face-to-face interaction (Feehan 2014).

It has further been suggested that wearables can be used to promote social causes. One initiative was the competition UNICEF ran for designers to generate ideas for what it calls "wearables for good," directed at improving the health and lives of children living in developing countries. The Wearables for Good Challenge website displays ideas by the winners, finalists, and some of the other competitors. These include a smart pendant that is first worn by a pregnant woman and then passed to her infant once it is born, used to record health and medical information such as vaccination and medication records, and a bracelet that can be dropped into water to purify it, which would also collect information about water quality (UNICEF 2017). Such initiatives represent a different perspective from those offered in most technological developer, start-up, and entrepreneurial discourses, in which the envisaged users of the wearables they are seeking to promote tend to be white, middle-class people who possess the cultural and economic capital to purchase and make use of these devices (Lupton 2016b; Schüll 2016).

A diverse range of techno-utopian and speculative imaginaries about the potential of wearables have therefore received public expression. Most of these are very positive about the benefits of wearables. These promotional imaginaries, therefore, draw on and attempt to generate affective forces, relational connections, and relational capacities when outlining the agential capacities of wearables. Underpinning many promotional narratives are suggestions that when people assemble with wearables, agential capacities will be generated that work to solve problems in people's lives, delight and enchant them by engaging them in playful relational connections with their bodies and other people, offer them greater control over risks such as poor health, and even contribute to the alleviation of socioeconomic disadvantage. Wearables are depicted as almost magical in their promised capacities to enhance people's lives.

In recent years, however, a counternarrative has emerged in market research reports and media coverage, in which the failure of wearables to reach predicted markets and to receive long-lasting use has been outlined. One market research report, for example, noted that among the people in the United States that the company had surveyed, one-third of consumers who have owned a wearable had stopped using the device within six months of receiving it (Ledger and McCaffrey 2014). Several other studies have reported on the apparent low interest by consumers in using self-tracking apps and wearable devices and how these devices have failed to meet developers' overly optimistic expectations in consumer adoption. Problems such as the cost of devices, their inaccuracy, and lack of interoperability have been highlighted in accounts of the failure of wearables and apps to reach their intended market (Patel, Asch, and Volpp 2015). Research has begun to appear that highlights lack of consumer enthusiasm for using wearables. For example, a study of Singaporean employees encouraged to use fitness trackers found that cash incentives motivated them to use the devices and increase their activity levels, but once these incentives stopped, use dropped away dramatically. No measurable health improvements were identified either, with or without incentives (Finkelstein et al. 2016).

Media reports have also noted the apparent decline of consumer interest in wearables, as revealed by sales and shipments figures. While sales for smartwatches such as Apple Watch appear to be healthy, the media have reported on the declining fortunes of one of the market leaders, Fitbit, and the slowing of growth in the wearable market for fitness trackers.

One example is an online news article published on the BBC News website, headlined "Has wearable tech had its day?" In the article, it is reported that smartwatch shipments are declining, and companies like Jawbone and Microsoft are leaving the wearable fitness tracker consumer market (Finley 2017).

Embodied Experiences of Using Wearable Devices

Empirical research that examines the ways in which people enact wearable devices offers some insights into how promotional imaginaries are taken up, resisted, reinterpreted, or rejected. From the feminist new material-ism perspective, humans are always imbricated within more-than-human assemblages that dynamically generate agential capacities as they move through the world and come into contact with different spaces and things (Lupton 2019). Wearables are intimate devices that are in constant physical contact with human bodies when they are used. They invite and generate affective forces and sensory-embodied engagements at numerous differ-ent levels. The first, and most obvious dimension, is that these devices are expressly designed to be worn on the body as prosthetics for registering and displaying bodily movements and functions. In addition, the personal data generated by these devices are themselves material objects that both record aspects of users' bodies and potentially work to change future bodily capaci-ties and attributes. Many wearables have an intended feedback mechanism, and have been designed accordingly as persuasive technologies, often seek-ing affective engagement as part of this function.

Some of these devices offer sensory engagements—sounds and haptic responses such as buzzes as well as data visualizations—which invite users to enter an interembodied and affective relationship. The Apple Watch, for instance, uses what Apple calls "taptics": signals that use force on the skin of the user to deliver feedback. Apple therefore promoted Watch on its release as "the most personal device we've ever created" (Colt 2014). Fur-thermore, wearables can become personalised via bodily contact with traces of the wearers' flesh and fluids—their sweat, skin flakes, blood, or bodily oils—or transformed in other ways through embodied contact—molding to the shape of the body part they touch, for example. Wearables' affordances mean that they can be brought into intimate embodied spaces that might otherwise be out of bounds for digital devices: the bed, the bathroom, the sexual encounter.

The very act of wearing a device itself enacts certain meanings and capacities. By placing a fitness band on the wrist, for example, a person is performing a type of subject position: the person who is interested in improving their fitness or learning about their body perhaps, or more broadly, the subject who wants to learn more about her or his body or who is conforming to the ideal of the responsible and entrepreneurial self (Lupton 2016b). Openly wearing such a device can provoke affective responses from others, including interest, intrigue, and excitement, particularly if the device is novel (Wilmott, Fraser, and Lammes 2017), but also disdain or even contempt. The experiences of Google with its Glass smart eyewear are salutary. Glass was announced by Google in 2012. It was heralded with much industry excitement (Encheva and Pedersen 2014) and media attention, with *Time* magazine nominating it as one of the best inventions of the year. Before its general release, Glass sets were sold to a limited number of "Glass Explorers" to test them. It soon became apparent that Glass wearers provoked negative reactions from onlookers. Glass wearers were viewed as "geeks," the headset appearing ridiculous and pretentious, with the term "Glassholes" used in some quarters to describe them. More seriously, others were concerned about being filmed by Glass wearers without their knowledge. Some public establishments began to ban Glass wearers. In the face of mounting criticism, in 2015 Google quietly shelved its plans to release the device to the general market (Swearingen 2015).

A growing body of literature, emerging mostly from human–computer interaction studies, sociology, and anthropology, has developed that examines people's experiences of using wearables. Researchers who have conducted interviews with long-term users of self-tracking devices have found that they often espouse the ideals of the self-responsibilized citizen, using these devices to exert a sense of control over their lives and to work toward self-improvement (Lupton and Smith 2018; Lupton 2018b). Some users refer to the pleasures of achieving a form of mindfulness and self-reflection in collecting and reviewing their data, or a way of resisting social norms or medical authority (Sharon and Zandbergen 2017; Lupton 2018b). A study using interviews with thirty people living in North America, Europe, and Asia who were long-term fitness-tracking device users (Fritz et al. 2014) found that most had integrated their devices deeply into their mundane routines. The metric feedback offered by the numbers about their physical activities was experienced as motivating, and, for most of these long-term users, had led to long-lasting behavior changes, such as walking more and sitting less. If they forgot to wear their device, these people were disappointed and frustrated that their physical activities were not being counted and recorded. They had become so accustomed to wearing them and constantly checking their data that it felt strange when they took them off. Many of these people, however, had lost their initial enthusiasm and excitement about the device as the novelty phase moved into routine use. They had learned from their devices how to estimate the steps they had taken that day, for example, or the calories they had expended.

Other researchers recruited seventeen people from a US-based technology company and invited them to purchase smart devices to use towards a goal they had identified for themselves (Lazar et al. 2015). Most participants chose health or fitness sensor devices, of which 80 percent were abandoned within two months. Like the habitual users in the study by Fritz and colleagues, the small number of participants in this study who persisted in using the wearable devices they had chosen did so because their devices had been successfully incorporated into their everyday routines and they had achieved some goals. Those people who had abandoned the use of their devices did so because it did not fit their self-perceptions, viewing the device as more appropriate for older people or for fitness fanatics, for example. Alternatively, they were not interested in the level of information the devices provided. The effort and time required to keep the devices charged or paired with their smartphone and to review the information they collected were also contributing factors to participants' decisions not to continue to use them. Several participants did not find the devices comfortable to wear on their bodies, particularly those who were unaccustomed to wearing jewellery or watches on their wrists, or who found devices like heart-rate monitors too tight around their chests, or who disliked the feeling of the devices becoming sweaty. For some people, the wearables were simply too obtrusive and obvious.

Understanding why people may relinquish use was the focus of research by Clawson and colleagues (2015). They reviewed advertisements for the sale of second-hand health-tracking devices on the US-based online classified-ad platform, Craigslist, to determine the reasons the sellers gave for not wanting them any longer. These researchers identified approximately 1,600 such advertisements over the course of one month. Analysis of the advertisements revealed that the sellers described many reasons for abandoning their devices. Some had been given the device as a gift rather than purchasing them, and therefore had not necessarily wanted to use the device in the first place. Others stated that they had achieved their goals in using the device and no longer needed it, while others were upgrading to a newer device or wanted to try a different fitness tracker—sometimes because their friends were using another type, and they wanted to try it too. The most common reason for abandonment, however, was a mismatch between the users' expectations and the capabilities of the device they had purchased. The researchers noted that a change in the user's life circumstances, such as a new baby, a new health condition, or meeting a fitness goal, was often provided as a reason for selling the device. They draw attention, therefore, to the dynamic and social elements of people's lives and the contexts in which they decide to take up wearable use and relinquish it.

Other studies have demonstrated that while using wearables for tracking fitness or activity levels may be motivating for some committed users, helping to spur them on, the metrics they generate can also be experienced as disappointing or shameful if users fail to reach goals or targets. Some people choose not to review their data while exercising because they may find their numbers discouraging or distracting (Patel and O'Kane 2015). People may also find that using a fitness-tracking device can diminish the enjoyment of exercise, rendering it more as work that must be productive rather than as a leisure activity enjoyed for its own sake (Etkin 2016). Our study of cyclists using self-tracking devices, including bike computers and wearables, to collect data on their rides (Sumartojo et al. 2016; Lupton et al. 2018) found that while the participants enjoyed the motivation and rewards they received from collecting and reviewing their data, incorporating these devices into everyday routines is a form of work. It requires people to ensure that they prepare their devices for tracking (for example, ensuring that they are charged, and that the GPS is working), remember to bring them on their cycling trips and turn them on. While some of these practices become habituated, and thus need little thought or attention, others require continual vigilance.

Wearable devices and their data can work to encourage users to take up and respond to defined values about what constitutes "health," "well-being," or "fitness." For example, Goodyear and colleagues (Goodyear, Kerner, and Quennerstedt 2019) found that the English school students in their study had oriented their ideas of physical fitness and health to the targets and norms set by the Fitbit they were using. The students asserted that they felt healthier if they met these targets and had often changed their habits to do so. They were encouraged to be competitive by comparing their Fitbit achievements with their friends who were also using the device. They commonly noted that they found the metrics generated by the device to be interesting and motivating when they first started using it. This interest and engagement were only sustained for a few weeks of the program, however. Some students quickly became bored with using the device, and in many cases, stopped. Others noted that if they began receiving notifications from the device that they had not met targets, they felt bad about themselves, which was another reason to give up using it. Some were resentful that the device did not adequately measure their physical activity or noted that it was quite easy to learn to "game" the device (by shaking one's hand while wearing the Fitbit, for example, to accumulate steps).

Autoethnographic accounts of using wearables have drawn attention to their ludic qualities and the pleasurable emotional rush of receiving notifications in the forms of haptic sensations, sounds, or visual imagery, or virtual rewards like badges (Fotopoulou and O'Riordan 2017; Wilmott, Fraser, and Lammes 2017). They have also highlighted some of the difficulties experienced in attempting to incorporate a smart device into the intimate domains of everyday life. Potential users may feel enchanted by the possibilities of a wearable device, but also disappointed, guilty, ashamed, or frustrated by its presence, if intended use is not achieved. These feelings were encountered in an autoethnographic study in which I was involved. My colleagues detailed their attempts to use the ŌURA smart ring, designed for wearing in bed to track sleep patterns. Despite their initial enthusiasm to try the ring, my colleagues unexpectedly experienced reluctance about wearing it in the intimate space of the bed (Salmela, Valtonen, and Lupton 2018).

Wearables can be experienced as disciplining devices. When fitness trackers are introduced in social settings in which people feel obligated or "pushed" (Lupton 2016a) to wear them, such as corporate wellness programs or competitions, the metrics generated can become a form of social currency and moral accounting (Gorm and Shklovski 2016). In contexts where people have little choice but to use wearables, such as workplaces or schools, they can feel resentful about the capacities for close surveillance these devices can exert. For example, the school students in Goodyear and colleagues' study (2019) experienced the Fitbit as another form of surveillance of their bodies by their teachers, and a way of pitting them against their peers. They resisted the use of the device as part of physical education at school, even while they accepted the norm of health and fitness established by the targets the device set. Moore's (2017) research on workers who were required to use wearables to track their productivity similarly found high levels of stress and dissatisfaction at being so closely monitored by their supervisors. Wearables can also bring work into other domains of life in an intrusive way: such as continual notifications about work emails on the Apple Watch when the wearer is attempting to enjoy a holiday (Wilmott, Fraser, and Lammes 2017).

As these studies demonstrate, the ubiquitous, mobile, and intimate affordances of wearables that are promoted so enthusiastically by their developers can be experienced as intrusive, or as a form of disciplinary surveillance. Furthermore, the agential capacities of playfulness, sensory engagement, and intimacy can become experienced as harassment. Here again, this research highlights the importance of the feminist new materialism's emphasis on affective forces and relational connections in opening or closing off agential capacities as these devices come together with humans.

Lively Data

In this more-than-human world of datafication, data are constantly on the move: generated, transmitted, used, and repurposed in different combinations (Lupton 2017). Digital data assemblages possess their own vitalities and forces (or "thing-power," in Bennett's words), requiring people who use wearables to monitor their bodies and lives to engage in another form of work: that of data sense-making (Lupton et al. 2018). When reviewing their data, people are continually making decisions about how accurate they are, how other conditions may have affected their metrics.

Thus, for example, in the study we conducted of cyclists using self-tracking devices to monitor their rides, we found that they considered such aspects as weather conditions, their state of health, or the type of bicycle they were using that day, and interpreted between the sensory engagements they experienced during their cycling trips and the information delivered by the wearable devices they were using (Lupton et al. 2018). Another ethnographic study of Swedish people using self-tracking wearables and apps similarly found that their data were understood in relation to the knowledge the participants already possessed through their bodily engagements with the world. The connections they were able to make between their bodily knowledge and the datafied knowledge contributed to how meaningful these data were (Fors and Pink 2017). As these studies demonstrate, the meaning of personal data generated by wearables, and what people can learn from them, is inextricably contextual and relational, for each wearable-user assemblage, and these conditions are always contingent and emergent.

The agential capacities of personal data to reveal aspects of people's lives to others offers another set of challenges for users. Most wearables are connected to cloud computing databases, extending people's personal data well beyond their bodies and into the internet. These data are open to use by third parties: the device developers and agencies to whom they may sell the data, and potentially surveillance agencies and cybercriminals. When data are transmitted from devices to cloud computing databases, and stored in digital archives, they are vulnerable to leakages, breaches, or hacking (Langley 2014; Shahmiri 2016). Different datasets about individuals can be combined to generate data profiles that can reveal many aspects of their lives and activities to a range of third parties, both legally and illicitly (Pasquale 2014).

Social research suggests that people who use devices like wearables to generate personal data are only just beginning to come to realize the almost limitless vital capacities of their information (for example, Chung et al. 2017; Patterson 2013). Across a range of studies I have conducted with Australian users of devices and apps that generated often very personal information about their bodies and lives (Lupton 2017; Lupton et al. 2018; Lupton and Smith 2018; Lupton 2018b, a), people were asked if they knew how the data that the device or app collected about them were used by others, and if they were concerned or worried about who might be viewing their data. Most people had spent little time thinking about these issues, reviewing terms and conditions or privacy policies for the devices and apps they used, or wondering how well their data were protected. They tended to view their personal data as having little value to others because of its mundane nature.

Conclusion

In this chapter, I have drawn on feminist new materialism theory to identify and analyze some of the interplays between key sociotechnical imaginaries and the affective forces, relational connections, and agential capacities of wearable devices. As I have shown, sociotechnical imaginaries make numerous claims for the potential of wearables. Empirical research of lived experiences demonstrates that the wearability of wearables, or the extent to which they can be seamlessly incorporated into embodied routines and "feel right," is vital to sustained use. Factors such as the device feeling uncomfortable on the body, looking unattractive, or not fitting well are important in whether a user will continue wearing it. But so too are the broader sociocultural meanings and contexts in which people purchase and use (or fail to use) wearables. Issues such as the spaces and places into which these devices are invited and how wearables participate in the wearer's social encounters and relational connections to things as well as other people, can all be important.

A range of agential capacities are created with and through these human–nonhuman assemblages. With human actors, these devices produce vital forces that contribute to a kind of thing-power. Simply wearing the device can enact subject positions that make people feel differently about themselves, potentially motivating them to behave differently. They can begin to align themselves to the norms and goals set by wearable software, striving to achieve the set values of health, productivity, or physical activity.

Wearables work with humans to generate flows of data about the user's body and activities. As I have shown, in some cases, viewing these data can motivate and inspire the device users, generating affective forces of pleasure, confidence, pride, and feelings of accomplishment when goals and targets are met, or when the numbers "look good." Their enactments of the wearable assemblage can inspire them to change their routines or maintain practices that work toward their goals. In other contexts, however, the sociotechnical imaginaries of these devices are not animated in everyday use. People may choose not to try them (as in the case of people who have been given unwanted devices as a gift) or may start to use them but find the devices disappointing because they are boring, inaccurate, or incur feelings of guilt or shame. These affective responses can also be understood as agential capacities, as they are relational forces generated by the wearable assemblage. Indeed, they may have the effect of motivating people to relinquish their use of wearables.

While an important body of literature has now been published on the lived experiences of using wearables, further research is required on how people make sense of the data generated by wearables and incorporate these data into their everyday lives. Drawing more attention toward what people make of the capacities of their lively data, as well as the other actors and agencies who are able to make use of or exploit that data, would also illuminate our understanding of the thing-power of wearables.

References

Barad, Karen. 2003. Posthumanist Performativity: Toward an Understanding of How Matter Comes to Matter. *Signs* 28 (3): 801–831. https://doi.org/10.1086/345321.

Barad, Karen. 2007. *Meeting the Universe Halfway: Quantum Physics and the Entanglement of Matter and Meaning.* Durham, NC: Duke University Press.

Bennett, Jane. 2004. The Force of Things: Steps toward an Ecology of Matter. *Political Theory* 32 (3): 347–372. https://doi.org/10.1177%2F0090591703260853.

Bennett, Jane. 2010. A Vitalist Stopover on the Way to a New Materialism. In *New Materialisms: Ontology, Agency and Politics*, edited by Diana Coole and Samantha Frost, 47–69. Durham, NC: Duke University Press.

Berg, Martin. 2017. Making sense with sensors: Self-tracking and the temporalities of wellbeing. *Digital Health* 3 (March 28). https://doi.org/10.1177/2055207617699767.

Braidotti, Rosi. 2002. *Metamorphoses: Towards a Materialist Theory of Becoming.* Cambridge: Polity.

Braidotti, Rosi. 2013. *The Posthuman.* Cambridge: Polity

Chung, Chia-Fang, Nanna Jensen, Irina A. Shklovski, and Sean Munson. 2017. Finding the Right Fit: Understanding Health Tracking in Workplace Wellness Programs. Paper presented at the 2017 CHI Conference on Human Factors in Computing Systems (CHI '17), Denver, CO, USA, May 6–11. https://doi.org/10.1145/3025453.3025510.

Clawson, James, Jessica A. Pater, Andrew D. Miller, Elizabeth D. Mynatt, and Lena Mamykina. 2015. No Longer Wearing: Investigating the Abandonment of Personal Health-Tracking Technologies on Craigslist. Paper presented at the 2015 ACM International Joint Conference on Pervasive and Ubiquitous Computing (UbiComp '15), Osaka, Japan, September 7–11. https://doi.org/10.1145/2750858.2807554.

Colt, Sam. 2014. Tim Cook Gave His Most In-Depth Interview to Date—Here's What He Said. *Business Insider Australia*, September 21. http://www.businessinsider.com.au/tim-cook-full-interview-with-charlie-rose-with-transcript-2014-9.

Encheva, Lyuba, and Isabel Pedersen. 2014. "One Day ...": Google's Project Glass, Integral Reality and Predictive Advertising. *Continuum* 28 (2): 235–246. https://doi.org/10.1080/10304312.2013.854874.

Etkin, Jordan. 2016. The Hidden Cost of Personal Quantification. *Journal of Consumer Research* 42 (6): 967–984. https://doi.org/10.1093/jcr/ucv095.

Feehan, Noah. 2014. Blush, a Social Wearable. *New York Times Labs*, January 15 http://blog.nytlabs.com/2014/01/15/blush-a-social-wearable/.

Finkelstein, Eric A., Benjamin A. Haaland, Marcel Bilger, Aarti Sahasranaman, Robert A. Sloan, Ei Ei Khaing Nang, and Kelly R. Evenson. 2016. Effectiveness of Activity Trackers with and without Incentives to Increase Physical Activity (TRIPPA): A Randomised Controlled Trial. *Lancet Diabetes & Endocrinology* 4 (12): 983–995. https://doi.org/10.1016/S2213-8587(16)30284-4.

Finley, Sarah. 2017. Is That Fitness Tracker You're Using a Waste of Money? *BBC News*, January 13. http://www.bbc.com/news/business-38594037.

Fors, Vaike, and Sarah Pink. 2017. Pedagogy as Possibility: Health Interventions as Digital Openness. *Social Sciences* 6 (2): 59. https://dx.doi.org/10.3390/socsci6020059.

Fotopoulou, Aristea, and Kate O'Riordan. 2017. Training to Self-Care: Fitness Tracking, Biopedagogy and the Healthy Consumer. *Health Sociology Review* 26 (1): 54–68. https://doi.org/10.1080/14461242.2016.1184582.

Fritz, Thomas, Elaine M. Huang, Gail C. Murphy, and Thomas Zimmermann. 2014. Persuasive Technology in the Real World: A Study of Long-Term Use of Activity Sensing Devices for Fitness. Paper presented at the SIGCHI Conference on Human Factors in Computing Systems (CHI '14), Toronto, ON, Canada, April 26–May 1. https://doi.org/10.1145/2556288.2557383.

Goodyear, Victoria A., Charlotte Kerner, and Mikael Quennerstedt. 2019. Young People's Uses of Wearable Healthy Lifestyle Technologies: Surveillance, Self-Surveillance and Resistance. *Sport, Education and Society* 24 (3): 212–225. https://doi.org/10.1080/13573322.2017.1375907.

Gorm, Nanna, and Irina Shklovski. 2016. Steps, Choices and Moral Accounting: Observations from a Step-Counting Campaign in the Workplace. Paper presented at the 19th ACM Conference on Computer-Supported Cooperative Work & Social Computing (CSCW '16), San Francisco, CA, USA, February 27–March 2. https://doi .org/10.1145/2818048.2819944.

Haraway, Donna. 2008. *When Species Meet.* Minneapolis: University of Minnesota Press.

Haraway, Donna. 2015. Anthropocene, Capitalocene, Plantationocene, Chthulucene: Making Kin. *Environmental Humanities* 6 (1): 159–165. https://doi.org/10.1215/ 22011919-3615934.

Haraway, Donna. 2016. *Staying with the Trouble: Making Kin in the Chthulucene.* Durham, NC: Duke University Press.

Jasanoff, Sheila. 2015. Future Imperfect: Science, Technology, and the Imaginations of Modernity. In *Dreamscapes of Modernity: Sociotechnical Imaginaries and the Fabrication of Power,* edited by Sheila Jasanoff and Sang-Hyun Kim, 1–33. Chicago: University of Chicago Press.

Langley, Matthew R. 2014. Hide Your Health: Addressing the New Privacy Problem of Consumer Wearables. *Georgetown Law Journal* 103 (6): 1641–1659. https:// georgetownlawjournal.org/articles/36/hide-your-health-addressing/pdf.

Lazar, Amanda, Christian Koehler, Joshua Tanenbaum, and David H. Nguyen. 2015. Why We Use and Abandon Smart Devices. Paper presented at the 2015 ACM International Joint Conference on Pervasive and Ubiquitous Computing (UbiComp '15), Osaka, Japan, September 7–11. https://doi.org/10.1145/2750858.2804288.

Ledger, Dan, and Daniel McCaffrey. 2014. *Inside Wearables: How the Science of Human Behavior Change Offers the Secret to Long-Term Engagement.* Published on Medium, April 21, 2017. https://medium.com/@endeavourprtnrs/inside-wearable-how-the -science-of-human-behavior-change-offers-the-secret-to-long-term-engagement -a15b3c7d4cf3.

Lupton, Deborah. 2016a. The Diverse Domains of Quantified Selves: Self-Tracking Modes and Dataveillance. *Economy and Society* 45 (1): 101–122. https://doi.org/ 10.1080/03085147.2016.1143726.

Lupton, Deborah. 2016b. *The Quantified Self: A Sociology of Self-Tracking.* Cambridge: Polity Press.

Lupton, Deborah. 2017. Personal Data Practices in the Age of Lively Data. In *Digital Sociologies,* edited by Jessie Daniels, Karen Gregory, and Tressie McMillan Cottom, 339–354. Bristol, UK: Policy Press.

Lupton, Deborah. 2018a. "Better Understanding about What's Going On": Young Australians' Use of Digital Technologies for Health and Fitness. *Sport, Education and Society.* Published online ahead of print. https://doi.org/10.1080/13573322.2018 .1555661.

Lupton, Deborah. 2018b. "I Just Want It to Be Done, Done, Done!" Food Tracking Apps, Affects, and Agential Capacities. *Multimodal Technologies and Interaction* 2 (2): 29. https://doi.org/10.3390/mti2020029.

Lupton, Deborah. 2019. The Thing-Power of the Human–App Health Assemblage: Thinking with Vital Materialism. *Social Theory & Health* 17 (2): 125–139. https:// doi.org/10.1057/s41285-019-00096-y.

Lupton, Deborah, Sarah Pink, Christine Heyes LaBond, and Shanti Sumartojo. 2018. Personal Data Contexts, Data Sense and Self-Tracking Cycling. *International Journal of Communication* 12:647–665. http://ijoc.org/index.php/ijoc/article/view/5925/2268.

Lupton, Deborah, and Gavin J. D. Smith. 2018. "A Much Better Person": The Agential Capacities of Self-Tracking Practices. In *Metric Culture: Ontologies of Self-Tracking Practices,* edited by Btihaj Ajana, 57–73. London: Emerald Publishing.

Moore, Phoebe. 2017. *The Quantified Self in Precarity: Work, Technology, and What Counts.* London: Routledge.

Núñez-Pacheco, Claudia, and Lian Loke. 2014. Aesthetic Resources for Technology-Mediated Bodily Self-Reflection: The Case of Eloquent Robes. Paper presented at the 26th Australian Computer–Human Interaction Conference (OzCHI '14), Sydney, NSW, Australia, December 2–5. https://doi.org/10.1145/2686612.2686613.

Pasquale, Frank. 2014. The Dark Market for Personal Data. *New York Times,* October 17. http://www.nytimes.com/2014/10/17/opinion/the-dark-market-for-personal -data.html.

Patel, Mitesh S., David A. Asch, and Kevin G. Volpp. 2015. Wearable Devices as Facilitators, Not Drivers, of Health Behavior Change. *Journal of the American Medical Association* 313 (5): 459–460. https://doi.org/10.1001/jama.2014.14781.

Patel, Misha, and Aisling Ann O'Kane. 2015. Contextual Influences on the Use and Non-use of Digital Technology While Exercising at the Gym. Paper presented at the 33rd Annual ACM Conference on Human Factors in Computing Systems (CHI '15). Seoul, Republic of Korea, April 18–23. https://doi.org/10.1145/2702123.2702384.

Patterson, Heather. 2013. Contextual Expectations of Privacy in Self-Generated Health Information Flows. Paper presented at the 41st Research Conference on Communication, Information, and Internet Policy. George Mason University School of Law, Arlington, VA, USA, September 27–29. http://papers.ssrn.com/sol3/papers .cfm?abstract_id=2242144.

Pedersen, Isabel. 2013. *Ready to Wear: A Rhetoric of Wearable Computers and Reality-Shifting Media*. Anderson, SC: Parlor Press.

Ryan, Janne. 2014. Gadi Amit on Designing Wearable Technology for the Quantified Self. *Radio National*, July 4. http://www.abc.net.au/radionational/programs/bydesign/gadi-amit-and-designing-for-the-quantitative-self/5572924.

Salmela, Tarja, Anu Valtonen, and Deborah Lupton. 2018. The Affective Circle of Harassment and Enchantment: Reflections on the ŌURA Ring as an Intimate Research Device. *Qualitative Inquiry* 25 (3): 260–270. https://doi.org/10.1177%2F1077800418801376.

Schüll, Natasha Dow. 2016. Data for Life: Wearable Technology and the Design of Self-Care. *BioSocieties* 11 (3): 317–333. https://doi.org/10.1057/biosoc.2015.47.

Shahmiri, Sara. 2016. Wearing Your Data on Your Sleeve: Wearables, the FTC, and the Privacy Implications of This New Technology. *Texas Review of Entertainment and Sports Law* 18 (1): 25–48. https://heinonline.org/HOL/P?h=hein.journals/tresl18&i=35.

Sharon, Tamar, and Dorien Zandbergen. 2017. From Data Fetishism to Quantifying Selves: Self-Tracking Practices and the Other Values of Data. *New Media & Society* 19 (11): 1695–1709. https://doi.org/10.1177%2F1461444816636090.

Sumartojo, Shanti, Sarah Pink, Deborah Lupton, and Christine Heyes LaBond. 2016. The Affective Intensities of Datafied Space. *Emotion, Space and Society* 21: 33–40. https://doi.org/10.1016/j.emospa.2016.10.004.

Swearingen, Jake. 2015. How the Camera Doomed Google Glass. *Atlantic*, January 15. https://www.theatlantic.com/technology/archive/2015/01/how-the-camera-doomed-google-glass/384570/.

UNICEF. 2017. Wearables for Good Catalogue. http://wearablesforgood.com/catalogue/.

Wilmott, Clancy, Emma Fraser, and Sybille Lammes. 2017. "I Am He. I Am He. Siri Rules": Work and Play with the Apple Watch. *European Journal of Cultural Studies* 21 (1): 78–95. https://doi.org/10.1177%2F1367549417705605.

4 Cyborg Experiments and Hybrid Beings

Kevin Warwick

Introduction

A cyborg is an entity made up of a biological and technological integration. Today the most common example of this is the merging together of a human with embedded technology of some kind into a new overall being. This, of course, raises issues as to the corresponding percentages of human and machine that make up the novel creature. Importantly, in a cyborg, a human and technology become an integrated system with capabilities different to and beyond the norm for a human.

Some people, such as the notable academic and anthropologist Gregory Bateson, regarded a blind person wielding a cane (Bateson 1972) as a cyborg, or a person with a hearing aid, or even someone who has benefitted from a hip replacement. There are many reported cases in which a person with a disability, who is aided by technology, is subsequently referred to as being a cyborg (Kafer 2013; Ellcessor 2017; Sparkes et al. 2018; Singer et al. 2019). In each of these cases, the technology is helping the individual overcome a self-identified problem. Recently there have also been many researchers in the field of wearable computers who have claimed to be cyborgs (Pentland 1998), the technology in this case being worn on the body.

We have seen numerous intrusions of technology into the human body. Cochlear implants and heart pacemakers are both commonplace and involve technology being readily accepted by the individual as being a necessary intrusion to enable them to have a richer existence in life. The individuals generally welcome the technology that is implanted because of the effects it has on their life.

In most of these examples—and there are many more, such as deep brain stimulation for those affected by Parkinson's disease (Camara et al. 2015)—the modifications are aimed at overcoming a problem (Hayles 1999). Any surgeons or medical personnel involved desire to implant all that can possibly be implanted and have no percutaneous wires, mainly to reduce the possibility of infection. This tends to reinforce an individual's concept of their own body and what it is capable of. The result for the individual is that when technology is implanted in their body, then they feel that that technology is a part of them. Conversely, when the enabling technology (such as a watch) is external to the body, then the person does generally not regard it, or anyone else for that matter, as being part of the individual.

The situation becomes much more difficult when technology is employed to enhance nonmedical bodily functions. Many examples of this already exist in terms of external devices, particularly in the military domain, such as infrared night sight incorporated into weapon-sighting systems or voice-controlled firing mechanisms introduced into the helmet of a fighter pilot. In her influential work (1985), Donna Haraway discussed these issues as part of the disruption of traditional categories. Cyborgs of this type, if indeed they are cyborgs, would appear to violate the human–machine distinction. The author disagrees here with Haraway, unless the technology is implanted, in which case he concurs completely. What I mean by this is that it's rather like someone riding a bicycle. They can move faster in certain circumstances, but they are still a human riding a bicycle. Perhaps their brain alters to some limited extent because of their ability, but it is still a human brain. However, when technology is implanted into the body, particularly into their nervous system or brain, their concept of selfhood changes. In this case, the individual has certain abilities, not some separate piece of technology.

Cyborgs represent a powerful ethical dilemma when an individual's consciousness is modified by the merging of human and machine. Essentially, it is not so much the physical enhancements or repairs that should be treated as cases for concern, but rather where the nature of an individual is changed by the linking of human and machine mental functioning. In the case of a human, this means linking technology directly with the human brain or nervous system, rather than by a connection that is either external to the nervous system but internal to the body, or even one that is external to both.

A range of cyborgs are considered in this chapter, chief among them being one in which the cyborg is formed by a human (or at least animal) and machine brain–nervous system coupling. Although this does refer to a relatively narrow definition with respect to all cyborg possibilities, many of the arguments that follow are dependent on such a definition. The critical point is that the brain is involved in the transition, rather than any modifications merely in the form of some physical addition.

Connections between technology and the human nervous system not only affect an individual person, raising questions as to the meanings of "I" and "self," but they also directly influence autonomy. An individual human being wearing a pair of glasses, whether they contain a computer or not, remains an autonomous being. Meanwhile a human whose nervous system is linked to a computer not only raises questions as to the concept of their individuality but also, when the computer is part of a network or at least connected to a network, allows their autonomy to be compromised.

It is this latter class of hybrid being that is of interest in this chapter. The main question arising from this discourse being: when an individual's consciousness is based on a part-human, part-machine nervous system, when they exhibit a hybrid form of consciousness, will they still hold to human values? This is acknowledging that machine consciousness is somewhat different from human consciousness, partly because of the structures and materials involved. Or rather, will hybrid beings hold values and an ethical standpoint that is more in keeping with their hybrid nature? Will such cyborg beings in the future regard humans, in a Nietzschean way (Nietzsche 1961), rather akin to how humans presently regard cows or chimpanzees?

On the other hand, some may prefer to look through Hollywood-style, philosophical pink glasses and see cyborgs as being "conducive to the long-range survival of humans" (Haraway 1985). It will be the cyborgs themselves, however, that will make the ultimate pro-human, anti-human decisions. Rather than humans surviving, as Haraway puts it, cyborgs will supersede them as predicted in various science-fiction scenarios (e.g., Parsons 2006; Nathanael 2019).

BrainGate Experiments

One type of human brain–computer interface, namely deep brain stimulation, employs electrodes for therapeutic purposes, to overcome the effects of Parkinson's disease (Pinter et al. 1999; Wu et al. 2010). Conversely, the possibility of using such interfaces for enhancement is not only an enticing prospect, but it could be a vitally important feature in the future.

The therapy versus enhancement question is not a simple one. In some cases, those who have suffered an amputation or sustained a spinal injury from an accident are able to regain control of devices via their (still functioning) neural signals (Donoghue et al. 2004). Meanwhile, stroke patients can be given limited control of their surroundings, as indeed can people with conditions such as motor neurone disease (Warwick 2013a; Warwick 2013b).

The situation is not straightforward in these cases, as everyone is given abilities that no human originally possesses; for example, the ability to move a cursor around on a computer screen using neural signals alone (Kennedy et al. 2004). The same question is encountered when it comes to blind individuals who could benefit from some extrasensory input, for instance, as is discussed further in this chapter, from a sonar system based on the same principle as bat echolocation: it does not repair their blindness but it allows them to make use of an alternative sense (Warwick 2013a).

Some interesting human research has been carried out using the micro-electrode array known as the Utah Array, now commercially referred to as the BrainGate. The individual electrodes (one hundred of them) are 1.5 mm long and taper to a tip with a diameter of less than 90 μm. This can be positioned directly in the brain or peripheral nervous system, enabling neural signals to be monitored and sensory signals to be applied as stimulation. Electrical activity from a few neurons monitored by the array electrodes has been decoded into a signal to direct cursor movements. This enabled an individual to position a cursor on a computer screen using neural signals for control in combination with visual feedback. The same technique was later deployed to allow the same individual recipient, who was paralysed, to operate a robot arm (Hochberg et al. 2006; Hochberg et al. 2012).

Recently the BrainGate implant was employed to enable a paralyzed individual to regain some control over his own arm (Bouton et al. 2016). A 24-year-old man who has a C5 paralysis due to a swimming accident received the BrainGate in his motor cortex, this being connected via a computer to a sleeve containing muscle-stimulating electrodes, allowing him to learn to move his own wrist and fingers to a limited extent.

The array in these cases has been used in merely a recording role for therapeutic purposes only. However, the first (in a chronological sense) use of the microelectrode array (shown in figure 4.1) has, I believe, considerably broader implications for attempts to extend the human recipient's capabilities.

Essentially this is what I am referring to when I talk about a cyborg—a human (myself) whose nervous system is directly linked to a computer network to form a hybrid being. In this way, an individual's capabilities can be considerably enhanced. I specifically chose to implant the BrainGate as it opened up the possibility of directly interfacing the nervous system/brain with a computer and hence the internet. Although some therapeutic possibilities were clearly in the cards, my main aim was to experiment into some human enhancements. To be clear, I did not need the implant for therapy myself, but rather it was implanted for scientific purposes.

The BrainGate microelectrode array was implanted into the median nerve fibres of a healthy human individual (me) in the course of two

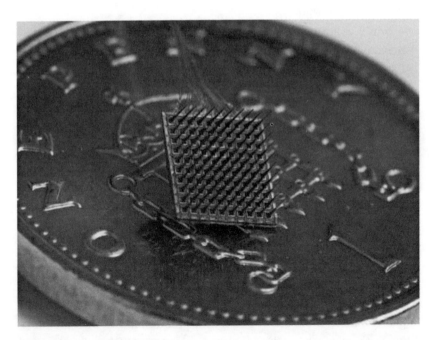

Figure 4.1
A one-hundred-electrode, 4 × 4 mm microelectrode array (BrainGate), shown on a UK one-pence piece for scale.

hours of neurosurgery at the Radcliffe hospital in Oxford, in order to test bidirectional functionality in a series of experiments. Stimulation current applied directly into my nervous system allowed information to be transmitted, while (motor) control signals were decoded from neural activity in the region of the electrodes (Warwick et al. 2003). Essentially, in this trial both efferent (motor) and afferent (sensory) signals were employed, thereby allowing for direct feedback. During the one-hundred-day implantation, a number of experimental trials were undertaken successfully using this setup (Warwick et al. 2004):

- Extrasensory (ultrasonic) input was successfully implemented.

- Extended control of a robotic hand across the internet was achieved, with feedback from the robotic hand's fingertips being sent back as neural stimulation to give a simple sense of force/grasp being applied to an object (this was achieved between Columbia University, New York (USA), and the University of Reading, England). This shows that an entity's brain and body can be in completely different places, merely connected by a network.

- A primitive form of telegraphic communication directly between the nervous systems of two humans (my wife assisted) was performed; see figure 4.2. When connecting brains directly in the same way this would become a form of thought communication.

- A wheelchair was successfully driven around, and speed controlled by means of neural signals alone using a simple menu interface.

- The color of jewelry was changed as a result of neural signals—also the behavior of a collection of small robots.

In most, if not all, of the above cases, the trial could be described as useful for purely therapeutic reasons, for example, the ultrasonic sensory input might be of use to an individual who is blind as was mentioned before, whereas telegraphic communication might be beneficial to people with certain forms of motor neurone disease. Each trial can, however, also be a potential form of enhancement beyond the human norm for an individual, what some refer to as Transhumanism. Indeed, I did not need to have the implant for medical reasons to overcome a problem; rather, the experimentation was carried out purely for the purposes of scientific exploration. It is therefore necessary to consider how far things should be taken.

Figure 4.2
My wife and I experimenting with neural implants for communication.

Human enhancement with the aid of brain–computer interfaces introduces all sorts of new technological and intellectual opportunities, but it also throws up a variety of different ethical concerns that need to be addressed (Warwick 2013a). While it might be reasonably expected that the vast majority of people are perfectly happy for interfaces of this kind to be used in therapy, it can be argued that the picture is not as clear when it comes to enhancement. But individual freedom must also be taken into account. If someone wants to stick a pin in their nose or finger, that is a matter for them. Should the situation be any different if they want to stick a hundred pins in their brain, even if it endows them with additional abilities?

Biohacking

The next area considered here is the use of implant technology for a variety of nonmedical purposes. The first of these is the implantation of a radio frequency identification device (RFID) as a form of identity. The device transmits by radio a sequence of pulses that represent a unique number/ code. The number can be preprogrammed to function rather like a PIN number on a credit card. If someone has an implant of this type, when it is activated the code can be checked by computer and the identity of the carrier thereby determined.

This type of device is in fact considered to some extent in chapter 5. However, I was the first human to experiment by implanting the technology, and for me it provided the impetus and reasoning that led on to my own BrainGate experiments, which I have just described. I therefore felt it critical to share this with you.

Such implants have already been used as a fashion item; to gain access to nightclubs in Barcelona and Rotterdam (the Baja Beach Club); as a high security device for the Mexican government; or as a source of medical information, having been approved in 2004 by the US Food and Drug Administration (Graafstra 2007; Foster and Jaeger 2007). Information about the medication an individual requires for conditions such as diabetes can be stored on the implant. Because it is implanted, the details cannot be forgotten, the record cannot be lost, and it will not easily be stolen.

An RFID implant does not have its own battery. It incorporates an antenna and a microchip enclosed in a silicon/glass capsule. The antenna picks up power remotely when it passes close to a larger coil of wire that carries an electric current. The power picked up by the antenna in the implant is used to transmit the number encoded on the microchip.

The size of the device, particularly the antenna, dictates the distance the implant needs to be from an energising coil in order to operate. If the implant is the size of a grain of rice, as many are nowadays, thereby enabling implantation simply by means of an injection, the coil needs to be placed adjacent to the implant, as closely as possible. With an implant of several centimeters in length, however, it's quite possible for successful pickup to occur over distances of one to two meters from the coil. Since there is neither a battery nor any moving parts, the implant requires no maintenance (Warwick 2013c).

Back in 1998, my university department was housed in what we had made into an intelligent building. With a smart card it was possible to cause events to occur under computer control at particular doorways. We found some RFID technology that could potentially be implanted, although it wasn't at all designed as an implant. The basis was that the RFID device would have the same effect as a smart card, but would, of course, be implanted.

As a result, an RFID implant was put in place in a human (me) for the first time on August 24, 1998, at Reading, England (see figure 4.3). It measured 22 mm long with a 4-mm diameter cylinder. The doctor who carried out the procedure, George Boulos, burrowed a hole in my upper left arm, pushed the implant into the hole, and closed the incision with two stitches.

The reason for selecting my upper left arm for the implant was that we were not sure how well it would work. We reasoned that, if the implant was not working well, I could easily wave my arm around in the hope that a stronger signal would be transmitted. The decision to place it in my arm was based on practical reasoning. It is therefore interesting that most

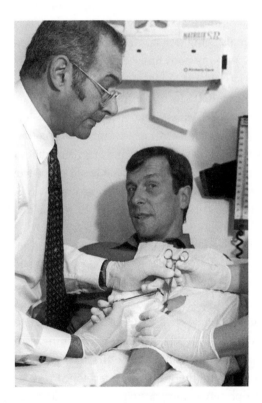

Figure 4.3
Author receiving an RFID implant (before James Bond!).

present-day RFID implants in humans are located in a similar place (the left arm or hand). In the James Bond film *Casino Royale* (the 2006 remake), even James Bond himself, played by Daniel Craig, had such a device implanted into his left arm (Warwick 2013c).

The RFID implant allowed me to control lights, open doors, and be welcomed with a "Hello" whenever entering the front door (Warwick and Gasson 2006). An implant of this kind could be used in humans for a variety of identification purposes—for example, as a credit card, a car key, or (as is already the case with some animals) a passport. As for potential future uses, it's really the point that whatever society is prepared or wishes to accept, combined with commercial development, will happen rather than usage and take-up being dependant on technological factors.

For me it meant that external signals were energizing the implant, and the implant in my body was responding by sending signals back to the computer. The follow-on from this, in my thinking, was "Okay, so what about changing the signals being transmitted from my body, and why could not the signals going into my body affect me in some way?" This led on to the use of the BrainGate, as just reported, which did exactly that.

As a follow-on to RFID technology, the use of implant technology to monitor people opens up a considerable range of issues. It is now realistic to talk of tracking individuals by means of implants using the Global Positioning System, a wide area network, or even a mobile telephone network. From an ethical point of view, it raises considerable questions when it is children, the elderly (e.g., those with dementia), or prisoners who are subjected to tracking, even though this might be deemed to be beneficial (Warwick and Gasson 2006).

Some related technology is described in the work of Neil Harbisson, who is color-blind. His work was originally referred to as the "Eyeborg" project. The technology developed involved a head-mounted sensor that translates color frequencies into sound frequencies (Ronchi 2009). Initially, Harbisson memorized the frequencies related to each color, but later he decided to permanently attach the eyeborg to his head, meaning a small camera faces forward from over his forehead and is connected to the back of his skull by a metal bar. Eventually, the project was developed further so that Harbisson was able to perceive color saturation as well as color hues. Software was then developed that enabled Harbisson to perceive up to 360 different hues through microtones and saturation through different volume levels (Harbisson 2008).

Another "Eyeborg" project has been carried out by Rob Spence, who replaced one of his eyes with an eyeball-shaped video camera. The prosthetic eye contains a wireless transmitter that sends real-time color video to a remote display. Spence lost his original right eye when playing with a gun on his grandfather's farm at the age of thirteen. He subsequently decided to build a miniature camera fitted inside his false eye.

The camera is not connected to his optic nerve and has not restored his vision in any way. Instead, it is used to record what is in his line of sight. The current model is low resolution, and the transmitter is weak, meaning that a receiving antenna has to be held against his cheek to get a good signal. A better-performance, higher-resolution model, complete with a stronger transmitter and receiver, is under development.

It is also well worth including here subdermal magnetic implants (Hameed et al. 2010). The procedure involves the controlled stimulation of mechanoreceptors in the finger by an implanted magnet manipulated through an external electromagnetic coil. Essentially any nonhuman sense can potentially be transformed into a touchy-feely sensation for an individual. For example, a blind person can have an accurate sense of distance to objects.

Both magnetic field strength and sensitivity are therefore important. However, implantation means that implant durability is an important requirement. Permanent magnets retain their magnetic strength over a long period of time and are robust to survive testing conditions. This restricts the type of magnet that can be considered for implantation. Hard ferrite, neodymium, and alnico magnets are available, inexpensive, and have been found, through appropriate testing, to be suitable for this purpose.

The magnetic strength contributes to the amount of agitation the implant undergoes in response to an external magnetic field and also determines the strength of the field that is present around the implant location. The skin on the human hand contains many low-threshold mechanoreceptors that allow humans to experience the shape, size, and texture of objects in the physical world through touch. The highest density of mechanoreceptors is found in the fingertips, especially those of the index and middle fingers. They are most sensitive to frequencies in the 200–300 Hz range.

The pads of the middle and ring fingers are the preferred sites for magnet implantation in the experiments that have been reported (Hameed et al. 2010). An interface containing a coil mounted on a wire frame and wrapped around each finger was designed for the generation of the magnetic fields to stimulate movement of the magnet within the finger. The general idea is that the output from an external sensor is used to control the current in the coil. As the signals detected by the external sensor change, they affect the amount of vibration experienced through the magnet (Warwick 2013c).

Experiments have been carried out in many application areas (Hameed et al. 2010; Harrison et al. 2018). The author has thus far supervised three research students who have received such implants, the first of whom was Jawish Hameed. Ultrasonic range information involves an ultrasonic sensor for navigation assistance. Distance information is encoded via the ultrasonic sensor as variations in the frequency of pulses. The mechanism constitutes a practical means of supplying accurate information about an individual's surroundings for navigational assistance.

An external ultrasonic sensor is attached to a coil of wire, which is wrapped around a finger containing an implanted permanent magnet. The output from the sensor dictates the current in the coil. As an object comes closer to the sensor, the current in the coil increases, causing the magnet to vibrate more fiercely in the finger. The individual involved can thereby feel the distance to objects. One potential position of the sensor(s) is on the brim of a baseball cap, as shown in figure 4.4, giving the individual an alternative distance-measuring system, very useful of course if the individual was blind as mentioned earlier.

Another sensor tested was an infrared detector. When operated in the same fashion as that just described for an ultrasonic sensor, it means that the temperature of objects dictates how much the magnet vibrates in the individual's finger. By pointing the infrared sensor at an object, the individual can "feel" how hot an object is even though it is quite remote.

Deep Brain Stimulation

An alternative treatment for Parkinson's disease using deep brain stimulation (DBS) started to be feasible when the relevant electrode technology became available from the late 1980/1990s onwards. Since then, some

Figure 4.4
Jawish Hameed using ultrasonics to stimulate his implanted magnet.

neurosurgeons have implanted neurostimulators connected to deep brain electrodes positioned in the thalamus, subthalamus, or globus pallidus of the brain to treat tremors, dystonia, and pain, as shown in figure 4.5.

A deep brain stimulation device contains an electrode lead with four or six cylindrical electrodes at different depths attached to an implanted pulse generator (IPG), which is surgically positioned below the collarbone. DBS has many advantages, for example, it is reversible. It is also much less dangerous than lesioning, and is highly successful in many cases (Warwick 2013c).

Ongoing research is aimed at developing an "intelligent" stimulator (Wu et al. 2010). Using an artificial intelligence network, this stimulator predicts when the tremors will begin (Warwick 2013c) so that the stimulator only needs to generate signals occasionally rather than continuously, thus operating in a similar fashion to a heart pacemaker. The job of the artificial intelligence system is to monitor the normal functioning of the human brain so that the system can accurately predict the onset of a Parkinson tremor,

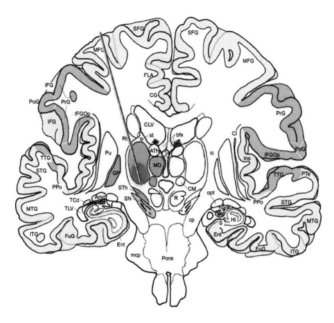

Figure 4.5
Positioning of DBS electrodes for Parkinson's disease.

several seconds before it actually occurs. In other words, the system's job is to outthink the human brain and stop it from doing what it "normally" wants to do (Warwick 2013c). Using artificial intelligence, however, it is also possible to model parts of the human brain and accurately characterize the type of functioning (in an electrical sense) in the brain. This is being used to provide a surgeon with extra information on the type of Parkinson's disease that each person has (Camara et al. 2019). However, ultimately it could be used directly to interact between the human brain and an external source, with the AI controlling brain functioning.

Another good and related example in terms of therapy is the work of Todd Kuiken (Kuiken et al. 2009). The first beneficiary of his technique was Jesse Sullivan, hailed in the media as the world's first "Bionic Man," who lost both of his arms as a result of an accident he sustained during his work as a high-power electrical lineman. His arms were replaced with robotic prosthetics so that he was able to control merely by thinking about using his original arms in the normal way. The method involved taking nerves that originally ran to Sullivan's arm and reconnecting them to muscles in his chest. When he thought about lifting an arm, for example, muscles in his chest contracted instead of muscles in the original arm. Electrodes connected externally on the chest muscles caused the prosthetic arm replacement to interpret such contractions as instructions to move in a particular way.

The technology described in this section has enormous potential for application in a broad spectrum of different fields. As an example, DBS can also be employed to overcome clinical depression. But restricting this technology to therapeutic purposes limits the need for philosophical and ethical argument. Conversely extending the scope for its application opens up numerous possibilities. For example, employing such methods to make individuals happy (by overcoming depression) draws attention to the possibility of recreational uses. Perhaps the most significant option would be their use to overcome negative character traits, and not merely to deal with bad habits or brain malfunctioning.

Growing Brains

Neurons can be cultured/grown under laboratory conditions on an array of noninvasive electrodes (in a small dish-like bowl). This can then be used to provide an attractive alternative to computer or human control with which to both construct a robot controller and investigate the operation of connected neurons over a substantial time period. The neurons connect to communicate with each other, and the resulting brain they create can be employed as the controlling device.

An experimental control platform, essentially a robot body, can move around within a defined area purely under the control of such a network/brain, and the effects of the brain, controlling the body, can be observed (Warwick et al. 2010a; Warwick et al. 2010b). So, a brain is grown and, when it is merely a few days old, it is given a body that allows it to sense the world around it and to move around in the world. Its capabilities therefore depend very much on what sort of robot body it is given.

Of course, this is interesting from a robotics perspective, but it also opens a different approach to the study of the development of the brain itself because of its sensory motor embodiment. This method allows investigations to be carried out into memory formation and reward/punishment scenarios—the elements that underpin the basic functioning of a brain (Warwick 2013b).

In most cases, the growth of networks of brain cells (typically around 100,000 to 150,000) in vitro involves first separating neurons obtained from foetal rodent cortical tissue. They are then grown (cultured) in a specialized chamber, where they can be provided with suitable environmental conditions (e.g., kept at an appropriate temperature of 37°C) and fed with a mixture of minerals and nutrients. An array of electrodes embedded in the base of the chamber (a flat multielectrode array, or MEA), as shown in figure 4.6, acts as a bidirectional electrical interface to and from the culture. This allows electrical signals to be delivered in order to stimulate the culture and also recordings to be made of the outputs from the culture (Xydas et al. 2011).

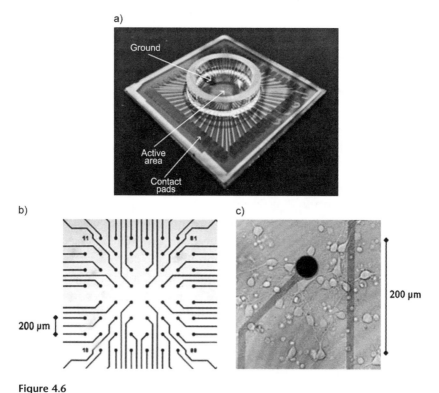

Figure 4.6
(a) A multielectrode array (MEA) showing the electrodes. (b) Electrodes in the center of the MEA seen under an optical microscope. (c) An MEA at ×40 magnification, showing neuronal cells in close proximity to an electrode.

The neurons in such cultures spontaneously connect, communicate, and develop, giving useful responses within a few weeks (after maybe 10 days) and typically continuing to do so for, at present, three months. The brain is grown in a glass specimen chamber lined with a flat 8 × 8 multielectrode array, which can be used for real-time recordings. This makes it possible to distinguish the firings of small groups of neurons by monitoring the output signals on the electrodes. A picture of the entire network's global activity can be formed in this way. It is also possible to electrically stimulate the culture via any of the electrodes to induce neural activity. In consequence, the multielectrode array forms a bidirectional interface with the cultured neurons (Chiappalone et al. 2007; DeMarse et al. 2001).

The cultured brain can then be coupled to a physical robot body (Warwick et al. 2010b); see figure 4.7. Sensory data fed back from the robot are subsequently delivered to the culture, thereby closing the robot–culture loop. In consequence, the processing of signals can be broken down into two discrete sections: (a) "culture to robot," in which live neuronal activity is used as the decision-making mechanism for robot control, and (b) "robot to culture," which involves an input-mapping process from the robot sensor to stimulate the culture (Xydas et al. 2011).

The actual number of neurons in a brain depends on natural density variations that arise when the culture is seeded in the first place. The electrochemical activity of the culture is sampled, and this is used as input to the robot's wheels. Meanwhile, the robot's (ultrasonic) sensor readings are converted into stimulation signals received as input by the culture, thereby closing the loop (Warwick 2013a).

Once the brain has grown on the array for several days, during which time it forms some elementary neural connections, an existing neuronal pathway through the culture is identified by searching for strong relationships between pairs of electrodes. These pairs are defined as those electrode combinations in which neurons close to one electrode respond to stimulation from the other electrode at which the stimulus was applied more than 60 percent of the time, and respond no more than 20 percent of the time to stimulation on any other electrode.

A rough input–output response map of the culture can then be created by cycling through the electrodes in turn. In this way, a suitable input/output electrode pair can be chosen to provide an initial decision-making pathway for the robot. Essentially the electrodes are poled to determine which electrodes the strongest passageways in the brain have developed between in the early development of the culture. This setup is then employed to control the robot body, for example, if the ultrasonic sensor is active, and we wish the response to cause the robot to turn away from an object that is located ultrasonically (possibly a wall) in order to keep moving (Warwick 2013c).

For experimental purposes, the intention is for the robot to follow a forward path until it reaches a wall, at which point the front sonar value decreases below a certain threshold, triggering a stimulating pulse. If the responding/output electrode registers activity, the robot turns to avoid the wall. In experiments, the robot turns spontaneously whenever activity is registered on the response electrode. The most relevant result is the occurrence of the chain of events: wall detection–stimulation–response. From a neurological perspective, of course, it is also interesting to speculate why there is activity on the response electrode when no stimulating pulse has been applied (Warwick 2013a).

As an overall control element for direction and wall avoidance, the cultured brain acts as the sole decision-making entity within the feedback loop. Clearly, the neural pathway changes that take place over time in the culture between the stimulating and recording electrodes are then an important aspect of the system. From a research point of view, investigations of learning and memory are generally at an early stage. However, the robot can be clearly seen to improve its performance over time in terms of its wall avoidance ability, in the sense that neuronal pathways that bring about a satisfactory action tend to strengthen purely though the process of habitually performing these activities—an example of learning due to habit (Hebb 1949).

However, the number of variables involved is considerable, and the plasticity process, which occurs over quite a period, is dependent on factors such as initial seeding and growth near electrodes as well as environmental transients such as temperature and humidity. Learning by reinforcement—rewarding good actions and punishing bad—is currently a major issue for research in this field (Warwick 2013a).

On many occasions the culture responds as expected, on other occasions it does not, and in some cases, it provides a motor signal when it is not expected to do so. But does it "intentionally" make a decision different from the one we would have expected? We cannot tell, but merely guess.

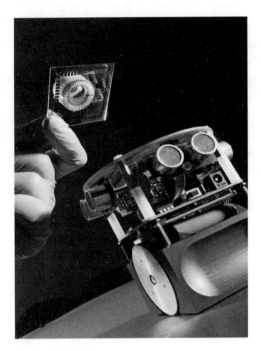

Figure 4.7
Brain and body—mobile robot shown in proximity to its cultured brain.

When it comes to robotics, it has been shown by this research that a robot can successfully have a biological brain with which to make its "decisions." The size of such a brain—100,000–150,000 neurons—is dictated purely by the limitations on the experimentation described. Three-dimensional structures are already being investigated and these permit the creation of cultures of up to 60 million neurons (Warwick 2013a).

The potential of such (rat brain robot) systems, including the range of tasks they can deal with, means that the physical body can take on different forms. It also can be assumed that such cultures will become larger, potentially growing to sizes of billions of neurons. On top of this, the nature of the neurons may be diversified. At present, rat neurons are generally employed in studies. However, human neurons are also being cultured, giving rise to a robot with a human neuron brain. If this brain then consists of billions of neurons, many social and ethical questions will need to be asked (Warwick 2010), especially regarding the rights of such creatures.

This type of cyborg is a hybrid of a biological brain and a technological robot body. One interesting question is whether or not such a brain is, or could be, conscious. Some, including the philosopher John Searle (Searle 1990), have concluded that consciousness is an emergent property; essentially, it is sufficient to put enough human neurons together with a high degree of connectivity, and consciousness will emerge. In the light of this argument, there is no reason robots with biological brains composed of sufficient numbers of human neurons should not be conscious. However, this leads to all sorts of follow on questions. For example, if a robot of this kind committed a crime, then who would be responsible—the robot itself?

Conclusions

Some argue that linking technology with humankind can merely be seen as humans acting as eccentric living beings. Any view of the appearance of superhumans can be seen as unwarranted "metaphysical" speculation (Coolen 2001). On the other hand, it could be felt that humankind is itself at stake (Warwick 1998; Cerqui 2001). A viewpoint can then be taken that either it is perfectly acceptable to upgrade humans with all the enhanced capabilities that this offers (Warwick 2002), or conversely it can be felt that humankind is just fine as it is and should not be tampered with (Cerqui 2001).

My own feelings are that, with the increasing pace and power of artificial intelligence and intelligent robots, upgrading humankind may be felt to be a necessary alternative. If you can't beat them, join them so to speak (Warwick 2013d). In any case, it seems a better ploy to have such technology working for you rather than against you. Questions however can then be raised as to what happens to those who do not wish to upgrade, thereby being left with relatively poor communication skills and abilities that are far inferior.

Perhaps the most important point is that by upgrading humans we are considering not merely a physical extension of human capabilities but rather a completely different basis on which the brain operates in a mixed human–machine fashion. Although it is undoubtedly true that physical extensions, such as an airplane, a pair of glasses, or even a wearable computer, in an assistive form of technology (Warwick et al. 2013), give humans capabilities that they would not themselves normally possess, when the nature of the brain itself is altered the situation is a very different one. Such an entity would have a different foundation on which any thoughts would be conceived in the first place. From an individualistic viewpoint, therefore, if I am myself upgraded I am happy with the situation. Those who wish to remain ordinary humans, however, may not be so happy.

We must be clear that by ultimately taking on board some of the advantages of AI, such as extra memory, high-powered mathematical capabilities—including the ability to conceive in many dimensions—the ability to sense the world in many ways, and communication by thought signals alone, such entities will be far more powerful, intellectually, than humans. It would be difficult imagining that an entity such as this would want to voluntarily give up its powers. It is also difficult to imagine that the entity would pay any heed to a human's trivial utterances.

It could be argued that humans are already digitally enhanced by current technology (Clark 2004) and to some extent this may, in any case, gradually alter morals. The big difference about the upgrading concept described here is that their brain is part human, part machine and hence the epicenter of moral and ethical decision making is no longer of purely human form, but rather it has a mixed human–machine basis.

One interesting aspect is that such an enhanced entity would most likely have a brain, which is not standalone, but rather, via its machine part, is connected directly to a network. One question, then: is it morally acceptable for a cyborg in the form of an enhanced entity to give up its individuality and become a node on an intelligent machine network? This is, of course, as much of a question for cyborgs as it is for humans.

This whole area is very exciting to be part of and is changing rapidly. But along with these changes comes a plethora of questions. Should every human have the right to be upgraded? If an individual does not want to upgrade, should they be allowed to defer, thereby taking on a role in relation to a cyborg, possibly rather akin to a chimpanzee's relationship with a human today?

This research is extremely exciting as there is so much to learn and many risks to be taken because, ultimately, we will only find out what is possible through experimentation. As a result, humanity will evolve in a technological way to become cyborgs, hybrid beings with abilities way beyond those of the humans of today.

References

Bateson, Gregory. 1972. *Steps to an Ecology of Mind*. New York: Ballantine.

Bouton, Chad E., Ammar Shaikhouni, Nicholas V. Annetta, Marcia A. Bockbrader, David A. Friedenberg, Dylan M. Nielson, Gaurav Sharma, Per B. Sederberg, Bradley C. Glenn, W. Jerry Mysiw, Austin G. Morgan, Milind Deogaonkar, and Ali R. Rezai. 2016. Restoring Cortical Control of Functional Movement in a Human with Quadriplegia. *Nature* 533 (7602): 247–250. https://doi.org/10.1038/nature17435.

Camara, Carmen, Kevin Warwick, Ricardo Bruña, Tipu Aziz, Francisco del Pozo, and Fernando Maestú. 2015. A Fuzzy Inference System for Closed-Loop Deep Brain Stimulation in Parkinson's Disease. *Journal of Medical Systems* 39 (11): 155. https://doi.org/10.1007/s10916-015-0328-x.

Camara, Carmen, Kevin Warwick, Ricardo Bruña, Tipu Aziz, and Ernesto Pereda. 2019. Closed-Loop Deep Brain Stimulation Based on a Stream-Clustering System. *Expert Systems with Applications* 126:187–199. https://doi.org/10.1016/j.eswa.2019.02.024.

Cerqui, Daniela. 2001. The Future of Humankind in the Era of Human and Computer Hybridisation: An Anthropological Analysis. In *Proceedings of the International Conference on Computer Ethics and Philosophical Enquiry (CEPE)*, edited by R. Chadwick, L. D. Introna, and A. Marturano, 9–48. Lancaster, UK: Lancaster University.

Chiappalone, Michela, Alessandro Vato, Luca Berdondini, Milena Koudelka-Hep, and Sergio Martinoia. 2007. Network Dynamics and Synchronous Activity in Cultured Cortical Neurons. *International Journal of Neural Systems* 17 (2): 87–103. https://doi.org/10.1142/S0129065707000968.

Clark, Andy. 2004. *Natural Born Cyborgs*. Oxford: Oxford University Press.

Coolen, Maarten. 2001. Becoming a Cyborg as One of the Ends of Disembodied Man. In *Proceedings of the International Conference on Computer Ethics and Philosophical Enquiry (CEPE)*, edited by R. Chadwick, L. D. Introna, and A. Marturano, 49–60. Lancaster, UK: Lancaster University.

DeMarse, Thomas B., Daniel A. Wagenaar, Axel W. Blau, and Steve M. Potter. 2001. The Neurally Controlled Animat: Biological Brains Acting with Simulated Bodies. *Autonomous Robotics* 11 (3): 305–310. https://doi.org/10.1023/A:1012407611130.

Donoghue, John P., Arto Nurmikko, Gerhard Friehs, and Michael Black. 2004. Chapter 63: Development of a Neuromotor Prosthesis for Humans. *Advances in Clinical Neurophysiology: Supplements to Clinical Neurophysiology* 57:592–606. https://doi.org/10.1016/S1567-424X(09)70399-X.

Ellcessor, Elizabeth. 2017. Cyborg Hoaxes: Disability, Deception, and Critical Studies of Digital Media. *New Media & Society* 19 (11): 1761–1777. https://doi.org/10.1177%2F1461444816642754.

Foster, Kenneth R., and Jan Jaeger. 2007. RFID Inside. *IEEE Spectrum* 44 (3): 24–29. https://doi.org/10.1109/MSPEC.2007.323430.

Graafstra, Amal. 2007. Hands On. *IEEE Spectrum* 44 (3): 18–23. https://doi.org/10.1109/MSPEC.2007.323420.

Hameed, Jawish, Ian Harrison, Mark N. Gasson, and Kevin Warwick. 2010. A Novel Human–Machine Interface Using Subdermal Implants. Paper presented at the IEEE 9th International Conference on Cybernetic Intelligent Systems, Reading, Berkshire, UK, September 1–2. https://doi.org/10.1109/UKRICIS.2010.5898141.

Haraway, Donna. 1985. A Manifesto for Cyborgs: Science, Technology, and Socialist Feminism in the 1980s. *Socialist Review* 80:65–108. https://doi.org/10.1080/0816464 9.1987.9961538.

Harbisson, Neil. 2008. Painting by Ear. *Modern Painters* (June): 70–73.

Harrison, Ian, Kevin Warwick, and Virginie Ruiz. 2018. Subdermal Magnetic Implants: An Experimental Study. *Cybernetics & Systems* 49 (2): 122–150. https://doi .org/10.1080/01969722.2018.1448223.

Hayles, N. Katherine. 1999. *How We Became Posthuman: Virtual Bodies in Cybernetics, Literature and Informatics.* Chicago: University of Chicago Press.

Hebb, Donald O. 1949. *The Organisation of Behaviour.* New York: Wiley.

Hochberg, Leigh R., Mijail D. Serruya, Gerhard M. Friehs, Jon A. Mukand, Maryam Saleh, Abraham H. Caplan, Almut Branner, David Chen, Richard D. Penn, and John P. Donoghue. 2006. Neuronal Ensemble Control of Prosthetic Devices by a Human with Tetraplegia. *Nature* 442 (7099): 164–171. https://doi.org/10.1038/nature04970.

Hochberg, Leigh R., Daniel Bacher, Beata Jarosiewicz, Nicolas Y. Masse, John D. Simeral, Joern Vogel, Sami Haddadin, Jie Liu, Sydney S. Cash, Patrick van der Smagt, and John P. Donoghue. 2012. Reach and Grasp by People with Tetraplegia Using a Neurally Controlled Robotic Arm. *Nature* 485 (7398): 372–375. https://doi .org/10.1038/nature11076.

Kafer, Alison. 2013. *Feminist, Queer, Crip.* Bloomington: Indiana University Press.

Kennedy, Philip, Dinal Andreasen, Princewill Ehirim, Brandon King, Todd Kirby, Hui Mao, and Melody Moore. 2004. Using Human Extra-Cortical Local Field Potentials to Control a Switch. *Journal of Neural Engineering* 1 (2): 72–77. https://doi .org/10.1088/1741-2560/1/2/002.

Kuiken, Todd A., Guanglin Li, Blair A. Lock, Robert D. Lipschutz, Laura A. Miller, Kathy A. Stubblefield, and Kevin B. Englehart. 2009. Targeted Muscle Reinnervation for Real-Time Myoelectric Control of Multifunction Artificial Arms. *Journal of the American Medical Association* 301 (6): 619–628. https://doi.org/10.1001/jama .2009.116.

Nathanael, Tanja. 2019. Doctor Who. In *Aliens in Popular Culture*, edited by Michael M. Levy and Farah Mendlesohn, 104–107. Westport, CT: Greenwood

Nietzsche, Friedrich. 1961. *Thus Spoke Zarathustra*. London: Penguin Classics.

Parsons, Paul. 2006. *The Science of Dr. Who*. Cambridge: ICON Books.

Pentland, Alex P. 1998. Wearable Intelligence. *Scientific American* 9 (4): 90–95.

Pinter, Michaela M., Monika Murg, Francois Alesch, Brigetta Freundl, Reinhard J. Helscher, and Heinrich Binder. 1999. Does Deep Brain Stimulation of the Nucleus Ventralisintermedius Affect Postural Control and Locomotion in Parkinson's Disease? *Movement Disorders* 14 (6): 958–963. https://doi.org/10.1002/1531-8257 (199911)14:6%3C958::AID-MDS1008%3E3.0.CO;2-E.

Ronchi, Alfredo M. 2009. *Eculture: Cultural Content in the Digital Age*. New York: Springer.

Searle, John. 1990. *The Mystery of Consciousness*. New York: New York Review of Books.

Singer, Merrill, Hans Baer, Debbi Long, and Alex Pavlotski. 2019. *Introducing Medical Anthropology: A Discipline in Action*. 3rd ed. Lanham, MD: Rowman & Littlefield.

Sparkes, Andrew C., James Brighton, and Kay Inckle. 2018. "It's a Part of Me": An Ethnographic Exploration of Becoming a Disabled Sporting Cyborg Following Spinal Cord Injury. *Qualitative Research in Sport, Exercise and Health* 10 (2): 151–166. https:// doi.org/10.1080/2159676X.2017.1389768.

Warwick, Kevin. 1998. *In the Mind of the Machine*. London: Arrow.

Warwick, Kevin. 2002. *I Cyborg*. London: Century.

Warwick, Kevin. 2010. Implications and Consequences of Robots with Biological Brains. *Ethics and Information Technology* 12 (3): 223–234. https://doi.org/10.1007/ s10676-010-9218-6.

Warwick, Kevin. 2013a. The Future of Artificial Intelligence and Cybernetics. In *There's a Future: Visions for a Better World*, edited by Nayef Al-Fodhan, 131–151. Madrid: BBVA Open Mind.

Warwick, Kevin. 2013b. The Disappearing Human–Machine Divide. *Approaching Religion* 3 (2): 3–15. https://doi.org/10.30664/ar.67511.

Warwick, Kevin. 2013c. Cyborgs—The Neuro-Tech Version. In *Implantable Bioelectronics: Devices, Materials, and Applications*, edited by Evgeny Katz, 115–132. New York: Wiley–VCH.

Warwick Kevin. 2013d. Cyborgs in Space. *Acta Futura* 6: 25–35. https://doi.org/10.2420/AF06.2013.25.

Warwick, Kevin, and Mark N. Gasson. 2006. A Question of Identity—Wiring in the Human. Paper presented at the IET Wireless Sensor Networks Conference, London, UK, December 4. https://doi.org/10.1049/ic:20060257.

Warwick, Kevin, Mark Gasson, Benjamin Hutt, Iain Goodhew, Peter Kyberd, Brian Andrews, Peter Teddy, and Amjad Shad. 2003. The Application of Implant Technology for Cybernetic Systems. *Archives of Neurology* 60 (10): 1369–1373. https://doi.org/10.1001/archneur.60.10.1369.

Warwick, Kevin, Mark Gasson, Benjamin Hutt, Iain Goodhew, Peter Kyberd, Henning Schulzrinne, and Xiaotao Wu. 2004. Thought Communication and Control: A First Step Using Radiotelegraphy. *IEEE Proceedings–Communications* 151 (3): 185–189. https://doi.org/10.1049/ip-com:20040409.

Warwick, Kevin, Slawomir J. Nasuto, Victor M. Becerra, and Benjamin J. Whalley. 2010a. Experiments with an In-Vitro Robot Brain. In *Instinctive Computing, Lecture Notes in Artificial Intelligence*, edited by Yang Cai, 1–15. New York: Springer.

Warwick, Kevin, Dimitris Xydas, Slawomir J. Nasuto, Victor M. Becerra, Mark W. Hammond, Simon Marshall, and Benjamin J. Whalley. 2010b. Controlling a Mobile Robot with a Biological Brain. *Defence Science Journal* 60 (1): 5–14. https://doi.org/10.14429/dsj.60.11.

Warwick, Kevin, Huma Shah, Anton Vedder, Elettra Stradella, and Pericle Salvini. 2013. How Good Robots Will Enhance Human Life. In *A Treatise on Good Robots*, edited by Krzysztof Tchoń and Wojciech W. Gasparski, 3–18. New York: Routledge.

Wu, Defeng, Kevin Warwick, Zi Ma, Jonathan G. Burgess, Song Pan, and Tipu Z. Aziz. 2010. Prediction of Parkinson's Disease Tremor Onset Using Radial Basis Function Neural Networks. *Expert Systems with Applications* 37 (4): 2923–2928. https://doi.org/10.1016/j.eswa.2009.09.045.

Xydas, D., J. Downes, M. Spencer, M. Hammond, S. Nasuto, B. Whalley, V. Becerra, and K. Warwick. 2011. Revealing Ensemble State Transition Patterns in Multi-Electrode Neuronal Recordings Using Hidden Markov Models. *IEEE Transactions on Neural Systems & Rehabilitation Engineering* 19 (4): 345–355. https://doi.org/10.1109/TNSRE.2011.2157360.

5 Überveillance and the Rise of Last-Mile Implantables: Past, Present, and Future

Katina Michael, M. G. Michael, Christine Perakslis, and Roba Abbas

Introduction

As the concept of the internet of things (IoT) gathers momentum to become the internet of things and people, many innovators are looking into smart technologies that are not only carried or worn but implanted beneath the skin to form an integral part of end-to-end network architecture. In some ways, the end user is the new "last mile" in the global interconnected network topology, formed since the rise of the IP-based core. Embodied computing technologies, such as implantable technologies in living things, become the final security and privacy frontier in a context where every object and subject is identifiable with an IPv6 unique address. Members of the biohacking community demonstrate how proximity implantables can be used in an organizational context for physical access control, in-building location tracking, and convenience-oriented applications. This chapter provides an historical overview of nonmedical implants and the state of play today, and it ponders applications in the future, as well as the corresponding implications. The narrative provides strong evidence toward the use of such embodied computing technologies as implantables as a means to making end users key nodes in a network. We also examine the repercussions of such technological developments in view of the benefits and risks of überveillance (embedded surveillance), together with the associated societal challenges.

From Luggables to Wearables and Implantables

Electronic-based physical access cards have been used to secure premises such as government buildings and large corporate offices since the inception of bar code and magnetic-stripe cards in the 1970s. Before they were clipped onto people in the form of physical badges, they were lugged around in pockets, purses, or wallets. Over time, for secure access control, these first-generation card technologies were replaced by more sophisticated system devices such as smart cards and biometrics, containing encrypted data and using techniques that were more difficult to dupe or to replicate (K. Michael 2003a).

An employee today wanting to gain access to their place of work typically carries a photo identity card in addition to a contactless smart card using radio-frequency technology, and may also use one of his/her unique physical characteristics (e.g., fingerprint, palmprint, iris, or face) for verification. Generally, the more information-sensitive the enterprise, the greater the security measures introduced to safeguard against fraudulent activities. Cards can nonetheless be lost or stolen, and photo identity badges can be counterfeited. This has led some innovators to consider the potential of radio-frequency identification (RFID) or implantable devices for employee identification, with the added possibility of using wireless networks to do location fixes on employees in large premises (e.g., manufacturing plants). Automatic identification devices can also provide access to militarized zones based on roles and privileges defined by administrator access control matrices.

RFID implantables are injected into the body and are theoretically not transferable, thus ensuring better security than traditional techniques. Microchip implants come in the form of tags or transponders that contain an integrated circuit. Animals have been implanted using the technology from the early 1990s to curb disease outbreaks and for total farm management (Trevarthen and Michael 2007).

Masters and Michael (2007) define three types of application areas for human-implantable microchips: (1) control (e.g., access control); (2) convenience (e.g., e-payment); and (3) care (e.g., accessing electronic health records remotely). A control-related human-centric application of RFID is any human use of an implanted RFID transponder that gives an implantee power over an aspect of their lives, or that gives a third party power over an implantee. A convenience-related application is any human use of an implanted RFID transponder that increases the ease with which tasks are performed. A care-related application is any use associated with medicine, health, or wellbeing (K. Michael and Masters 2004).

But how did implantables appear to suddenly enter the automatic iden-tification landscape? The normalization of RFID bracelets began around the mid-1980s for home detention, extended supervision orders, and prison inmate tracking and monitoring. This is not atypical of emerging technolo-gies, which are often tested on smaller minority groups. 3M championed the development of a "one piece" GPS monitoring system that integrates tracking, communication, and mapping technologies. The company noted that the system, attached to the leg, has the ability to define inclusion and exclusion zones and provide an animated birds-eye-view mapping func-tionality. Implantables have the added advantage of being discreet, in that they are not outwardly visible. For example, parolees on extended supervi-sion orders who might be implanted would be given the opportunity to undergo rehabilitation without the added stigmatization from observers (K. Michael et al. 2009). Similarly, persons who have been charged with a crime but not yet tried or convicted could be granted bail and monitored elec-tronically via implantables without the risk of observers presuming their guilt. However, there remain a great deal of ethical dilemmas around the question of trespassing the outer body and invading the inner person.

The notion of insertables (user removable embedded devices) has been introduced into the literature by Heffernan et al. (2017), at times to chal-lenge the concept of an implantable (third-party removable embedded device) and elsewhere to signify a new breed of device that can be removed by a user. A number of examples come to mind, like Rich Lee's (Arthur 2013) "implanted" ear buds that can send music directly to one's ears and can eas-ily be removed, or BrickHouseSecurity's "Squelch" micro bluetooth spy ear-piece that is fitted deep within the ear so it is invisible, and is removed with the aid of a super strong magnet (BrickHouseSecurity 2009; 2018). "Pure" insertables may be removable by the user, granting personal autonomy, but they still go deeper than a detachable wearable that can be stripped off the outer layer of the skin without the aid of a magnet. More often than not, an insertable requires some device to eject it from its in-body docking location (e.g., ear, mouth, nose, uterus [Michael and Monteleone 2019]).

Background: The Human Implant Controversy

RFID bracelets are in use in such closed campus facilities as Disney's Magic Kingdom for access control and electronic payments. Some banks, like

Barclays Bank, also piloted the use of a wristband for RF/NFC-enabled transactions. Bracelets and bands have also been used in prisons (to track inmates, security guards, and visitors, providing access to particular zones), and also for hospitals (to track medical staff and visitors through "contact and trace" programs, such as during the SARS epidemic) (K. Michael and Masters 2006). The technology can work to give access to specific rooms or inversely to keep people within certain perimeters (e.g., to keep new-born babies from being stolen from postnatal wards). The potential of RFID implantable devices for employee identification was demonstrated in a commercial context in two well-known cases: the Baja Beach Club in Barcelona, Spain (2004–2009), and Citywatcher.com in Cincinnati, Ohio, in the United States (2006–2008).

In the case of the Baja Beach Club, both employees and club patrons were given the opportunity to receive implants. The employees used the implants to gain access to restricted areas in the Club (e.g., IT systems and administration records), and the club patrons used the implants for e-payment and to gain access to "very important patron" (VIP) lounge areas within the Club. In Citywatcher.com, all employees of the small business were given an opportunity to acquire an implant for access control, and a total of four employees were implanted. In both instances, implantation was not mandatory. The cases demonstrated that implantable devices can work just as well as contactless proximity cards for physical access control to premises (K. Michael and M. G. Michael 2010). Both programs have now been discontinued, but there has been a flurry of activity particularly in the United States, Australia, Sweden, Germany, and the Netherlands pursuing the potential for such embodied computing technologies involving connected humans.

Some of the issues that were prevalent in both organizational deployments had more to do with overcoming usability issues than with social, ethical, or legal concerns, since both commercial programs were on an opt-in basis (M. G. Michael and K. Michael 2007; Kumar 2007; Kargl et al. 2008; Wang and Loui 2009; Clarke 2010). The Citywatcher.com project preceded the State of Ohio's legislation against the enforced chipping of employees but regardless was in accordance with it, given that it was entirely voluntary (Friggieri et al. 2009). The biggest hurdles had to do with (1) the actual location of the implantable device in the human body as designated by the vendor (at the back of the triceps in the upper right arm); (2) the location of the RFID readers (too high for some members of the population); and (3) the complexity of getting the implants embedded into willing participants, as it required a number of personnel to be engaged in the end-to-end procedure (IT manager, nurse or doctor, end-user, management for witnessing consent, etc.).

When interviewed and explicitly asked about social, ethical, or legal dilemmas and the risks related to the implantation of humans, representatives from both Baja Beach Club and Citywatcher.com stated that there were no risks or that risks were of a very limited nature (K. Michael 2009a; K. Michael 2009b). Representatives of both companies touted the benefits, convenience, rewards, and future prospects above and beyond any perceived risks. They were also passionate about the possibility that one day, *all* humans might never have to worry about carrying wallets, that credit card fraud would diminish, and that identity fraud would be eradicated. When asked about some of the major challenges such as the cloning of implants, electronic viruses on implants (Gasson 2010), the need for continual upgrades, dysfunctional implants, and members of the community who did not wish to opt in, both interviewees seemed untroubled by the problems this might pose. Dissent by members of the community over implantables for citizens or employee ID was seen as (1) generally limited to Christian fundamentalists who harbored concerns over the infamous "number of the beast"; (2) those who (genuinely) had "something to hide"; or (3) those that would raise complaints against just about anything. Indeed, according to the interviewees, all risks were simply considered to be teething problems of an emerging technology and would be overcome in the very short term, similarly to the security controls introduced since the inception of the internet. The risk versus reward question was not a point of contention—the rewards would outweigh any plausible risks, according to the key informant interviewees (K. Michael and M. G. Michael 2013).

The problem with implants, from the perspective of the individual body's interaction with the technology, has for the most part to do with (1) permanency (depending on the site and length of implantation); (2) the requirement for a third party to enact removal upon request; (3) the bearer's capacity to understand how the device may be interacting with the space around them with or without their consent; (4) the device's insecurity; and (5) enforceability when considering the implantation of minors, persons suffering from cognitive disorders or dementia, and others in dependent relationships (K. Michael and M. G. Michael 2009, 512). The human-centric implant controversy has to do with the potential for all human beings to be implanted with what seemingly looks like a liberating technology in embedded beneath-the-skin implants (i.e., you do not need to carry keys, wallets, cards, or proof of ID). But microchip implants are in reality a technology of controls, limits, and rights. The controversy will become especially rife if the majority of society enjoys the perceived benefits of using implants, with the minority deciding to live "off the grid." There is a great deal of literature on the digital divide, but the divide that implants might cause is particularly radical and has not been commensurately addressed. The introduction of potentially culture-shifting techniques is invariably surrounded by clashes of policy, law, society, and philosophical and religious beliefs.

We have seen the enactment of antichipping laws in the United States (Friggieri et al. 2009) to guard against the possible abuse or misuse of embedded technologies within various relationship contexts—parent/child, employer/employee, doctor/patient, state/citizen, and so on. In fact, the State of Ohio outlawed enforced implantation of employees in SB 349, *A Bill To Prohibit an Employer from Requiring an Employee of the Employer to Insert into the Employee's Body a Radio Frequency Identification Tag.* Legislation in this space has continued to be drafted over the last two decades, albeit with a focus on enforced "injection" rather than any other means of inward bodily identification. National-level governing bodies like the Federal Communication Commission (FCC) in the United States have had little to say regarding non-health-related implants. Their primary concern is likely to be around the best use of spectrum domestically and the prospective revision of regulation in the context of the new technology, rather than governance of the human body.

A significant specter of embodied computing technologies, which is beyond the individual physical issues, is *überveillance* (M. G. Michael and K. Michael 2007). Überveillance is now commonly defined as "ubiquitous or pervasive electronic surveillance that is not only 'always on' but 'always with you,' ultimately in the form of bodily invasive surveillance" (Australian Law Dictionary 2010). The concept is linked to Friedrich Nietzsche's vision of the Übermensch, who is a person with powers beyond those of an ordinary human being (M. G. Michael and K. Michael 2010). Überveillance is analogous to Big Brother implanted in you, for example heart, pulse, and temperature sensor readings emanating from the body in binary data wirelessly, or even through amplified eyes, such as an inserted contact lens "glass" that might provide visual display and access to the internet or social networking applications (M. G. Michael and K. Michael 2013). Überveillance brings together all forms of watching from above and below, from machines that move to those that stand still, from animals and from people, acquired involuntarily or voluntarily, using obtrusive or unobtrusive devices (K. Michael et al. 2010). The network infrastructure underlies the ability to collect data directly from the sensor devices worn by the individual, and big data analytics ensures an interpretation of the unique behavioral traits of the individual, implying not just predicted movement but intent and thought (K. Michael and Miller 2013).

It has been said that überveillance is that part of the veillance puzzle that brings together the *sur*, *data*, and *sous* to an intersecting point (Stephan et al. 2012). In überveillance, there is the "watching" from above component (*sur*), there is the "collecting" of personal data and public data for mining (*data*), and there is the watching from below (*sous*), which can draw together social networks and strangers, all coming together via wearable and implantable devices on/in the human body (M. G. Michael et al. 2008). Überveillance can be used for good in the practice of health, for instance (Guta, Gagnon, and Jacob 2013), but we contend that independent of its application for nonmedical purposes, it will always have an underlying control factor (Masters and Michael 2005).

Implanting Humans for Nonmedical Applications (1997–2006)

The first known person to be implanted with a transponder for the purposes of demonstrating identification was Eduardo Kac in 1997 (K. Michael 2003a). Kac, a multimedia, communications, and biological artist produced a work entitled *Time Capsule*, which depicted him self-injecting an implant into his ankle, "web-scanning" the transponder, and then logging on to register himself on an animal database. In the following year, Kevin Warwick's experiment *Cyborg 1.0* had a profound impact on what could be achieved using implantable technologies (Warwick 2002a). Warwick was the first person to be implanted with a functional transponder for nonmedical research purposes (K. Michael 2003b). This experiment allowed a computer to monitor Warwick as he moved through halls and offices at his workplace using a unique identifying signal emitted by the implanted chip. He could operate doors, lights, heaters, and other computers without lifting a finger. Warwick's experiments, including *Cyborg 2.0* in 2002, demonstrated the potential for RFID implants to be used in convenience, care, and control-oriented applications. The experiments were sponsored by Nortel Networks, alongside Tumbleweed Communications, Computer Associates, and Fujitsu (Warwick et al. 2003). In *Cyborg 2.0*, Warwick had a one-hundred-electrode array surgically implanted into the median nerve fibres of his left arm (Warwick 2002b). Most notably, Warwick was able to control an electric wheelchair just by using a neural interface linked to his implant. Here, Warwick showed the potential of Brain-to-Computer Interfaces (BCI) but also of Brain-to-Brain Interfaces (BBI).

While Warwick was demonstrating the many use cases of implantables, Kac was pointing to the ethical dilemmas and what he called "trauma" in the creation of technology. According to Kac (1997), the "physical trauma ... amplifies the psychological shock generated by ever-faster cycles of technological invention, development, and obsolescence." Thus, Kac preempted philosophical debate on the question of implants with his *Time Capsule* work, and Warwick demonstrated the implant as an identity and location-finding capability, propelling further debate on the impending possibilities. Kac and Warwick saw years into the future.

In 1999, between Warwick's *Cyborg 1.0* and *Cyborg 2.0* experiments, British Telecom's Peter Cochrane wrote *Tips for Time Travellers*, in which he described a microchip implant as a "soul catcher chip" (Cochrane 1999, 7, 57). The year Cochrane's monograph was published, the Auto-ID Center consortium at MIT formally began researching the internet of things, a term coined by former Procter and Gamble assistant brand manager Kevin Ashton (Auto-ID Labs 1999).

At about the time of Warwick's *Cyborg 2.0* experiment in Britain in March 2002 came the unrelated establishment of the VeriChip Corporation in the United States, following the terrorist attacks of September 11, 2001. Scott Silverman, the CEO of VeriChip, was often quoted describing the need for implants, especially for first responders. He noted the possibility of such a device tethered to an electronic bracelet being able to help first responders get out of hopeless situations, like a burning tower that was about to collapse (Applied Digital Solutions 2003). Executives at VeriChip were implanted in early 2002 before the VeriChip implantable RFID had received FDA approval (FDA 2004). Having observed widespread testing of

RFID implants in animals for so many years with generally beneficial outcomes in farm operations, Applied Digital Solutions embarked on human implantables through their subsidiary VeriChip.

The VeriChip campaign to *Get Chipped* was launched in early 2003. There were a number of Veri centers where the procedure could take place in the United States. There was even a high-tech ChipMobile bus fully equipped to perform the implant procedure "on the road." About the size of a grain of rice, the VeriChip was the world's first subdermal commercial RFID microchip for use in humans. In theory, an implantee could be identified in a wi-fi network, such as in a workplace or on a university campus. Radio-frequency energy from the reader triggers the dormant VeriChip to send a signal containing the unique ID number. The exchange of data is transparent and seamless. Thus, for example, an individual could be identified by RFID, giving emergency services potentially life-saving access to the implantee's medical data and history. It is estimated there were over 2,000 recipients of the VeriChip (Lewan 2007).

In April 2002, the Jacobs family volunteered to be the first consumers to receive a VeriChip. On May 11, 2002, the Jacobs chipping procedure was broadcast live on American television (BBC 2002). VeriChip then implanted some high-profile people, including Rafael Macedo de la Concha (Mexico's Attorney General) and a number of his staff, citing security purposes (Gardner 2004). The company also drew political figures like Tommy Thompson, US Secretary of Health and Human Services (2001–2005) and candidate for the 2008 US presidential election, who ultimately also served a two-year directorship on the board of VeriChip (Albrecht and McIntyre 2005). In 2004 and 2006, Baja Beach Club and Citywatcher.com engaged in VeriChip programs, and a host of private "Veri-chippings" were conducted with members of the public, included Alzheimer's patients (ABC News 2007) and persons suffering from medical conditions and allergies.

Other new cyborg initiatives occurred independently of corporate interests, among them the case of Neil Harbisson in 2004, who was the first person to implant an antenna into his head. Harbisson's device "sends audible vibrations in his skull to report information to him. This includes measurements of electromagnetic radiation, phone calls, music, as well as video or images which are translated into audible vibrations" (Harbisson 2010). He is also said to have the ability to receive signals and data from satellites.

As use cases of implantables in real-world contexts have increased, legislation has continued to lag behind. Yet there were early signs that some debate by government entities would be necessary over how these new forms of embodied computing technologies might enter the mainstream and what that might mean for society. The EU Opinion No. 20 on "Ethical Aspects of ICT Implants in the Human Body" was published, written by the European Group on Ethics in Science and New Technologies (EGE), chaired by the Swedish philosopher Göran Hermerén, and adopted on March 16, 2005 (EGE 2005). Among the group were key members Professors Rafael Capurro and the late Stefano Rodotà.

Citizen scientists continued to self-experiment with RFID beneath the skin and share their learning with one another using the internet. On March 22, 2005, Amal Graafstra of the United States was implanted with his first RFID tag. Graafstra (2007) and others like him (e.g., Mikey Sklar and Jonathan Oxer) pioneered noncommercial human implantables for custom-built home applications and were dubbed do-it-yourselfer RFID implantees (DIYers) by observers. Many of the early DIYers belonged to the Tagged Forum, which was set up to accommodate fellow tinkerers at the beginning of 2006. It became the "go-to" place for learning about how to tinker with RFID implants and what applications to build with them. The Forum soon attracted more attention than it wanted, targeted with posts proclaiming members were heralding in the "mark of the beast" (Rev. 13:16–18). As a result, the forum went underground and was left alone, away from public gaze.

For Graafstra, the VeriChip transponder sold to the public within a commercial setting represented completely different privacy challenges than the glass tags embedded in his own body (K. Michael and M. G. Michael 2009, 427–450). In fact, he was clearly not in favor of getting an implant that possessed antimigration coating, and that was under the control of a third party, injected so deep into the body (Graafstra et al. 2010). In 2006, Graafstra authored his own book, *RFID Toys*, written primarily for "tech-heads" who wanted to adapt their social living spaces for convenient interactivity (Graafstra 2006). Graafstra then branched out with several transaction-based start-ups that make use of a fully cryptographic piece of embeddable technology. His retail arm gathered momentum, supplying to resellers across the globe who specialize in personal chippings (K. Michael 2016). Graafstra claimed in 2016 that he had sold over 10,000 RFID injector kits for humans globally (Graafstra et al. 2016).

The period from 1997 to 2006 was a time of intense novelty, early hype, and proposing a future that very few genuinely wished to engage with (K. Michael 2015, 5–7, 17). A limited number of academics, some keen bio-hackers, and radical start-ups had taken seriously the idea of microchipping people. Things would begin to change drastically when some big brands began to openly engage with the broader concept of a paperless and cash-less society.

Human-centric Implantable Use Cases (2007–2017)

Well known to most in the auto-ID industry were two IBM commercials produced in the mid-2000s, exhibiting RFID for "grab and go" shopping at a smart supermarket (IBM 2007) and increased visibility in the supply chain (IBM 2008). The "cutesy" nature of these commercials was a step away from the original "shock and awe" of the Applied Digital Solutions VeriChip "Get Chipped" campaigns, which were a response to national security (i.e., 9/11) and America's healthcare crisis (Applied Digital Solutions 2006).

It was not just IBM who had noted major change on the horizon through the embedding of RFID in humans and objects, but also Gartner, Micro-soft Research, CISCO, Nokia, AutoDesk Research, Ericsson, MYOB, VISA, American Express, and InQTel (Wood 2004; Perusco et al. 2006; Storey 2014; Francis 2015; Chan 2016; IQT 2017) and smaller companies like Xega (Rosenberg 2008; Opam 2011). Executives of large multinationals were beginning to consider the possibility of an "on-off" RFID embedded tag that the user could control through an external I/O switch on the surface of their body (Perusco et al. 2006).

In a survey of 10,000 PricewaterhouseCoopers (PWC) employees across major economies, 70 percent of PWC personnel said they would consider using "treatments to enhance their brain and body if this improved their employment prospects" (Hannan and Fox Koob 2017). Other studies (Michael et al. 2017a), like that conducted by Lloyd's Bank, conclude that 7 percent of Britons would take up chip implants for banking (Boden 2015), and a survey by BITKOM of 1,000 respondents in Germany found that 23 percent would accept having a microchip implanted in their body if that would bring concrete benefits as a result (EDRi 2010).

Much of the change in acceptance of such technologies has come from building up banking systems infrastructure for electronic transactions. Interoperability has been key in all of this, and historically just one example among many was the (EMV) Europay, MasterCard, and VISA alliance (K. Michael 2003a). Traditional banking was shaken beyond mere "standards" and "specifications"—a wave of full-blown deregulation of the telecommunications and banking sectors washed across the globe. It had become evident that traditional providers were being pressured by nontraditional players (Allen and Barr 1997). Credit card companies now had competitors who were ICT giants.

Penetrating the New Last Mile—The Human Body

Companies like Cochlear in 2017 have described the potential to fuse their hearing implantable device with a service that delivers entertainment-like music straight to the ear (Hinchliffe 2017). This is the blurring of the prosthetic with the amplified, the medical with the entertainment, as noted in a TEDxUWollongong scenario (K. Michael 2012).

End users have always been depicted in network diagrams as the last node—from the core to the edge to access nodes and finally to the end user's home, workplace, or roaming location. Whereas desktop, laptop, tablet, and cellphone have been traditionally the devices depicted in these architectural diagrams, we *now* are witnessing the growth of embedded devices in things and people. These typically have been prosthetic devices like heart pacemakers, but since 2010 we are now seeing nonmedical devices come to the fore. On the human side, implantable devices like smart integrated circuits (IC), radio-frequency identification (RFID), near-field communications (NFC), light emitting diodes (LEDs), and magnets have broken through the final frontier: the body. No longer are we identifying just an individual, but we can decorporealize the person, to the implants in their heart, in their hip, hand, knee, and even the brain. Such transformations involve more than just sporting an implant, although the outward bodily transfigurations cannot help but have an inward-facing metaphysical and existential impact on the human person, as studies of tattooing have learned (Grognard 1994).

While the argument has been made by many that identity tokens do not have to be embedded to render the end user a "last mile" node, there is something starkly different about a device that one cannot remove on one's own. And while theoretically "not transferable," the RIFD tag or transponder can be cloned and can be "killed" using a number of different well-known security attacks (Sirotich 2007). The tag can also overtly or covertly be interrogated with or without your permission via inconspicuous readers installed in shopping malls or even lamp posts. Although an implantable cannot inform the individual of who has accessed its unique ID, the blockchain may well register all flows in a future based on smart city principles. The following are current use-cases of such embodied computing technologies as implantables that might point to mass market applications.

Ticketing

Andreas Sjöström of Sojeti boarded a Scandanavian Airlines flight from Stockholm Arlanda Airport to Paris using nothing but his NFC chip as a boarding pass (Sjöström 2016). Soon after, SJ Rail announced that its SJ Priority clients could have their ticket validated using their implantable (Weller 2017). Interestingly, since Sjöström's experiment, he has written a blogpost on why "NFC chip implants are a bad idea," citing such reasons as: it solves no real problem, doesn't work well, takes more time, limited usage, and serious health issues (Sjöström 2017).

Security

Microchip implants for the purposes of personal security were utilized in Mexico by the Xega company as early as 2008 (New Scientist staff and Reuters 2008). As the rate of kidnappings has continued to rise, Mexicans have considered "identification chips" as one preventive measure. By 2008, Xega claimed to have 2,000 clients of the VeriChip implant in Mexico at a cost of an upfront fee of US $4,000 plus an annual fee of US $2,200. Of course, there is no "tracking" capability in this chip; at best, the implant would act as an identifier if a mutilated body were discovered post crime.

Ingestible chips have also been showcased at the 2013 D11 Conference (Kulaiay 2013) by (then) Google's Regina Dugan (formerly the nineteenth director of DARPA and now at Facebook's renowned lab, Building 8) for the purposes of ensuring that only verifiable users gain access to applications and computer devices. In essence, this is a daily "security" pill you could take. The same year chipmaker Freescale, who produces the chipset for the Fitbit, had created an Advanced RISC Machine (ARM)-powered functional, swallowable chip (Maly 2013). This is also a high-powered computer you can swallow.

Amal Graafstra of Dangerous Things, previously mentioned as a front-runner during the first phase of nonmedical implantation, has been working on an implantable solution based on an NXP NFC chip (Dangerous Things 2015). The Vivokey is based on a NFC platform for identity, security, cryptography, and payment applications. In February 2019, he officially launched Vivokey's Spark cryptobionic implant. Graafstra also implanted an Arduino device in his forearm in September 2016 for self-testing purposes, to be used for the storage of encrypted critical information.

Additionally, access control chips are used at the Epicenter building in Sweden for physical access control to the building, to photocopiers, and even to computers (Epicenter 2017). The Swedish company Biohax was responsible for conducting those chippings for security (Biohax International 2017). Of interest to those in the security community at large, is how two of the most insecure devices, RFID and NFC technology, are being touted for "security purposes" (Halamka et al. 2006).

Health and Monitoring

Proteus (*Medgadget* 2015) proposed that a tiny transmitter accompany all pharmaceuticals, to allow for remote monitoring of patients with adherence to prescribed medications. This would involve some form of behavioral tracking with markers denoting human activity graphs (*Wired UK* 2014) showing when individuals stood, sat, slept, and engaged in exercise. As previously mentioned, the personal health record (PHR) implantable device patent filed by Digital Angel Corporation, known as the VeriChip, was approved by the Food and Drug Administration in the United States in 2004 (FDA 2004). Among those VeriChipped were people suffering from allergies and diabetes as well as Alzheimer's patients living in aged care facilities. Future work commences to make these biomedical developments increasingly important in terms of health outcomes with micrometer-scale, magnetic-resonance-coupled, RFID-carrying wireless sensors small enough to fit in cells (Hu et al. 2017).

E-payment

E-payment would in effect signify the end of "paper" cash and possibly be linked to bitcoin initiatives. Three Square Market (32M) has begun to use implantable devices as a cashless e-payment solution for its vending machines (Darrow 2017). They are purportedly working with American

Express, who are handling the credit transactions. Some vending machines are now designed with no slots for coins, and analysts are now systematically studying specific vending machine transaction patterns linked to credit cards. With greater convenience to users, it would not be such a leap to get patrons to use a vending machine to purchase their favorite soft drink or packet of chips using implants. This highly convenient payment method could emerge as an example of addiction-by-design vending (Schüll 2012). Likewise, the introduction of paywave-based NFC "tap and go" point of sale (PoS) machines has meant that the number of user transactions with plastic cards has dramatically increased in frequency (Elsworth 2014), with some in severe credit debt claiming that the "value" of real money is being lost psychologically, and their ability to control their spending is diminishing. Facebook's cryptocurrency campaign to support a cashless society through the Libra Association may further exacerbate the potential reach of implantables in a cashless society, evading the problems that existed with card not present fraud.

As investigated by researchers (K. Michael 2009a; K. Michael and M. G. Michael 2010), the Baja Beach Club in Barcelona, Spain, accepted payments for goods in their club using a VeriChip implantable. VISA was also working with the University of Technology Sydney (UTS) on future e-payment scenarios (Francis 2015). Biohackers are talking up the potential to use implantables for bitcoin transactions and to aid in blockchain registers. In fact, implants are the ultimate blockchain facilitator, as they are "easy" and always available at the point of transaction, even if it is a remote transaction via a computer console or smartphone.

Criminals and VIPs

There have been a number of high-profile law enforcement and government officials who have called for individuals to be chipped if they are sex offenders (Berry 2011), high-risk persons to society (ABC News 2011), illegal immigrants, and suspected terrorists (*Express Tribune* Correspondent 2015). In 2016, the president of Indonesia, Joko Widodo, passed the directive known as *perppu*, where judges of pedophilia and rape cases are able to enforce the chipping of an offender for all their lives, providing trackability by police (Martel 2016). This follows a bill that was presented in 2008 in the Indonesian province of Papua for some carriers of HIV to be implanted (Associated Press 2008). On the other side of the spectrum are high-profile officials, considered very important persons, who have adopted microchip implants. Among these, as already noted was the Mexican Attorney General (*Wired* 2004) and some of his staff.

Multifunctional Input/Output Device

Several biohackers and companies are experimenting with embedded computer devices with a multiplicity of sensors, on-board cryptographics, more memory, and faster processing speeds. Grindhouse Wetware's Tim Cannon has a Circadia in his left forearm that reads physiological characteristics such as temperature and sends the information remotely to a tablet (Motherboard 2013). Autodesk Research (Holz et al. 2012) also in 2012 experimented with an implantable user interface that had a number of on-board sensors (Holz 2017) including tap sensor, tactile button, pressure sensor, LED, speaker, and vibration motor. The Autodesk Research presented at a CHI conference was significant for its multifunctionality and outside-the-box thinking for computer inputs, though it raised some particularly grave issues for self-experimentation from a participant-observer view. Photography published with the paper shows some radical aesthetic intrusion into the forearm of the experimenter, with a note indicating that people should not try this at home: "Throughout this paper, illustrations have been used in place of actual photographs of the specimen, to ensure ethical and professional standards are maintained" (Holz et al. 2012).

The use-cases of implantable devices have continued to expand from their original demonstrations of Projects Cyborg 1.0 (Warwick 1998) and Cyborg 2.0 (Warwick 2002b), conducted by Kevin Warwick and Mark Gasson. Initially these chips were for identity, location, and interactivity, but they have grown to be so much more. The question remains whether we want to buy in to a future of locked-in principles. While the cool, convenience, and care factors are significant, the control dimension is ever present (Masters and Michael 2005). Who would really want a device that is embedded and cannot easily be removed, registering their every move back to base overtly, or even covertly? For now, the chips most implantees carry are passive devices, but it will not be long before we want more interactivity and turn to semiactive or fully active devices that can do precision location using ultra-wideband (UWB), Bluetooth (BLE), or even NFC technology tethered to smartphones, depending on the context.

Certainly, we have had prosthetic devices that are, for the greater part, life sustaining (e.g., heart pacemakers) or preventative devices (e.g., birth control implantables), such as the Implanon (Implanon USA 2016). However, individuals who are required to anchor down to a brand, or multiple brands, a bank, a telecoms provider, or even a government ID, are likely to disfavor implants.

Some members of the biohacking movement are experimenting with microchipping themselves and others to figure out what else they might do when government ID is heralded in. What might such experimentation achieve if not ultimately propelling us toward a government ID based on implantables? We have seen the biohackers give in to the glitz of big ICT, credit card giants, telecoms vendors, and even DARPA (K. Michael et al. 2017b). This seems to override the biohacker ethic steeped in citizen science, and we already see the complexities take place before us; that is, biohackers now talking to business and trailblazing big ideas. Wetware Grindhouse is talking about hacking the brain next (Mallonnee 2012).

The Implications of Human-centric Implants

Following are some of the major repercussions of implanting the body using miniaturized computer hardware. These concerns apply not just to such embodied computing technologies as injectables but also to swallowable devices and other such technologies that may sit under the skin. There are other relevant issues that space will not allow us to cover in this chapter, including that implants do not always work well (despite what proponents claim), the growing concerns over health issues and spectrum issues, the potential for electromagnetic interference, and multibrand ownership problems.

Security

When using extremely insecure technologies (Reynolds 2004), such as RFID and NFC, for the purposes of physical access control, security issues inevitably arise. No doubt, as these technologies proliferate, people could be drawn against their will to unlock front doors, computer desktops, tablet devices, smartphones, and more, even while asleep (Dehghan 2017). Additionally, there has been no way of tracking unique ID numbers outside a closed campus environment unless a global register is enacted independent of manufacturer. This could lead to a form of unique lifetime identifier for each person, and the things they possess or interact with, and their corresponding social networks. In 2004, Gartner (Reynolds 2004) published several reports indicating that RFID was very insecure. Some people have got around this by claiming that we will still require two-factor authentication with implantables—the embedded ID token, and a biometric or even a password—but this defeats the purpose. RFID and NFC tags can be read and even written to by just about any reader device or smartphone. As previously mentioned, RFID tags can be cloned (Halamka et al. 2006) and hacked (MKme Lab 2014) and also "killed" (Roberti 2014). Biohackers defend the insecurity of the RFID tag by stating that most implants are passive and can be triggered not further than 10 centimeters away, but this ignores that some RFID passive tags have a read range of 10 meters (BlueBite 2019). Civil libertarians and privacy experts point to this as offering even greater precision to identify or locate individuals at the point of the transaction. Moreover, there are NFC readers in smartphones; and we are continuously interacting with our phones. It would not be difficult to precisely identify and locate an implantee with fixed or mobile readers.

Privacy

There are various rights connected to privacy, including location privacy, bodily privacy, and information privacy (Clarke, 1988). No doubt the greatest privacy invasions will come when sensors we bear pick up everything we say, see, and think, and send this data back to hive minds for processing (Ward 2019). High tech beneath the skin is highly intrusive to our overall physical and mental privacy. Individuals who bear implantables have a very limited personal capacity to remove these devices. Removal could mean, at least over time, that we are *persona non grata* or even a "nonperson."

The more data that will be amassed on the databases linked to the implants, the greater the willingness for identity theft and stored personal details. Risks to privacy include surveillance by family members, employers, insurers, stalkers, and governmental agencies. Premises could be rigged up with readers in restrooms, walkways, and flooring to track human movement and the tracking would be continuous via multiple stakeholder vectors, not discrete as it is presently defended.

Enslavement

There is an effectively limitless amount of control that comes with 24/7 monitoring of what may become akin to black box recorders in the body. For now, we have GPS tags that can be worn by recipients (refer to Abbas et al. 2017 for outcomes of GPS-based observational study), such as the "fight recorder" (Defence Science and Technology Group 2017), and devices such as those made by Myriota, enabling machine-to-machine connectivity in the internet of things (Myriota 2018). Although embodied computing technologies such as implantables may seem to introduce greater convenience and care, the dimension of control will be prevalent. The enslavement will also come from those who have access, and for this purpose a given *axis of access*, into the surveillance that could be established by the techno-elite who will be the primary drivers behind the push for singularitarianism. An electronic apartheid could ensue; the technological chasm between the haves and have-nots could be irreconcilable. For the majority of the populace, there could be no "taking a break" from the onslaught of surveillance. The ontological implications, that is, questions directly dealing with the nature of being, are likely to be enormous.

Social e-Inclusion

If we enslave ourselves to a series of future upgrades, as we have seen with smartphones, new and graded societies of people will emerge who can afford varying levels of embodied computing technologies and entry into the higher axis points of new technologies. They will have memory chips to make them smarter and more employable, drug delivery chips to help them live longer, and chips that link them up to neural interfaces and digital speeds for maximum throughput. Those who cannot afford a life of continual upgrades will have access to multifunctional or multiapplication chips that ration and control their e-payments, and everyday applications like ticketing. Others still, depending on the economic system and government, will simply walk around with a unique lifetime identifier, likely DNA codes, used to identify them as "living," perhaps fundamentally robbed of autonomy. Brand ownership will also dictate who can do what with the device(s), and who has read or write access. Perhaps those who can afford it will get more than one chip to serve specific functions; perhaps others who are uninsurable, due to health status or crimes, will have one chip that governs their holistic actions. Already some biohackers have noted the limited space in their hands as they continue to upgrade and hybridize.

Human Rights

Humans could also be reduced to "things" in an "internet of things," where people will be tagged (2017), tracked, and traced like objects. Implants could curb freedom and perhaps even aspects of free will. We have seen what numbered "brands" did to humans who were minorities in that state-sponsored Holocaust; unleashing something even more sophisticated nowadays, using electronic identification implantables, would magnify social sorting on a scale never before seen or imagined. Every piece of data gathered, as we develop and grow, and every related piece of data to family or friends, could be analyzed. These are the fundamental building blocks of the dystopia often written about and discussed in recent decades.

Two important pieces of international law are the *Universal Declaration of Human rights* (especially article 3), and *International Covenant on Civil and Political Rights* (especially articles 7–9). In 2007, researchers (Albrecht 2007) attempted to introduce a Bodily Integrity Act, but it did not come to pass. In the field of human rights, violation of the bodily integrity of another is regarded as unethical, intrusive, and even criminal. This is why law enforcement cannot take an individual's DNA sample without their consent for less-serious offences, otherwise seeking a compulsion order from a judge for more-serious crimes (K. Michael 2009c).

In terms of risks to one's health, nonmedical devices are a personal liability, given the unknown consequences over long-term use. The VivoKey's warning to buyers and recipients reads: "While the VivoKey Spark transponder has undergone several quality checks during manufacture and has been put through a battery of tests with various private labs, it has not been tested or certified by any government regulatory agency for implantation or use inside the human body. Use of this device is strictly at your own risk" (VivoKey 2019).

Discussion: When Medical and Nonmedical Implants Converge

Evaluating Border Crossings in an Interconnected World

We are rapidly moving into the uncharted territory of pervasive technology with an interconnected world of thinking machines. As a vast array of embedded smart devices will be connected to the internet of things and people (IoTaP), technology will be far more intelligent and ubiquitous. Fueled by *calm technology*, devices will free humans from the effort of human-to-machine (H2M) interactions, as well as elements of everyday decision making. Technology will think and act for us behind the lines of visibility. The reach of technology now can extend from the sky (surveillance) to the street (dataveillance, as described by Clarke [1988]) to the person around you (sousveillance, as noted by Mann and colleagues [2003]) to within you (überveillance, as noted by M. G. Michael [2006]), and back to the sky (figure 5.1). Information exchanges can now move seamlessly and automatically in and through us, and across multiple platforms in each of the converging veillances.

To determine privacy violations in the context of the veillances, researchers (Perakslis et al. 2014) examined "borders of privacy" as defined by Gary T. Marx in 2001. Marx proposed four borders. *Natural Borders* relate to materially observable elements such as walls, doors, clothing, facial expressions, and oral conversations. *Social Borders* relate to expectations such as

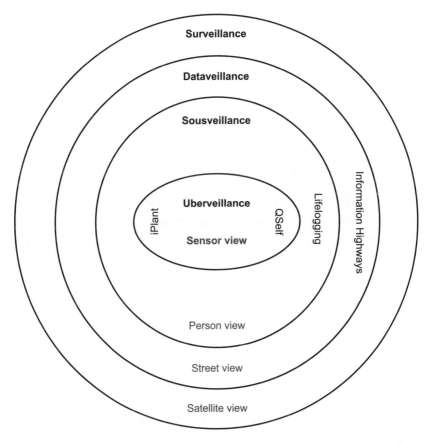

Figure 5.1
The Veillances: Watching or Being Watched.

confidentiality with professionals or family and friends, and freedom from invasion of privacy by others in the social system. *Spatial or Temporal Borders* relate to expectations such as the right to delineate between various areas of an individual's life (work, personal, religious spheres) or at various points in time, and rights to maintain decoupled spheres. *Borders Due to Ephemeral or Transitory Effects* relate to expectations such as the right to have information forgotten, or to delete permanently a past extemporaneous or regrettable action.

The four privacy borders were set against the backdrop of the four veillances and contemplated Marx's concentric circles of information about a human (i.e., individual, private, intimate, and sensitive information). The convergence of the veillances creates an urgent need to address embodied computing technologies that can listen to the inside of humans (e.g., body and thought), quantify our behavior through algorithms, or modify our biochemistry. Thus, researchers (Perakslis et al. 2016) proposed a fifth border, the *physio-psychological border*, defined as "the boundaries of the internal realm of the individual's human system such as physiological and psychological; the expectations of personal autonomy and self-determination of his or her human system, including ownership of the information."

Six Principal Risks of Pervasive Implantable Technologies

Perakslis et al. (2014) have explored these emerging pervasive systems relative to embodied computing technologies and have proposed risks, as well as three overarching attributes to consider: intelligent, unobtrusive, and ubiquitous. Juxtaposing these with the four veillances in order to harvest risks, the authors had proposed six principal risks:

1. Insightfulness: With data gleaned across all veillances, devices will assess humans in multiple contexts, capacities, and times, allowing the system to have a precise and profound understanding of a human in their past, present, and future states.

2. Imperceptibility: Users will be mostly unaware of what is collected, by whom, for how long, how it is synthesized with other data, and who owns the data.

3. Incomprehensibility: Terms and conditions are often murky and/or mutable, and the everyday consumer is not likely to comprehend the wide-ranging system, nor the associated risks across multiple organizations sharing data.

4. Indelibility: Our digital footprints are likely to leave an indelible history of analyzable behaviors, especially if we do not own our data, or if it is shared and stored elsewhere in the veillances.

5. Invasiveness: As we allow devices to listen inside of us and communicate back and forth between the veillances, we are likely to create systems in which not only are our behaviors predicted but even our intent. Dignity is likely to be at risk, even if unintentionally.

6. Involuntariness: Opting in to technology is becoming a requirement to participate in society, to belong and benefit socially or financially.

Pervasive technologies violate all of the aforementioned borders of privacy and so society must enter into the debate to address these issues. History has shown that commonly, consequences are delayed; false senses of security often exist in early stages.

When Metadata is "All" of You: Analogue to Digital

Überveillance (M. G. Michael and K. Michael 2010) can undeniably lead to misinformation, misinterpretation of data, and the manipulation of information. Data gathered for one purpose, no doubt could be retrospectively used, for unrelated functions. Of course, such embodied computing technologies as implantables are just one view of the world (Ms. Smith 2017); the other is what we are doing to our surroundings and the sensors we are embedding wall-to-floor in buildings, in clothing and textiles, in cars and trucks, in private toilets and public lamp-posts. Smart they may well be, but this data will send endless streams back to base for law enforcement big data software to trawl and record and act upon (Merrill 2015).

Perhaps there could be *nowhere* to hide as smart materials in infrastructure interact with smart sensors in people. Would this be all in the name of smart cities and sustainable living paradigms? Perhaps there would be proactive profiling of the masses or targeted populations, like never before envisioned. The coalescence of sensors meeting network infrastructure will mean a world that is more secure in some respects, but also far more less secure if humans have no anonymity, or where creativity and diverse thinking will be curbed for utilitarian dreams, or where ever greater corruption could take place using digital audits that no one can conclusively prove fake. This is possibly the greatest paradox of überveillance: at the very point where we have the greatest visibility of individual day-to-day proceedings, we will also experience the greatest risk. Although benefits of such technologies have been enjoyed at some levels (e.g., medical implants), they have not eliminated or reduced wars, terrorism, famine, or poverty. However, especially in health care, these incredible strides forward are surely welcome and encouraged. Therefore, we are arguing for responsible and discerning engineering where its applications and consequences are well thought out and broadly scrutinized.

If we continue down this technological path unchecked and without rigorous ethical considerations, the result will be severe disruption, with society enabled by technology embedded subcutaneously. There is so much we do not know yet that will take decades to discover—are these devices really safe for the integrity of the *body* and the soundness of the *mind*? Particularly if we understand these components of our life to be highly networked and integrated.

Conclusion

The universal application of such embodied computing technologies as implantables with überveillant consequences can no longer be dismissed as "conspiracy theory," especially as we inch toward a society whereby end users or individuals are becoming the final security and privacy frontier, or the "last mile" in the internet of things and people (IoTaP). The repercussions of these technological developments, such as security, privacy, and human rights challenges, have yet to be fully appreciated. This chapter provides historical context illustrating the advent and rise of salient embodied computing technologies and urges individuals to question and challenge existing assertions regarding the wider benefits of such converging technologies, especially as humans become key nodes in a global network. While the researchers agree that there are many potential health, entrepreneurial, security, and other gains to be had, caution should be exercised. In addition, responsible and discerning engineering is encouraged. Failure to address such issues is likely to result in the realization of an überveillance society that will be plagued with misinformation, misinterpretation of data, and the manipulation of information. This could prove to be one of the greatest ironies of our information age.

References

Abbas, Roba, Katina Michael and MG Michael. 2017. What Can People Do With Your Spatial Data?: Socio-Ethical Scenarios. In A. Marrington, D. Kerr and J. Gammack (Eds.), *Managing Security Issues and the Hidden Dangers of Wearable Technologies*, 206–237. Hershey, PA: IGI Global.

ABC News. 2007. Alzheimer's Patients Lining Up for Microchip. ABC News, August 28. https://web.archive.org/web/20070914185245/http://abcnews.go.com/GMA/OnCall/story?id=3536539.

ABC News. 2011. Top Cop's Wishlist: Microchipped Crooks. ABC News (Australia), January 24. http://www.abc.net.au/news/2011-01-24/top-cops-wishlist-microchipped-crooks/1915814.

Albrecht, Katherine. 2007. Bodily Integrity Act. CASPIAN. https://web.archive.org/web/20150226125030/www.antichips.com/anti-chipping-bill-v07-numbered.pdf.

Albrecht, Katherine, and Liz McIntyre. 2005. *Spychips: How Major Corporations and Government Plan to Track Your Every Purchase and Watch Your Every Move*. Nashville: Nelson Current.

Allen, Catherine A., and William J. Barr, eds. 1997. *Smart Cards: Seizing Strategic Business Opportunities*. New York: McGraw-Hill.

Applied Digital Solutions. 2003. Implantable Personal Verification Systems. https://web.archive.org/web/20031202233328/http://www.adsx.com/prodservpart/verichip.html.

Applied Digital Solutions. 2006. The VeriChip: HealthLink Information. https://youtu.be/Ms-XLxIi7Xo.

Arthur, Charles. 2013. Music to Your Ears? Try a Headphones Implant Like Rich Lee. *Guardian*, July 5. https://www.theguardian.com/technology/2013/jul/04/headphones-implanted-ear-grinder-rich-lee.

Associated Press. 2008. HIV Carriers Face Microchip Implants in Indonesia's Papua Province. *Guardian*, November 25. https://www.theguardian.com/world/2008/nov/24/indonesia-aids.

Australian Law Dictionary. 2010. Overview: Uberveillance. *Oxford Reference*. http://www.oxfordreference.com/view/10.1093/oi/authority.20110803110446167.

Auto-ID Labs. 1999. Auto-ID Labs: The Leading Academic Research Network on the Internet of Things. https://www.autoidlabs.org/.

BBC. 2002. US Family Gets Health Implants. *BBC News*, May 11. http://news.bbc.co.uk/2/hi/health/1981026.stm.

Berry, Petrina. 2011. Microchip, Castrate Sex Offenders: MP. *Sydney Morning Herald*, March 24. http://www.smh.com.au//breaking-news-national/microchip-castrate-sex -offenders-mp-20110324-1c7uw.html.

Biohax International. 2017. Home Page. Biohax International. https://www.biohax .tech/.

Medgadget. 2015. Proteus Swallowable Smart Pills FDA Approved to Measure Medica- tion Adherence. July 6. https://www.medgadget.com/2015/07/proteus-swallowable -smart-pills-fda-approved-to-measure-medication-adherence.html.

Blue Bite. 2019. RFID vs NFC. October 10. https://www.bluebite.com/nfc/rfid-vs-nfc.

Boden, Rian. 2015. Half of Brits Expect to Replace Cash with New Technologies. *NFC World*, August 28. https://www.nfcworld.com/2015/08/28/337345/half-of-brits -expect-to-replace-cash-with-new-technologies/.

BrickHouse Security. 2009. Designed for Secret Service, the Invisible Bluetooth Ear- piece Is Finally Available to the Public. YouTube video published October 22, 2:26. https://youtu.be/OO0_CmhMF9k.

BrickHouse Security. 2018. Wireless Ear Receiver (Squelch). BrickHouse Security Official Site. https://www.brickhousesecurity.com/audio-surveillance/squelch/.

Chan, Stephanie. 2016. Monique Morrow Aims to Give Others Identity—And Her Identity Is Built On Helping Others. *The Network: Cisco's Technology News Site*, Sep- tember 7. https://newsroom.cisco.com/feature-content?type=webcontent&articleId =1785844.

Clarke, Roger. 1998. Information Technology and Dataveillance. *Communications of the ACM* 31 (5): 498–512. https://doi.org/10.1145/42411.42413.

Clarke, Roger. 2010. What Is Uberveillance? (And What Should Be Done About It?). *IEEE Technology and Society Magazine* 19 (2): 17–25. https://doi.org/10.1109/MTS .2010.937030.

Cochrane, Peter. 1999. *Tips for Time Travelers*. New York: McGraw-Hill.

Dangerous Things. 2015. NFC Compatible Archives. https://dangerousthings.com/ category/compatibility/nfc-compatible/.

Darrow, Barb. 2017. Something Big Brother Would Love? A Company Will Implant Microchips in Employees. *Fortune*, July 24. http://fortune.com/2017/07/24/ microchips-employees/.

Defence Science and Technology Group. 2017. "Black Box" for Soldiers to Capture Crucial Data on the Battlefield. Australian Department of Defence Science and Technology, September 7. https://www.dst.defence.gov.au/news/2017/09/07/black -box-soldiers-capture-crucial-data-battlefield.

Dehghan, Saeed Kamali. 2017. Qatar Airways Plane Forced to Land after Wife Discovers Husband's Affair Midflight. *Guardian*, November 8. https://www.theguardian.com/world/2017/nov/08/qatar-airways-plane-forced-to-land-after-wife-discovers-husbands-affair-midflight.

EDRi (European Digital Rights). 2010. Survey on Chip Implants in Germany. March 10. https://edri.org/edrigramnumber8-5study-human-chips-germany/.

EGE (European Group on Ethics in Science and New Technologies). 2005. Ethical Aspects of ICT Implants in the Human Body: Opinion Presented to the Commission by the European Group on Ethics. http://europa.eu/rapid/press-release_MEMO-05-97_en.pdf.

Elsworth, Sophie. 2014. Australia Hooked On Tap and Go Payments: Visa payWave. News Corp Australia Network, February 8. http://www.news.com.au/finance/money/australia-hooked-on-tap-and-go-payments-visa-paywave/news-story/abbc91388c52d1ae5eab0a321cb7fbcc.

Epicenter. 2017. Home page. Epicenter Stockholm. https://weareepicenter.com/stockholm/.

FDA (US Food and Drug Administration). 2004. Class II Special Controls Guidance Document: Implantable Radiofrequency Transponder System for Patient Identification and Health Information—Guidance for Industry and FDA Staff. December 10. https://www.fda.gov/regulatory-information/search-fda-guidance-documents/class-ii-special-controls-guidance-document-implantable-radiofrequency-transponder-system-patient.

Francis, Hannah. 2015. Chip Implants Beneath the Skin Bring a New Meaning to "Pay Wave." *Sydney Morning Herald*, May 29. http://www.smh.com.au/digital-life/digital-life-news/chip-implants-beneath-the-skin-bring-a-new-meaning-to-pay-wave-20150528-ghbq71.html.

Friggieri, Angelo, Katina Michael, and M. G. Michael. 2009. The Legal Ramifications of Microchipping People in the United States of America—A State Legislative Comparison. Paper presented at the 2009 IEEE International Symposium on Technology and Society, Tempe, AZ, USA, May 18–20. https://doi.org/10.1109/ISTAS.2009.5155900.

Gardner, W. 2004. RFID Chips Implanted in Mexican Law-Enforcement Workers. *InformationWeek*, July 15. https://www.informationweek.com/rfid-chips-implanted-in-mexican-law-enforcement-workers/d/d-id/1026195.

Gasson, Mark N. 2010. Human Enhancement: Could You Become Infected with a Computer Virus? Paper presented at the 2010 IEEE International Symposium on Technology and Society, Wollongong, NSW, Australia, June 7–9. https://doi.org/10.1109/ISTAS.2010.5514651.

Graafstra, Amal. 2006. *RFID Toys: Cool Projects for Home, Office, and Entertainment.* Indianapolis: Wiley Publishing.

Graafstra, Amal. 2007. Hands On: How Radio-Frequency Identification and I Got Personal. *IEEE Spectrum,* February 28. https://spectrum.ieee.org/computing/hardware/hands-on.

Graafstra, Amal, Katina Michael, and M. G. Michael. 2010. Social-Technical Issues Facing the Humancentric RFID Implantee Sub-Culture through the Eyes of Amal Graafstra. Paper presented at the 2010 IEEE International Symposium on Technology and Society, Wollongong, NSW, Australia, June 7–9. https://doi.org/10.1109/ISTAS.2010.5514602.

Graafstra, Amal, Jonathan Oxer, Meow Ludo, and Katina Michael. 2016. "Augmented Australia" panel at the launch of *Deus Ex: Mankind Divided.* ATP Innovations, Redfern, NSW, Australia, September 24.

Grognard, Catherine. 1994. *The Tattoo: Graffiti for the Soul.* Madrid: Promotional Reprint Company.

Guta, Adrian, Marilou Gagnon, and Jean Daniel Jacob. 2012. Using Foucault to Recast the Telecare Debate. *American Journal of Bioethics* 12 (9): 57–59. https://doi.org/10.1080/15265161.2012.699140.

Halamka, John, Ari Juels, Adam Stubblefield, and Jonathan Westhues. 2006. The Security Implications of VeriChip Cloning. *Journal of the American Medical Informatics Association* 13 (6): 601–607. https://doi.org/10.1197%2Fjamia.M2143.

Hannan, Ewin, and Simone Fox Koob. 2017. Worker Chip Implants "Only Matter of Time." *Australian,* August 3. http://www.theaustralian.com.au/business/technology/worker-chip-implants-only-matter-of-time/news-story/1f9f9317cc84f365410a089566153f51.

Harbisson, Neil. 2010. Cyborg Project: A Transmedia Project. http://cyborgproject.com/.

Heffernan, Kayla J., Frank Vetere, and Shanton Chang. 2017. Towards Insertables: Devices inside the Human Body. *First Monday* 22 (3). http://firstmonday.org/ojs/index.php/fm/article/view/6214/5970.

Hinchliffe, Emma. 2017. This Made-for-iPhone Cochlear Implant Is a Big Deal for the Deaf Community. *Mashable,* July 26. http://mashable.com/2017/07/26/cochlear-implant-iphone/.

Holz, Christian. 2017. Implanted User Interfaces. http://www.christianholz.net/implanted_user_interfaces.html.

Holz, Christian, Tovi Grossman, George Fitzmaurice, and Anne Agur. 2012. Implanted User Interfaces. In *Proceedings of the ACM SIGCHI Conference on Human*

Factors in Computing Systems (CHI '12), edited by Ed H. Chi and Kristina Höök, 503–512. New York: ACM. https://doi.org/10.1145/2207676.2207745.

Hu, Xiaolin, Kamal Aggarwal, Mimi X. Yang, Kokab B. Parizi, Xiaoqing Xu, Demir Akin, Ada S. Y. Poon, and H.-S. Philip Wong. 2017. Micrometer-scale magnetic-resonance-coupled radio-frequency identification and transceivers for wireless sensors in cells. *Physical Review Applied* 8:014031. https://doi.org/10.1103/PhysRev Applied.8.014031.

IBM. 2007. The Future Market: Business Innovations. YouTube. https://www.youtube .com/watch?v=eob532iEpqk (video no longer available due to copyright claim).

IBM. 2008. Inventory Off Track: IBM Can Help. YouTube video uploaded June 26, 0:31. https://youtu.be/oAvQcYcvyaw.

Implanon USA. 2016. Implanon. Merck Sharp & Dohme B.V. https://web.archive .org/web/20160314170416/http://www.implanon-usa.com/en/consumer/index .xhtml.

IQT. 2017. National Security: Identify, Adapt, Deliver. In-Q-Tel. https://www.iqt.org/ sectors/national-security/.

Kac, Eduardo. 1997. Event in Which a Microchip (Identification Transponder Tag) Was Implanted in the Artist's Left Ankle. Time Capsule, Casa das Rosas Cultural Center, São Paulo, Brazil. http://www.ekac.org/timec.html.

Kargl, Frank, Elaine Lawrence, Martin Fischer, and Yen Yang Lim. 2008. Security, Privacy and Legal Issues in Pervasive eHealth Monitoring Systems. Paper presented at the 7th International Conference on Mobile Business, Barcelona, Spain, July 7–8. https://doi.org/10.1109/ICMB.2008.31.

Kulaiay, Mohamed. 2013. Regina Dugan at D11 2013. YouTube, June 1. https:// www.youtube.com/watch?v=fzB1EcocAF8.

Kumar, Vikas. 2007. Implantable RFID chips: Security versus ethics. In *The Future of Identity in the Information Society, IFIP International Federation for Information Processing, Vol. 262*, edited by S. Fischer-Hubner, P. Duquenoy, A. Zuccato, and L. Mariucci, 151–157. Berlin: Springer.

Lewan, Todd. 2007. Chips: High-Tech Aids or Tools for Big Brother? Debate Rages over Proliferation of Ever-More-Precise Tracking. *NBC News*, July 23. http://www .nbcnews.com/id/19904543/ns/technology_and_science-security/t/chips-high -tech-aids-or-tools-big-brother/.

Mallonnee, Laura. 2012. The DIY Cyborgs Hacking Their Bodies for Fun. *Wired*, June 8. https://www.wired.com/story/hannes-wiedemann-grinders/.

Maly, Tim. 2013. Freescale's Insanely Tiny Arm Chip Will Put the Internet of Things inside Your Body. *Wired*, February 26. https://www.wired.com/2013/02/freescales -tiny-arm-chip/.

Mann, Steve, Jason Nolan, and Barry Wellman. 2003. Sousveillance: Inventing and Using Wearable Computing Devices for Data Collection in Surveillance Environments. *Surveillance & Society* 1 (3): 331–355. https://doi.org/10.24908/ss.v1i3.3344.

Martel, Frances. 2016. Indonesia: President OKs Chemical Castration, Microchip Implant for Pedophiles. *Breitbart*, May 26. http://www.breitbart.com/national-security/2016/05/26/indonesia-oks-chemical-castration-pedophiles/.

Marx, Gary. 2001. Murky Conceptual Waters: The Public and the Private. *Ethics and Information Technology* 3 (3): 152–169. https://doi.org/10.1023/A:1012456832336.

Masters, Amelia, and Katina Michael. 2005. Humancentric Applications of RFID Implants: The Usability Contexts of Control, Convenience and Care. Paper presented at the Second IEEE International Workshop on Mobile Commerce and Services, Munich, Germany, July 19. https://doi.org/10.1109/WMCS.2005.11.

Masters, Amelia, and Katina Michael. 2007. Lend Me Your Arms: The Use and Implications of Humancentric RFID. *Electronic Commerce Research and Applications* 6 (1): 29–39. https://doi.org/10.1016/j.elerap.2006.04.008.

Merrill, Whitney. 2015. Whitney Merrill: Predicting Crime in a Big Data World. Presentation given at 32C3 Gated Communities, December 30, 31:51. https://youtu.be/_du5F4chi-g.

Michael, Katina. 2003a. The Technological Trajectory of the Automatic Identification Industry: The Application of the Systems of Innovation (SI) Framework for the Characterisation and Prediction of the Auto-ID Industry. PhD diss., University of Wollongong School of Information Technology and Computer Science. https://ro.uow.edu.au/theses/309/.

Michael, Katina. 2003b. The Automatic Identification Trajectory. In *Internet Commerce: Digital Models for Business*, edited by Elaine Lawrence, Stephen Newton, Brian Corbitt, John Lawrence, Stephen Dann, and Theerasak Thanasankit, 131–134. Milton, Australia: John Wiley & Sons.

Michael, Katina. 2009a. The Baja Beach Club IT Manager. http://www.katinamichael.com/interviews/2015/3/20/baja-beach-club-it-manager.

Michael, Katina. 2009b. The Microchip Implant Consultant. http://www.katinamichael.com/interviews/2015/3/20/gary-retherford-the-microchip-implant-consultant.

Michael, Katina. 2009c. The Implications of the European Court of Human Rights' Ruling Against the UK's Policy of Keeping Fingerprints and DNA Profiles and Samples of Innocents. Unpublished manuscript, University of Wollongong.

Michael, Katina. 2012. Microchipping People: Associate Professor Katina Michael at TEDxUWollongong. Filmed May 29 in Wollongong, NSW, Australia. TEDx video, 14:31. https://youtu.be/fnghvVR5Evc.

Michael, Katina. 2015. Mental Health, Implantables, and Side Effects. *IEEE Technology and Society Magazine* 32 (2): 5–17. https://doi.org/10.1109/MTS.2015.2434471.

Michael, Katina. 2016. RFID/NFC Implants for Bitcoin Transactions. *IEEE Consumer Electronics Magazine* 5 (3): 103–106. https://doi.org/10.1109/MCE.2016.2556900.

Michael, Katina, Anas Aloudat, M. G. Michael, and Christine Perakslis. 2017a. You Want to Do What with RFID? Perceptions of Radio-Frequency Identification Implants for Employee Identification in the Workplace. *IEEE Consumer Electronics Magazine* 6 (3): 111–117. https://doi.org/10.1109/MCE.2017.2684978.

Michael, Katina, and Amelia Masters. 2004. Applications of Human Transponder Implants in Mobile Commerce. Paper presented at the 8th World Multiconference on Systemics, Cybernetics and Informatics, Orlando, Florida, USA, July 18–21. https://ro.uow.edu.au/infopapers/384/.

Michael, Katina, and Amelia Masters. 2006. Realized Applications of Positioning Technologies In Defense Intelligence. In *Applications of Information Systems to Homeland Security and Defense*, edited by Hussein A. Abbass and Daryl Essam, 167–195. Hershey, PA: Idea Group.

Michael, Katina, and M. G. Michael. 2007. Homo Electricus and the Continued Speciation of Humans. In *Encyclopedia of Information Ethics and Security*, edited by Marian Quigley, 312–318. Hershey, PA: IGI Global.

Michael, Katina, and M. G. Michael. 2009. *Innovative Automatic Identification and Location-Based Services: From Bar Codes to Chip Implants*. Hershey, PA: IGI Reference.

Michael, Katina, and M. G. Michael. 2010. Implementing "Namebars" Using Microchip Implants: The Black Box beneath the Skin. In *This Pervasive Day: The Potential and Perils of Pervasive Computing*, edited by Jeremy Pitt, 163–206. London: Imperial College London Press.

Michael, Katina, and M. G. Michael. 2013. The Future Prospects of Embedded Microchips in Humans as Unique Identifiers: The Risks versus the Rewards. *Media, Culture & Society* 35 (1): 78–86. https://doi.org/10.1177%2F0163443712464561.

Michael, Katina, M. G. Michael, and Roba Abbas. 2009. The Dilemmas of Using Wearable Computing to Monitor People: An Extended Metaphor on the Tracking of Prison Inmates and Parolees. Paper presented at the Australia and New Zealand Society of Criminology Conference—Crime and Justice Challenges in the 21st Century: Victims, Offenders and Communities. Perth, WA, Australia, November 22–25.

Michael, Katina, M. G. Michael, Jai C. Galliot, and Rob Nicholls. 2017b. Socio-Ethical Implications of Implantable Technologies in the Military Sector [Guest Editorial]. *IEEE Technology and Society Magazine* 36 (1): 7–9. https://doi.org/10.1109/MTS.2017.2670219.

Michael, Katina, and Keith W. Miller. 2013. Big Data: New Opportunities and New Challenges. *Computer* 46 (6): 22–24. https://doi.org/10.1109/MC.2013.196.

Michael, Katina, and Rebecca Monteleone. 2019. Microchipping People is a "Bad Idea": An Interview with Andreas Sjostrom. *IEEE Technology and Society Magazine* 38 (2): 18–21, 39.

Michael, M. G., and Katina Michael. 2007. A Note on "Überveillance." In *The Second Workshop on the Social Implications of National Security: From Dataveillance to Uberveillance and the Realpolitik of the Transparent Society*, edited by Katina Michael and M. G. Michael, 9–25. Wollongong, Australia: University of Wollongong.

Michael, M. G., and Katina Michael. 2007. Uberveillance. 29th International Conference of Data Protection and Privacy Commissioners—Privacy Horizons: Terra Incognita, Location Based Tracking Workshop, Montreal, Canada. http://works.bepress.com/kmichael/146/.

Michael, M. G., and Katina Michael. 2009. Uberveillance: Definition. In *Macquarie Dictionary*, 5th ed., edited by S. Butler, 1094. https://works.bepress.com/kmichael/178/.

Michael, M. G., and Katina Michael. 2010. Toward a State of Überveillance. *IEEE Technology and Society Magazine* 29 (2): 9–16. https://doi.org/10.1109/MTS.2010.937024.

Michael, M. G., and Katina Michael, eds. 2013. *Uberveillance and the Social Implications of Microchip Implants: Emerging Technologies*, 463. Hershey, PA: IGI Reference.

Michael, M. G., Sarah J. Fusco, and Katina Michael. 2008. A Research Note on Ethics in the Emerging Age of überveillance. *Computer Communications* 31 (6): 1192–1199. https://doi.org/10.1016/j.comcom.2008.01.023.

MKme Lab. 2014. RFID with Arduino—Some Fun Hacking Cards. YouTube video published April 20, 7:43. https://youtu.be/Up-DSf98UFE.

Motherboard. 2013. Experimenting with Biochip Implants. YouTube video published October 31, 7:30. https://youtu.be/clIiP1H3Opw.

Ms. Smith. 2017. Cops Use Pacemaker Data to Charge Homeowner with Arson, Insurance Fraud. *CSO.* January 30. https://www.csoonline.com/article/3162740/security/cops-use-pacemaker-data-as-evidence-to-charge-homeowner-with-arson-insurance-fraud.html.

Myriota. 2018. Home page. http://myriota.com/.

New Scientist Staff and *Reuters.* 2008. Mexicans Get Microchipped over Kidnapping Fears. *New Scientist*, August 22. https://www.newscientist.com/article/dn14589-mexicans-get-microchipped-over-kidnapping-fears/.

Opam, Kwame. 2011. RFID implants Won't Work If You've Been Kidnapped in Mexico. *Gizmodo*, August 23. https://www.gizmodo.com.au/2011/08/rfid-implants-wont-work-if-youve-been-kidnapped-in-mexico/.

Perakslis, Christine, Jeremy Pitt, Katina Michael, and M. G. Michael. 2014. Pervasive Technology: Principles to Consider. *Ethics in Biology Engineering & Medicine: An International Journal* 5 (4): 79–93. https://doi.org/10.1615/EthicsBiologyEngMed .2015013104.

Perakslis, Christine, Katina Michael, and M. G. Michael. 2016. The Converging Veillances: Border Crossings in an Interconnected World. *IEEE Potentials* 35 (4): 23–25. https://doi.org/10.1109/MPOT.2016.2569724.

Perusco, Laura, Katina Michael, and M. G. Michael. 2006. Location-Based Services and the Privacy–Security Dichotomy. Paper presented at the 3rd International Conference on Mobile Computing and Ubiquitous Networking, London, England, October 11–13. https://works.bepress.com/mgmichael/9/.

Reynolds, Martin. 2004. RFID Implants Need Better Privacy Protection. Gartner Research, October 19. https://www.gartner.com/doc/456911/rfid-implants-need -better-privacy.

Roberti, Mark. 2014. How Can I Kill an RFID Tag Implant? *RFID Journal*, May 22. http://www.rfidjournal.com/blogs/experts/entry?11028.

Rosenberg, Mica. 2008. Satellites Track Mexico Kidnap Victims with Chips. *Reuters*, August 21. https://www.reuters.com/article/us-mexico-crime-chips/satellites-track -mexico-kidnap-victims-with-chips-idUSN2041333820080822.

Schüll, Natasha. 2012. *Addiction by Design: Machine Gambling in Las Vegas.* Princeton, NJ: Princeton University Press.

Sirotich, Matthew. 2007. ePassport Security under the Microscope. In *The Second Workshop on the Social Implications of National Security: From Dataveillance to Überveillance and the Realpolitik of the Transparent Society,* edited by Katina Michael and M. G. Michael, 257–280. Wollongong, Australia: University of Wollongong.

Sjöström, Andreas. 2017. NFC Chip Implants Are a Bad Idea. Andreas Sjöström official site, December 3. http://andreassjostrom.com/nfc-chip-implants-are-a-bad-idea/.

Sjöström, Andreas. 2016. Boarding a Flight with an NFC Implant. YouTube video published January 8, 8:42. https://youtu.be/ORDjQU5pBc0.

Stephan, Karl D., Katina Michael, M. G. Michael, Laura Jacob, and Emily P. Anesta. 2012. Social Implications of Technology: The Past, the Present, and the Future. *Proceedings of the IEEE* 100 (Special Centennial Issue): 1752–1781. https://doi.org/ 10.1109/JPROC.2012.2189919.

Storey, Greg. 2014. Bringing the Ease of Contactless Payments to the Virtual Marketplace. Presentation given at The Future of Payments—Technology & Innovation, Sydney, Australia, September 19. http://fst.net.au/conferences/technology -innovation-future-payments.

Express Tribune Correspondent. 2015. Plan to Track Fourth Schedule Suspects Using Chip Implants Meets Scathing Criticism. *Express Tribune*, March 14. https://tribune.com.pk/story/852977/plan-to-track-fourth-schedule-suspects-using-chip-implants-meets-scathing-criticism/.

Trevarthen, Adam, and Katina Michael. 2007. Beyond Mere Compliance of RFID Regulations by the Farming Community: A Case Study of the Cochrane Dairy Farm. Paper presented at the Sixth International Conference on Mobile Business, Toronto, Canada, July 9–11. https://doi.org/10.1109/ICMB.2007.21.

VivoKey. 2019. VivoKey Spark [Cryptobionic Implant]. DangerousThings.com. https://dangerousthings.com/product/vivokey-spark/.

Wang, Jessa Liying, and Michael C. Loui. 2009. Privacy and Ethical Issues in Location-Based Tracking Systems. Paper presented at the 2009 IEEE International Symposium on Technology and Society (ISTAS 2009), Tempe, AZ, USA, May 18–20. https://doi.org/10.1109/ISTAS.2009.5155910.

Ward, Jacob. 2019. Why Data, Not Privacy, Is the Real Danger. *NBC News*, February 4. https://www.nbcnews.com/business/business-news/why-data-not-privacy-real-danger-n966621.

Warwick, Kevin. 1998. Project Cyborg 1.0. Kevin Warwick official website. http://www.kevinwarwick.com/project-cyborg-1-0/.

Warwick, Kevin. 2002a. *I Cyborg*. London: Century.

Warwick, Kevin. 2002b. Project Cyborg 2.0: The Next Step towards True Cyborgs? Kevin Warwick official website. http://www.kevinwarwick.com/project-cyborg-2-0/.

Warwick, Kevin, Mark Gasson, Benjamin Hutt, Iain Goodhew, Peter Kyberd, Brian Andrews, Peter Teddy, and Amjad Shad. 2003. The Application of Implant Technology for Cybernetic Systems. *JAMA Neurology* 60 (10): 1369–1373. https://doi.org/10.1001/archneur.60.10.1369.

Weller, Chris. 2017. A Swedish Rail Line Now Scans Microchip Implants in Addition to Accepting Paper Tickets. *Business Insider*, June 20. https://www.businessinsider.com.au/swedish-rail-company-scans-microchip-tickets-17-6-2017-6.

Wired. 2004. Mexican Officials Get Chipped. July 13. https://www.wired.com/2004/07/mexican-officials-get-chipped/.

Wired UK. 2014. Andrew Thompson: Digital Drugs Will Transform Healthcare. YouTube video published May 2, 14:46. https://youtu.be/3aId6jSDSg0.

Wood, Ken. 2004. Ubiquitous Computing at Microsoft Research in UK. *Channel 9*, September 29. https://channel9.msdn.com/Blogs/TheChannel9Team/Ken-Wood-Ubiquitous-computing-at-Microsoft-Research-in-UK.

6 Designing Technological Comportment: On Wearable Technology, Digital Rituals, and Non-Users

Marcel O'Gorman

> I would call this comportment toward technology which expresses "yes" and at the same time "no," by an old word, releasement toward things.
>
> —Martin Heidegger, "Discourse on Thinking" (1966, 54)

In March 2014, I found myself standing just inside the entrance of a massive carnival tent in downtown Phoenix, dressed in a black cassock and wearing a long gray wig. With arms outstretched, I entreated passers-by to confess their digital sins and lock away their devices in a repurposed Catholic tabernacle box. My friend and colleague wore a similar disguise, supporting my efforts by preaching the Analog Word: "Know thyself—not thy selfies!" We, the Ministers of the Digital Tabernacle, had descended upon the Carnival of the Future to profess digital abstinence. This performance fills me with a sort of monkish self-loathing; perhaps in part because of the ludicrous get-up, but more so because it suspends the performers in a state of technological ambivalence, even to the point of hypocrisy. That said, I have come to understand this project, which I have since performed several times, as a wearable intervention; beyond the wig and cassock, the disguise also includes an Autographer lifelogging camera,[1] worn around the neck and modified to look like a shiny black cross (see figure 6.1).[2] This device allows the performers to document willing and not-so-willing penitents as they confess their "digital sins," one photo for every thirty seconds. Why would a preacher of digital abstinence make such explicit and hypocritical use of an invasive digital device?

Before tackling this question directly, it is useful to consider the broader context of digital wearables that promote forms of abstinence. There has been a notable surge recently in the invention of such devices. The most

Figure 6.1
Lifelogging Cross for Digital Tabernacle, 2014

common example might be apps for the Apple Watch, such as the Livestrong Myquit Coach or the more adventurously titled Get Rich or Die Smoking app. These products help a smoker monitor consumption, earn rewards for good behavior, and access a support network, among other functions. But they are not strictly designed for a wearable device. On the other hand, there is the QT-Watch, a designated device for smoking cessation designed by a medical doctor who specializes in the treatment of nicotine addiction. Among other features, the QT-Watch sports a small button on the face with a cigarette graphic on it, used to count the number of times a user lights up during the day. A far more sophisticated device is the SmartStop, a watch-like wearable that serves as a transdermal nicotine delivery platform. As I write this, the researchers are seeking to miniaturize the SmartStop into a light wristband with Bluetooth connectivity that not only administers doses of nicotine, but also links the wearer to an addiction support app, much like the ones mentioned above.

For those seeking abstinence from harder substances such as alcohol and illicit drugs, wearables become more creative and, not surprisingly, more invasive. In 2015, researchers at the University of Texas at Dallas developed (what looks like an Arduino-based) "Wearable biochemical sensor for monitoring alcohol consumption lifestyle through Ethyl glucuronide (EtG) detection in human sweat" (Selvam et al. 2016). The hacked-together device uses LED lights to indicate whether the wearer is in a state of "abstinence" (green), "mild alcohol consumption" (yellow), or "binge drinking" (red) (Selvam et al. 2016). Since then, more refined versions of alcohol-deterring wearables have been developed at other laboratories across the United States, including one at Florida International University that targets binge drinking on college campuses (Kregting 2017). This particular watch-like invention "picks up vapors from the skin and sends the data to a server. If the alcohol reading is high, via an app, a designated loved one gets an alert to check in on the user" (Kregting 2017).

Meanwhile, researchers at the University of Massachusetts Medical School have tested a wrist-worn biosensor on four emergency department patients to monitor their illicit drug habits (Carreiro et al. 2015). The wearable provides real-time detection of skin conductivity, skin temperature, and acceleration. Although it was designed to study the health-related behaviors of drug addicts, and not to promote abstinence, other products are being developed for this very purpose. The start-up company Behaivior (note that the AI is not a typo), founded at Carnegie Mellon University, is developing a biosensor wearable that alerts a recovering addict when heart rate, stress level, or even geographical location suggests that a relapse may be imminent. Rather than attempting to detect drug use directly, the Behaivior device is proactive; it "screens users for whether they are in a prerelapse craving state, and therefore at higher risk of relapsing in the near future" (Behaivior n.d.). Much like the alcohol-sensing device described above, an accompanying app will allow friends or family members to access live data from the device wearer and possibly plan an intervention.

Finally, an account of digital wearables that promote abstinence would be incomplete without consideration of sexual abstinence. As with smokers, there are apps designed for sex addicts, including the Abstain! app developed by Hungry Wasp LLC for Apple devices.[3] Once again, these apps are not designed specifically for wearable applications; in fact, dedicated wearables that promote sexual abstinence seem to be uncharted territory. Surprisingly, a search for "chastity wearables" on Google did not yield a tidal wave of sites marketing chastity rings for Christian teens, but instead produced many links to Evotion, a company that sells 3D-printed chastity belts for men. While these wearables—which look like overdetermined modernist sculptures or possibly lingerie designed for naughty Star Wars Storm Troopers—are not digital, what's instructive about them is that they are not designed to promote chastity at all. In fact, they might be viewed as ironic devices that harness abstinence, so to speak, for the sake of promoting a more controlled, or perhaps ritualistic access to sexual pleasure. More to the point, these chastity belts share something crucial in common with all the other abstinence wearables discussed thus far: quite simply, they are all built on the assumption that abstinence is not a permanent condition, but a temporary state that serves a specific purpose, whether it be health improvement, legal vigilance, or sexual stimulation.

In *All or Nothing: A Short History of Abstinence in America*, Jessica Warner defines abstinence as "a principled and unerring refusal to engage in a particular activity" (Warner 2006, xi). "Going without something for a short period of time," suggests Warner, "is not abstinence" (xi). The problem with this rigid definition—which to be fair is based on Warner's account of the nineteenth-century Temperance movement—is that it does not take into account the possibility of temporary or even ritualistic forms of abstinence. Consider, for example, the words that God spoke to Aaron regarding abstinence in the mobile Tabernacle that was central to the Israelites' exodus from Egypt:

> 8 And the Lord spake unto Aaron, saying,9 Do not drink wine nor strong drink, thou, nor thy sons with thee, when ye go into the tabernacle of the congregation, lest ye die: it shall be a statute for ever throughout your generations:10 And that ye may put difference between holy and unholy, and between unclean and clean;
> (Leviticus 10:9)

This is not an all-or-nothing commandment, but a site-specific form of abstinence that more closely reflects our own contemporary rituals of moderation. For example, a raging carnivore might abstain from eating meat while having a weekly lunch date with a vegan friend. Here, abstinence is integrated into a temporary ritualistic practice, much in the same way that Catholics might not eat meat on Fridays during the season of Lent, but are free to feast on Friday flesh for the rest of the year. This brings us back to Digital Tabernacle, which is an attempt to co-opt some of the discursive and ritualistic practices of abstinence specific to Catholicism, and put them in the service of a critical intervention that asks people to contemplate not God, but their own digital habits.

The focus on ritual here is central to my broader research on digital abstinence, which seeks in part to understand how digital devices inspire ritualistic behaviours[4] and how, in turn, new rituals might be developed to encourage moderation of digital device usage. In *The Craft of Ritual Studies*, Ronald Grimes provides practical advice for students of ritual, whether they are junior undergraduates or scholars seeking to integrate ritual studies into their own field of research. Frustrated with the tendency of ritual studies scholars to provide reductive or self-conflicting definitions of ritual, Grimes promotes a more experimental approach, as encapsulated in the following bicycle-inspired passage: "Borrow or invent a definition and, imperfect as it is, work with it. Figure out what it facilitates and it inhibits. Repair it if you can, and keep on pedaling. If that doesn't work, trade it in on a new model" (Grimes 2014, 190). Consider, for example, Victor Turner's definition of ritual as "formal behaviour prescribed for occasions not given over to technological routine that have reference to beliefs in mystical (or non-empirical) power" (1970, 19). While this technosensitive definition would help distinguish between digital rituals and simple user routines prescribed by designers, it ignores the fact that ritual itself is a form of technique. As Barry Stephenson suggests in his description of the *Liji* or Confucian *Book of Rites*, "Ritual is a device and technique for generating and maintaining order, good will, and a sense of belonging" (B. Stephenson 2015, 102). In seeking to define digital ritual, it would be best to keep this concept of technique in mind, perhaps combining it with an axiom from Jonathan Z. Smith: "Ritual is, first and foremost, a mode of paying attention" (1992, 103). More specifically, as Stephenson puts it, ritual is "a different way of framing attention between what one is doing and what one is thinking or feeling" (2015, 84). I have chosen to pedal along with ritual theories that focus on attention because they work well in the context of digital culture, which comes with its own demands on the attentional capacities of device users.

With this conception of ritual in hand, I want to consider the possibility of creating new digital rituals that encourage users to pay attention in a different way than what is dictated by the consumer devices at their disposal. Grimes uses the word "counter-ritual," noting that "ritualists can perform 'against,' taking issue with, or providing alternatives to rituals that exclude them and values they cherish" (2014, 303).[5] Grimes even provides a checklist that can help suggest how new ritual actions might be invented, a process he calls *ritualizing* (2014, 193). Actions can be transformed into rituals by:

- traditionalizing them—for instance, by claiming that they originated a long time ago or with the ancestors;
- elevating them by associating them with sacredly held values—those values that make people who they are and that display either how things really are or how they ought to be;
- repeating them—over and over, in the same way—thus inscribing them in a community and/or the self;
- singularizing them, that is, offering them as rare or even one-time events;
- prescribing their details so they are performed in the proper way;
- stylizing them, so they are carried out with flair;
- entering them with an extraordinary attitude or in a special state of mind—for example, contemplatively or in a trance;
- invoking powers to whom respect or reverence is due—gods, royalty, and spirits, for example;
- attributing to them special power or influence;
- situating them in special places and/or times; or
- having them performed by specially qualified persons (2014, 194).

Digital Tabernacle provides one example of how new rituals might be invented to promote digital abstinence by traditionalizing, elevating, repeating, singularizing, prescribing, stylizing, and performing specific actions.

The concept of inventing rituals for digital abstinence is, of course, not exclusive to the Ministers of the Digital Tabernacle. High-tech burnouts can find solace at one of many, highly ritualistic, digital detox camps that have sprouted up around the United States during the past decade. One of the most prominent retreats, Camp Grounded, offers the following rationale for a digital detox on its website, elevated by reference to "sacredly held values" (Grimes 2014, 194): "In an era of constant technological acceleration and innovation, an over abundance of screen time, information overload, tech-driven anxiety, social media everything, internet addiction, a constant sense of FOMO (fear of missing out), selfies, and being endlessly tethered and always available—many have referred to us as the ultimate decelerator. We help you slow down. We remind you to look up" (Digital Detox n.d.). Similarly, in 2008, attendees of a retreat organized by Reboot, an organization guided by Jewish traditions, conceived of the Sabbath Manifesto, described on the Reboot website as "a creative project designed to slow down lives in an increasingly hectic world" (n.d.). As part of this mandate, Reboot also launched a ritualistic National Day of Unplugging, "a 24 hour period—running from sundown to sundown—and starts on the first Friday in March. The project is an outgrowth of The Sabbath Manifesto, an adaption of our ancestors' ritual of carving out one day per week to unwind, unplug, relax, reflect, get outdoors, and connect with loved ones" (reboot n.d.). Like Camp Grounded, the National Day of Unplugging focuses on concepts like authenticity and presence, while promoting an attention to time that is not determined by technocratic demands (Digital Detox n.d.). Reboot has even designed a small "sleeping bag," a wearable worn by handheld devices themselves, which can be used as part of a digital Sabbath ritual (n.d.).

This sleeping bag brings us closer to the conception of a wearable that might be central to a ritualistic performance of digital abstinence. A distant cousin of this bag has been marketed successfully by a San Francisco–based start-up called Yondr, which has invented a neoprene pouch with a magnetic enclosure designed to ensure the non-use of handheld devices at specific events. People at the event lock their device in a Yondr case and take it with them into the venue. On the way out, they use a small unlocking station to liberate the device from the pouch. Yondr is essentially prescribing a new ritual practice that targets the attention of audiences attending a live show. Championing the catchphrase "be here now," Yondr claims to have "a simple purpose: to show people how powerful a moment can be when we aren't focused on documenting or broadcasting it" (Yondr n.d.). The list of performers who have used Yondr includes Chris Rock, Alicia Keys, and Guns N' Roses. Nightclubs, schools,[6] and churches are also making use of the product. David Sax writes in a *Guardian* article that Yondr, which he calls a "cell phone straightjacket," might help us reclaim a more enjoyable, tech-free version of reality (Sax 2016). Otherwise, "putting screens between that reality, and our selves, instantly creates a pixilated poverty of a rich analog experience" (Sax 2016). What Yondr demonstrates is that phenomenological questions about presence, reality, and the self—as ill-guided as these questions may sometimes be—may be plied for the sake of designing digital abstinence wearables that mobilize new rituals of moderation. Then again, one might challenge this argument by noting that the Yondr pouch is technically not wearable, nor is it digital, especially when compared, for example, to a product like the ill-fated Ivanka Trump Chargeable Handbag. What, then, would a digital abstinence wearable look like?

Taking a cue from the rhetorical strategies of Yondr, Digital Sabbath, Camp Grounded, and other proponents of digital abstinence, students in one of my design classes recently pitched their concept for a product called OneWatch. This is a timepiece with only one arm that takes twenty-four hours to go through a full rotation. Students justified the design of the watch by pitching it as a form of resistance to Taylorism: "In sales, factories, and athletics, the faster a person completes a task, the more they are rewarded, be it with financial bonuses, promotions, or trophies. To be more efficient at these tasks, people for generations have worked at breaking down each movement of an activity into simple mechanics or techniques that can be quickly and easily taught and mastered" (Fryer-Davis 2017, 2). Digital technology, as the author notes, has only exacerbated this problem; wearable devices are an explicit symbol of what we have come to know as the quantified self, which is the apotheosis of Taylorism. The OneWatch on the other hand, inspired by the work of Jacques Ellul and Lewis Mumford among others, "is designed to abstract time and counter its structured nature" (Fryer-Davis 2017, 2). The watch is not meant to be worn all day every day, but as a way of creating a special time that is not governed by efficiency. Put otherwise, when worn as part of a ritual practice of technical resistance, this wearable promotes the concept of *illud tempus* introduced by Mircea Eliade (1959, 169). The inventors of the OneWatch are attuned to the possibility that "profane temporal duration can be periodically arrested" through the designation of a sacred time, a time out of time (Eliade 1959, 71).

The OneWatch might best be described as a *counterfunctional object*, a term coined by James Pierce and Eric Paulos, who suggest that "extreme functional limitations can be a valuable source of new positive possibilities" (Pierce and Paulos 2014, 375). For example, designers of the OneWatch, by making the timepiece less precise than a traditional watch, are urging users to disconnect from efficiency-driven conceptions of time that can lead to anxiety, competition, and obsession with productivity (Fryer-Davis 2017). Counterfunctional objects can be especially useful to creatively explore and possibly critique the design of contemporary technologies. In the case of Pierce and Paulos, the target object is not the smartwatch, but the digital camera. The authors have designed and tested a series of counterfunctional cameras, including the following: an Ultra-Low Resolution Camera that critiques the "overabundance of high-resolution images in a digital era" (Pierce and Paulos 2014, 377); an Inaccessible Digital Camera that provokes the user to destroy the camera in order to access the photo data; a Capsule Camera that shows the number of photos taken but does not have a viewfinder or display, thus encouraging delayed gratification and surprise (Pierce and Paulos 2014, 380). Drawing on language that echoes the digital abstinence camps cited already, Pierce and Paulos ask the following question: "In an age of faster, smarter and more numerous multi-functional technologies, what value can emerge based on technological absence, inability and inhibition?" (2014, 376).

This brings us to the Digital Chastity Belt designed by one of my MA students, Adam Cilevitz, for his final thesis project. The crudely designed wearable was hacked together using a standard men's belt, a clip-on phone case, an Arduino microcontroller, and parts coaxed out of a novelty electric shock pen. The user is intended to wear the belt with a handheld device inserted in the case over the pelvic region. When the lid to the case is opened, a surprising shock is delivered to the user's crotch. Not surprisingly, this counterfunctional device produced more laughs than it did shocks, and this response adequately reflects the designer's intentions. As Adam put it in an essay that accompanied the project, the Digital Chastity Belt "ambivalently comment(s) on the rhetorics of cell phone addiction and digital abstinence, while proposing a practical—if not extravagant and ironically excessive—method for framing and managing this addiction" (Cilevitz 2015, 3). Cilevitz suggests that his project explores the pleasures and pains of handheld device usage, a concept he wryly encapsulates in the word *phonamism*, drawing on the Biblical tale of Onan, whose name has become synonymous with masturbation (i.e., onanism) (Cilevitz 2015, 4).

Cilevitz's ethos in approaching this design project is instructive since it characterizes a critical practice of making that explores digital culture by means of humour, irony, and above all, ambivalence. We want to heed the pop wisdom of "be here now," but we also want to be everywhere all at once. We want to avoid appearing narcissistic, but we also want to record our experiences to share with others and store for ourselves. What's more, we know better than to embrace naïve notions of presence, reality, and the self guided by a vague form of technological determinism, but at the same time, we often get the sense that contemporary ethical, environmental, social, psychological, and health-related problems may be exacerbated by digital technologies. Digital abstinence wearables provide opportunities to mobilize this ambivalence for the sake of engaging in critical reflection on technoculture. Digital Chastity Belt, like the OneWatch and the lifelogging cross of Digital Tabernacle, provides an example of how to turn a wearable device into an object-to-think-with that promotes discussion of how to comport ourselves digitally.

It's essential to note that Cilevitz's reference to "digital addiction" is also ironic and ambivalent (Cilevitz 2015, 3), a result of his own inability to come to terms with this pop psychological prognosis. As dana boyd suggests in *It's Complicated: The Social Lives of Networked Teens*, the term *addiction* is used in a cavalier fashion by teens to identify media usage habits that they might view as excessive, or more accurately, as abnormal (boyd 2014, 85). But mainstream media leans on the specter of addiction to engage in a more technologically determinist rhetoric that sensationalizes tech-related behaviours. As boyd puts it, "It is easier for adults to blame technology for undesirable outcomes than to consider other social, cultural, and personal factors that may be at play" (boyd 2014, 79). Echoing this concern, Laura Portwood Stacer adds that the "addiction metaphor might actually work to naturalize 'normal' degrees of use among most of the population. Consumer culture and the corporations which power it are thus left unproblematized" (Portwood-Stacer 2012, n.p.). What's more, by loosely applying a rhetoric of addiction to media usage habits, there is a danger of trivializing forms of addiction that are verifiably life-threatening and unquestionably destructive. For example, "Fear mongering stories," boyd suggests, "often point to accounts of internet addiction boot camps[7] in China and South Korea, where the compulsion allegedly rivals alcoholism, drug addiction, and gambling" (boyd 2014, 78). As with verifiable addictions, it is unproductive to lay the blame on a single cause for the specific digital behaviours of an individual; when social and psychological problems are tangled up with digital technologies, it is best to consider the specific web of circumstances in which users—and more to the point here, *non-users*—find themselves enmeshed.

In the introduction to *How Users Matter*, Nelly Oudshourn and Trevor Pinch make a point of focusing on the concept of *non-users* as an important category in the sociological study of technological design and production. Most of the authors in *How Users Matter* decry what's known as the top-down or executive function of technological design, aiming instead "to go beyond a rhetoric of designers being in control" (Oudshourn and Pinch 2003, 15). Oudshourn and Pinch's introduction, titled "How Users and Non-Users Matter," references the work of various authors in the anthology who suggest that one way out of this rhetoric is to focus explicitly on non-users. "Instead of representing resistance and non-use as irrational, heroic, or involuntary," these authors argue that non-use behaviours "should be considered as rational choices shaping the design and (de)stabilization of technologies" (Oudshourn and Pinch 2003, 19). Further, the authors note that non-use is "most likely to occur in situations in which the prescribed uses and the symbolic meanings attached to the technology by its producers and its promoters do not correspond to the gender relations, the cultural values, and the identities of specific groups of people" (Oudshourn and Pinch 2003, 19). This situational conception of non-use is corroborated by Christine Satchell and Paul Dourish in their article "Beyond the User: Use and Non-Use in HCI," where they set out "to recognize 'the user' as a discursive formation rather than a natural fact, and then to examine the circumstances in which it arises, the forces that shape it and the uses to which it is put" (Satchell and Dourish 2009). They provide a framework for this approach by identifying "six forms of non-use: lagging adoption, active resistance, disenchantment, disenfranchisement, displacement, and disinterest" (Satchell and Dourish 2009).[8]

The non-use wearables I have discussed thus far seem to fit best into the category of *active resistance* identified by Satchell and Dourish. One might also imagine digital non-use wearables fitting into any of the other categories, perhaps simultaneously. For example, the mode of resistance motivating Yondr is obviously based on a perception of handheld devices as distracting and somehow producing an inauthentic experience. But this resistance function of the non-use device is complicated by the way in which Yondr also secures the intellectual property rights, and hence the profits, of mainstream performers.[9] It would be inaccurate, for example, to suggest that users of Yondr are actively engaging, for example, in what Laura Portwood Stacer has called "conspicuous non-consumption" rooted in a rejection of neoliberal values (Portwood-Stacer 2012, n.p.). Rather, it might be more precise to label these non-users as a *disenfranchised* community. The Digital Chastity Belt presents an even more complex case. While the design seems to reflect *active resistance* and possibly *disenchantment*, the overt eroticism of the device, in addition to the designer's ironic approach, suggest instead what I would call an *ambivalent resistance*, motivating a critical design approach that leaves room for the designer to surrender control over the meaning and functionality of a device, for the sake of exploring a complex technocultural issue. Returning to Digital Tabernacle, I have observed that the project functions not only by asking participants and performers to confront their ambivalence toward technology, but also their ambivalence toward the religious symbols and rituals that are co-opted in the process. Most importantly, all of these projects focus less on the question of "How do we wear technology?" than they do on a much more complex and nuanced question: "How do we comport ourselves technologically?"

The notion of ambivalent resistance bears a close resemblance to Martin Heidegger's conception in "Discourse on Thinking" of *Gelassenheit*, which he defines loosely as "releasement toward things" (Heidegger 1968, 54). Heidegger relied on this concept to compose an uncharacteristically gleeful passage about how to get along in a world of rampant technological innovation. The passage is worth quoting at length, for reasons that should become obvious to the reader:

> We can use technical devices, and yet with proper use also keep ourselves so free of them, that we may let go of them any time. We can use technical devices as they ought to be used, and also let them alone as something which does not affect our inner and real core. We can affirm the unavoidable use of technical devices, and also deny them the right to dominate us, and so to warp, confuse, and lay waste our nature.
>
> But will not saying both yes and no this way to technical devices make our relation to technology ambivalent and insecure? On the contrary! Our relation to technology will become wonderfully simple and relaxed. (Heidegger 1968, 54)

Needless to say, this passage lays bare not only Heidegger's technological determinism, but also his essentialist conception of the human as a thing with an "inner and real core" and a stable "nature" (Heidegger 1968, 54). What's more, he suggests that technical devices have a stable essence and a specific way in which they "ought to be used" (54). Having acknowledged these obvious philosophical problems with the passage, what I want to rescue from it is a relaxed approach to technical devices that is at once ambivalent and easy-going, yet critical and discerning. Moreover, what Heidegger describes here is a specific focus on how we pay attention to things, or how we attend to attention more generally, which is a central question that can be used to guide the creation of digital abstinence devices.

Along these lines, we may just as well consult the Amish, who also champion a concept of *Gelassenheit* that guides their adoption of new technologies. In the case of the Amish, *Gelassenheit* also refers to a sort of releasement, but a releasement toward the will of God, a letting-go that was made infamous when victims of the Nickel Mines School Shooting in Lancaster County, Pennsylvania, openly forgave the violent perpetrator and made peace with his family. As Donald Kraybill suggests in *The Riddle of Amish Culture*, "the symbols of *Gelassenheit* articulate surrender, bond the community together, and mark off boundaries with the larger society" (2001, 54–55). When it comes to technological adoption, Amish ambivalence can lead to such interesting inventions as a counterfunctional Linux-based computer that will allow word processing and other desktop publishing functions, but will not connect to the outside world via the Internet (Kraybill, Johnson-Weiner, and Nolt 2013, 316).

Still, it is too easy to romanticize the Amish approach to technological adoption—a process that novelist Neal Stephenson has coined as *Amistics* (2015, 611)—because they are able to work within a space and time of their own design, carefully selecting technologies as they see fit, as long as they don't negatively impact their very clear-cut value system, which is held together by a strict set of rituals. Of course, most of us lack such a rigid set of values, nor do we necessarily want one, and few would be willing to give up electric lights in their home for the chance to live in a world without presidential tweets. The Amish focus on rituals, such as their eight-hour communion service, which involves a confession of sins and a foot-washing ceremony, brings us back to the concept of comportment. As Ronald Grimes suggests, "Rituals model bodily comportment outside rituals by prescribing actions inside rituals" (Grimes 2014, 307). What the Amish demonstrate is that it is possible, even within the well-oiled machine of contemporary technocapitalism, to carve out a culture that marches to the beat of its own nonelectric drum. That is not to say that the Amish are not technical people, nor do they eschew efficiency, as the counterfunctional computer example demonstrates. But they are not afraid to resist techniques of efficiency that they deem as somehow harmful, and they do so by relying on ritual techniques that enforce the values that make technology non-use a part of their daily lives.

In *The Technological Society*, Jacques Ellul defines technique as "the totality of methods rationally arrived at and having absolute efficiency in every field of human activity" (Ellul 1967, xxv). This definition still holds today, especially as we consider the focus of wearable computing on quantifying the self and integrating the human more efficiently into digital networks. But as I have argued elsewhere, it is important to recall that technics are not a recent product of human society.[10] The human, following the work of André Leroi-Gourhan and others[11] who have followed his him, is always already technical, thanks to our prosthetic relationship to tools. In the words of Leroi-Gourhan, "The whole of our evolution has been oriented toward placing outside ourselves what in the rest of the animal world is achieved inside by species adaptation" (Leroi-Gourhan 1993, 20). David Wills has proposed a theory of *dorsality* that involves looking back to our technical origins as a way of putting our technical future into perspective. More to the point, Wills insists that "We should reserve the right to *hold back*, not to presume that every technology is an advance" (Wills 2008, 6). If we adhere to the theory of co-evolution, it is possible to conclude that every technology is a wearable technology. This prompts me ask yet another, final question: What are we wearing *on our backs* today, and how does this impact our species as a whole? This is not an obtuse question but the basis for a politically inflected understanding of wearable computing that is not driven forward blindly by a naïve conception of progress. Wearables are an overt reminder that we are technical animals, and that we have the ability to shape our comportment by carefully selecting the techniques to which we will adapt. Bearing in mind that the etymological root of comportment brings us to the French word *porter* (to wear)[12] and to the Latin word *portare* (to carry), with all of its evolutionary implications, I have attempted here to develop a way to think about wearable technology and comportment at the very same time.

Notes

1. The Autographer was developed in 2013 by a start-up called OMG Life, which is now defunct. I accessed the devices on an early release basis for my own research on memory and technology.

2. This invention was inspired in part by the ibelive, developed in 2005, which is a T-shaped cap that fit onto the base of an iPod shuffle to turn it into a glossy white cross. The inventor, Scott Wilson, provided the following text to pitch his product: "Inspired by the world's obsession with the iPod, iBelieve is a replacement cap and lanyard for your Shuffle. Now you can profess your devotion with a fashionable symbol of faith. Join the fastest growing religion on the planet" (Wilson n.d.).

3. According to a post on the antimasturbation subreddit called "nofap," the developers of Abstain! "thought of naming [the app] Fapstronaut but decided on Abstain! to conform to the app store guidelines" (Systemride 2013).

4. My focus is not on how digital media can foster existing rituals, such as for example, a funeral in Second Life. For a consideration of this topic, see Ken Hillis, *Online a Lot of the Time: Ritual, Fetish, Sign*. Ronald Grimes, to whom I owe a debt of gratitude for schooling me in ritual studies, also discusses telepresent rituals in *The Craft of Ritual Studies*.

5. It seems appropriate here to mention the nineteenth-century Luddites, who attempted to resist technological change by inventing new rituals that fostered social cohesion, including the invention of Ned Ludd himself. For a more detailed discussion of Luddism in the context of critical digital design, see my chapter entitled "The Making of a Digital Humanities Neo-Luddites" in *Making Things and Drawing Boundaries: Experiments in the Digital Humanities* (forthcoming).

6. I am currently leading a research project with the Vision and Attention Lab at University of Waterloo to study the impact of Yondr on student task performance in an undergraduate classroom.

7. A group of students in my recent course on Non-Use pitched a digital detox boot camp that poked fun at the rhetoric of Chinese Internet addiction camps. Their design included a uniform for campers that was essentially an oversized Yondr case.

8. Sally Wyatt provides her own categorization of non-users in her article "Non-Users Also Matter: The Construction of Users and Non-Users of the Internet." These include resisters, rejecters, the excluded, and the expelled (Wyatt 2003, 76). While no list of non-user categories can be complete, I have chosen to reference the list of Satchell and Dourish as it offers a more capacious rubric for identifying non-use behaviors.

9. As noted in a *New York Times* article by Janet Morrissey, "Lesser-known bands might be more hesitant to try Yondr, as many rely on fans posting photos and videos to promote their shows" (Morrissey 2016).

10. See for example, *Necromedia*, especially chapter 1: "Necromedia Theory and Posthumanism."

11. See Bernard Stiegler, *Technics and Time 1: The Fault of Epimetheus*. Stiegler's adoption of Leroi-Gourhan for the study of contemporary technoculture has been mobilized widely in posthumanist texts, including David Wills's *Dorsality: Thinking Back through Technology and Politics*, Cary Wolfe's *What Is Posthumanism*, Mark B. N. Hansen's *New Philosophy for New Media*, and my own book, *Necromedia*.

12. This etymological link between wearables and the French word *porter* has caused a great deal of consternation for translators. Obviously, the French translation into *portable*, which literally means portable in English, and which is used to designate a laptop or handheld device, does not suffice. This issue has been explored at length by Julien Cadot, who attempted to address it, fruitlessly as it happens, with the Académie Française (Cadot 2015).

References

Behaivior. n.d. What We Do. http://www.behaivior.com/what-we-do.

boyd, danah. 2014. *It's Complicated: The Social Lives of Networked Teens*. New Haven, CT: Yale University Press.

Cadot, Julien. 2015. Comment traduire wearable? L'Académie Française nous a répondu. *Numerama*, October 27. http://www.numerama.com/tech/128374-comment -traduire-wearable-lacademie-francaise-nous-a-repondu.html.

Carreiro, Stephanie, David Smelson, Megan Ranney, Keith J. Horvath, R. W. Picard, Edwin D. Boudreaux, Rashelle Hayes, and Edward W. Boyer. 2015. Real-Time Mobile Detection of Drug Use with Wearable Biosensors: A Pilot Study. *Journal of Medical Toxicology* 11 (1): 73–79.

Cilevitz, Adam. 2015. *Hands Off: Phonamism and the Digital Chastity Belt*. Master's thesis, University of Waterloo.

Digital Detox, About. n.d. http://digitaldetox.org/about/.

Eliade, Mircea. 1959. *The Sacred and the Profane*. New York: Harcourt.

Ellul, Jacques. 1967. *The Technological Society*. New York: Vintage Books.

Fryer-Davis, Peter. 2017. OneWatch by Timeless Design. Term paper, University of Waterloo.

Grimes, Ronald. 2014. *The Craft of Ritual Studies*. New York: Oxford University Press.

Hansen, Mark B. N. 2004. *New Philosophy for New Media*. Cambridge, MA: MIT Press.

Heidegger, Martin. 1968. *Discourse on Thinking*. Translated by John M. Anderson and E. Hans Freund. New York: Harper and Row.

Hillis, Ken. 2009. *Online a Lot of the Time*. Durham, NC: Duke University Press.

Kraybill, Donald B., Karen M. Johnson-Weiner, and Steven M. Nolt. 2013. *The Amish*. Baltimore: Johns Hopkins University Press.

Kraybill, Donald B. 2001. *The Riddle of Amish Culture*. Baltimore: Johns Hopkins University Press.

Kregting, Martin. 2017. Engineers at FIU Develop Wearable Sensor to Battle Excessive Drinking. *ICT & Health*, June 19. https://www.ictandhealth.com/news/newsitem/article/engineers-at-fiu-develop-wearable-sensor-to-battle-excessive-drinking.html.

Leroi-Gourhan, André. 1993 [1964]. *Gesture and Speech*. Trans. A. Bostock Berger. Cambridge, MA: MIT Press.

Morrissey, Janet. 2016. Your Phone's on Lockdown: Enjoy the Show. *New York Times*, October 15. https://nyti.ms/2e6otmu.

Mumford, Lewis. 1934. *Technics and Civilization*. New York: Harcourt.

O'Gorman, Marcel. 2017. The Making of a Digital Humanities Neo-Luddite. In *Making Things and Drawing Boundaries: Experiments in the Digital Humanities*, edited by Jentery Sayers, 116–127. Minneapolis: University of Minnesota Press.

O'Gorman, Marcel. 2015. *Necromedia*. Minneapolis: University of Minnesota Press.

Oudshoorn, Nelly, and Trevor Pinch, eds. 2005. *How Users Matter: The Co-Construction of Users and Technology*. Cambridge, MA: MIT Press.

Pierce, James, and Eric Paulos. 2014. Counterfunctional Things: Exploring Possibilities in Designing Digital Limitations. Paper presented at the 2014 Conference on Designing Interactive Systems. Vancouver, BC, Canada, June 21–24. https://doi.org/10.1145/2598510.2598522.

Portwood-Stacer, Laura. 2012. How We Talk about Media Refusal, Part 1: "Addiction." *Flow Journal*, July 29. https://www.flowjournal.org/2012/07/how-we-talk-about-media-refusal-part-1.

Sabbath Manifesto. n.d. http://www.sabbathmanifesto.org/about.

Satchell, Christine, and Paul Dourish. 2009. Beyond the User: Use and Non-use in HCI. Paper presented at the 21st Annual Conference of the Australian Computer–Human Interaction Special Interest Group: Design (OZCHI '09). Melbourne, Victoria, Australia, November 23–27. https://doi.org/10.1145/1738826.1738829.

Sax, David. 2016. At Your Next Concert: Stop Filming, Start Listening. *Guardian*, July 17. https://www.theguardian.com/commentisfree/2016/jul/17/musicians-concert-phone-etiquette-silicon-valley.

Salvam, Anjan Paneer, Sriram Muthukumar, Vikramshankar Kamakoti, and Shalini Prasad. 2016. A Wearable Biochemical Sensor for Monitoring Alcohol Consumption

Lifestyle through Ethyl Glucuronide (EtG) Detection in Human Sweat. *Scientific Reports* 6 (March 21): 23111. https://doi.org/10.1038/srep23111.

Smith, Jonathan Z. *To Take Place: Toward Theory in Ritual*. Chicago: University of Chicago Press, 1992.

Stephenson, Barry. 2015. *Ritual: A Very Short Introduction*. New York: Oxford University Press.

Stephenson, Neal. 2015. *Seveneves*. New York: William Morrow.

Stiegler, Bernard. 1998. *Technics and Time 1: The Fault of Epimetheus*. Trans. Richard Beardsworth and George Collins. Stanford, CA: Stanford University Press.

Systemride. 2013. Abstain! App. Reddit, December 12. https://www.reddit.com/r/NoFap/comments/1sr8q2/abstain_app/.

Turner, Victor. 1970. *The Forest of Symbols: Aspects of Ndembu Ritual*. Ithaca, NY: Cornell University Press.

Warner, Jessica. 2006. *All or Nothing: A Short History of Abstinence in America*. Toronto: McLelland & Stewart.

Wills, David. 2008. *Dorsality: Thinking Back Through Technology and Politics*. Minneapolis: University of Minnesota Press.

Wilson, Scott. n.d. iBelieve: Apple iPod Art in Chicago Museum. *Obama Pacman*, March 2, 2010. http://obamapacman.com/2010/03/ibelieve-apple-ipod-homage-chicago-art-institute-museum/.

Wolfe, Cary. 2010. *What is Posthumanism?* Minneapolis: University of Minnesota Press.

Wyatt, Sally. 2003. Non-users Also Matter: The Construction of Users and Non-users of the Internet. In *How Users Matter: The Co-construction of Users and Technology*, edited by Nelly Oudshoorn and Trevor Pinch, 67–80. Cambridge, MA: MIT Press.

Yondr. n.d. Our Vision. Overyondr. http://overyondr.com/.

7 The Big Toe's Resistance to Smart Rehabilitations

Gary Genosko

Introduction

Big toe computing points beyond the keyboard, tabletop mouse, and the world of fingers, palms, and hand-held devices. Extrapolating from the theory of French writer Georges Bataille (1995, 87) in his essay "Big Toe," gathered in the *Encyclopaedia Acephalica* circa 1929, the interface of the most human yet base part of the human body and computing, both personal and wearable, confounds the low with the high and produces a condition in which the computational intervenes to overcome the horror evoked by the lowly, flat, dirty foot with chipped nails. For Bataille, having lost its prehensile character, the human big toe is idiotic, especially compared with fingers, which are long, light, nimble, and intelligent; distorting while echoing Darwin, no less, on the "great toe" as the most "characteristic peculiarity" of the human, in its nonopposability and hence condition for bipedalism, it remains that in evolutionary terms the big toe is "distinctively human" (Beaumont 2015, 873). Yet, for all the nobility of the human, whose head is elevated and distant from the feet that are stuck in the mud, the civilized big toe insistently imposes its ignobility where least expected, and it troubles our encounter with our own humanity, adding an ineradicable degree of murkiness to our intelligence.

Together, let's imagine another world of computing in which big toe–eye coordination, like the pioneering work of the Eudaemons—a group of graduate students, overeducated and underemployed, described by Thomas Bass in his neglected book *The Eudaemonic Pie* (2000[1985])—initiated a transversal and interruptive reterritorialization by hacking roulette in Vegas casinos as an homage of sorts to Claude Shannon's dream of machine intelligence. But the facts are hard to face—feet are having a hard time reentering the space dominated by hands and thumb-labor. But devices like the Wii, and arcade-style floor mounted games like *Dance Dance Revolution,* reengage feet in the way that floor-based board games like Twister did for an earlier generation. Certainly, Lady Gaga has done her part in bringing feet back into the picture, with an extraordinary array of extreme booties and pumps. Big toes languish, most often wrapped in fabric, hidden from view, crushed together with other smaller toes in stupid shoes, out of step in a smart universe. We need to regain feet by refocusing attention on every-day pedals, from sewing machines, pianos, and other musical instruments. From skateboards to hoverboards, toe pressure is absent from behind the heels (back axis), and this makes standing sideways in a crouch the most stable position to be in. Toe control is the name of the game on a hover-board, to be sure (Christie 2016).

This investigation is, however, predicated on a simple observation: that embodied computing is born in a *hustle* at the origins of the infor-mation age in Shannon's (and Turing's) dreams of intelligent machines. Here, then, I want to regain both feet and the base seductive power of the big toe in computing by looking at wearable computing's early misadven-tures, before turning to Bataille's lessons about big toes for the digital age, as well as some promising inventions, and how Bataille's rogue surrealism can assist in thinking ourselves under the table, to wallow joyfully in the office dust.

Smartness and Footwear

In his creative explorations of countersurveillance technologies and per-sonalization of computing in the development of wearable webcams, Toronto-based engineer, and master of sousveillance, Steve Mann reminds us of one of the key reference points of smart clothing: embedded within the history of timing circuits designed in the 1960s and 1970s to win at casinos (primarily against roulette wheels), the inspirational shoe designed and tested in the field by the Eudaemons, whose exploits were described in Bass's aforementioned book. Photographing the original shoe through his own WearComp system, Mann describes an epiphany in which humanistic technology frees the spirit of the inventive risk-taking individual, perhaps standing on his or her head with feet raised in the air. While I have elsewhere criticized Mann's philosophies as homespun, sociologically naïve, and mis-directed when it comes to conceptualizing power relations (Genosko 2005), his enthusiasm for the big toe–triggered shoe is genuine and insightful, and I share in it wholeheartedly. His eye is neither on whether or not it worked—even in its single functionality—nor if it recouped costs, but in the spirit of his own early inventions, his question concerns the degree to which "the human was given the opportunity to inject himself into an oth-erwise predetermined, and often unfriendly and sterile environment [of the casino]" (Mann and Niedzviecki 2001, 58). Mann knows his shoes, and he returns to them periodically, reporting his disappointment at the discourse of futurity that couched the so-called smart shoe or "Schmoo" presented by designer Karim Rashid in 2000 (Mann and Niedzviecki 2001, 94) and com-missioned by the San Francisco Museum of Modern Art.

The early history of embodied computing is not linked to fashion and design but to gambling as its primary examples, beginning with Edward O. Thorp and information theorist Shannon's wristwatch-like "time calcula-tion apparatus" (Mann and Niedzviecki 2001, 56) circa 1961 (described at length by Bass as "cigarette pack-sized"), and in the late 1970s the shoe-based microprocessor, with "tactile inputs," for analyzing the quadrant of numbers upon which a roulette ball would come to rest. Shannon is, argu-ably, the greatest gadgeteer of the twentieth century, and the breakthrough of inputting data with the big toes firmly regains analog computing as a pedal-powered domain. But Mann ends with the Eudaemons and jumps decades later ahead to his own head-mounted WearComp, essentially a visual-editing memory system.

The shoe computers of the Eudaemons were controlled by means of microswitches activated by the big toes of the right and left feet: "D. steps out of the car and stands with his big toes positioned over the micro-switches in his left and right shoes. His left toe is expert at motoring the computer among subroutines in its program. His right toe is trained for tapping in data" (Bass 2000[1985], 6). Bass's descriptions of Doyne's [James Doyne Farmer] toe work is remarkable: "Once the parameters are adjusted and the computer is clicked into its playing mode, Doyne's left toe takes a break. The right foot can handle the rest ... with his right toe become an autonomous unit, bouncing over its microswitch like a frog's leg pithed for a demonstration of galvanic electricity" (Bass 2000[1985], 11). Toes need to be flexed. "Toe-operated microswitches" demanded concentration and accuracy (2000[1985], 13). It was not done "casually." These toes cannot be taken for granted. They need to be practiced. The big toe may also be restorative. Consider the role it plays in the performance of actress Uma Thurman's role as Beatrix Kiddo (the Bride) in *Kill Bill* (dir. Q. Tarantino 2003). She overcomes her partial paralysis by concentrating on her bare feet, telling herself over and over again, to "wiggle your big toe." This experiment repurposes the big toe—having lost, due to lack of practice, many of its few remaining abilities. A practiced big toe may learn to grab and hold objects. This is evident in the case of persons with upper-extremity disabilities, namely shortened arms. But the repetitive actions required by the two toes do not result in nimble feet.

Nevertheless, the elevation of the foot—the lowness of which does not compare favorably with the head, for instance—to a cerebral role means that it sheds some of its baseness and acquires in connection with the computer it manages a new, albeit somewhat incongruous, status. But the foot itself has been subject to tortuous compression, and used as a signifier of filthiness, as Bataille reminds us. The toes described by Bass required special socks; no mention of nail care is made. The ignominy of corns and bunions is avoided. The independence of the right toe is underlined by Bass, but at the same time he restricts its autonomy to a science experiment scenario. Even here constraints are front and center. The specter of experimentation looms large.

There is something of the toe's baseness that cannot be so easily shaken. Bass's image of a pithed frog's leg subjected to electrical charges renders the toe ludicrous—an animated, but not exquisite, corpse. It is hard to realize any aspirations with such an image of the toe's disorderliness, having invoked the spirit of Luigi Galvani in the late eighteenth century and his wild hypotheses of animal electricity held in the leg muscles of a dissected frog like a battery pack (Schlesinger 2010). The idea of an advanced system of computation placed in one's shoe and operated by one's big toes is fundamentally derisive. And in the end, the toe must wallow in the sweat dirt in which it is culturally held because the project fails to produce consistent results and is beset by technical problems. The attempt to crack roulette fails, after a pretty good early run, in the instability of its technologies. These toes jammed themselves. Yet, isn't this inescapable baseness what makes the big toe so seductive? And the pleasure one derives from Bass's book is in direct proportion to the failures of the toe-switches. The toes go back into their regular socks and disappear, after a few moments of hopeful elevation by beating the house to a special rank in the obscure early history of embodied computing. And when Mann reproduces a photograph, through WearComp, of the famous shoe, there are no toes in sight. Any sense of stupidity that clings to toes cannot coexist with the evidence it provides for Mann of ingenious design and individual spirit. In bathing it in "a high contrast purple videographic glow," Mann (Mann and Niedzviecki 2001, 57) sterilizes the object as if a carbolic wash were required to even photograph it. Mann may insist on humanistic technology, but he has no place for "the most human *part* of the human" (Bataille 1995, 87). Yet, surely this is Bass's point about the pithed frog's leg: its autonomy as a part is revealed only in the scrambling of the living frog's brain for the sake of the study of its physiology. Bad biological practice preps the bouncing and twitching big toe gone rogue. Perhaps Bataille is acutely correct in pointing out that feet simply cannot escape some damage. And Bass is ambivalent about the accomplishments of the big toes at stake because he loosens Doyne's right big toe from the steadiness and intelligence that operating such a computer required.

Recent literature on wearware pays scant attention to shoes. But when it does, it is for the sake of a really high-tech shoe, and this discourse of progress grinds the earlier models underfoot.The enhanced e-shoe displaces the big toe in favor of the heel and the sole. Returned to its baseness, the big toe even loses contact with the gay dissipations of gambling. Any number of scientific reports on gait analysis and sports engineering involving foot operations may be dredged from the literature, beginning with the late '90s foot interfaces with vibrating soles ("Fantastic Magic Slippers") to the generations of WARAJI sandals (Walking, Running, and Jumping Interface; see Barrera et al. 2004) that turn the hands-focused problem of VR inputs downward toward the feet. This downward trend will come to settle in a perverse object, the Toe Mouse.

It seems that the big toe, our most human part according to Bataille, does think after all; hands are normally thoughtful, and fingers investigative and expressive, yet big toes possess kinematic characteristics that make them, as the Eudaemons believed, excellent for inputting data. Smartness is in this toe and not merely in the shoe. The Japanese team around Noriko Tanaka based at the Osaka Electro-Communication University that developed and tested the concept of the Toe Mouse, found that a big toe could be used effectively by able-bodied and disabled persons alike as a hands-free mouse (Tanaka et al. 2007). The study concluded that dragging and clicking with the big toe could be accomplished comfortably, and that task completion times diminished during testing. Still, a cultural fascination with big toes in Japan is not a universal, and European sensibilities may be ruffled by erotic transformations of big toes into penises in some popular Japanese imaginaries; here, the Osaka team refer to the big toe as a "foot thumb," demonstrating the extent of the figurative effort to rehabilitate the lowly digit, to smarten it up. But does this promising development restrict our exit from the digiverse of thumbs and fingertips? After all, it was not developed and marketed. It failed.

French prehistorian André Leroi-Gourhan would have appreciated our predicament. In *Gesture and Speech* (1993 [1964]), Leroi-Gourhan argued that, in evolutionary terms, the liberation of the hands is the condition upon which neurological adaptation took place. However, over the course of technological development into the age of cybernation with automatic control systems and eventually posthuman artificial intelligence, there is a regression of the hands. Leroi-Gourhan did not see the rise of the desktop keyboard, mobile media, and hand-held devices. Even if his theory of hand regression is wrong, he did not mobilize the big toe in the name of an embodied cybernetics. Leroi-Gourhan is also associated, after all, with his consideration of the opposable big toe—the most stereotypical feature of the ape-human—and an important point of divergence between the primate and human foot. He does not regain the big toe in the wake of the thesis of the "regression of the hand" (1993[1964], 405), perhaps because its encounter with the most advanced technologies would have produced too much discord. This discord was for Bataille a motivating factor in his meditations on the big toe. Leroi-Gourhan could not have imagined that sedentariness would become so productive, and that the "transposed *Homo sapiens*" who would emerge in time would revert to a big toe computing.

Those who recount the development and success of BlackBerry emphasize the gestural semiotics of the "Prayer Position"—shoulders hunched, head bowed over the unit, with thumbs-a-poppin' (Sweeny 2009, 9; McQueen 2010, 193). The BlackBerry–iPhone struggle (and subsequent pad wars) seems to be reduced to thumb size, with the big-thumbed Mac enthusiasts complaining about the tiny keyboard and the BlackBerry addicts recoiling at the thought of tapping on glass (with the release of the PlayBook this changed little): "Apple fanboys with big thumbs took up the master's call [Steve Jobs], complaining about the BlackBerry's 'cramped little QWERTY'" (Sweeny 2009, 142). So-called "thumb-dancing" (Sweeny 2009, 213) on the tiny keyboard, angled at 40 degrees for the thumb tips (McQueen 2010, 117), especially under the table in a meeting or at a family dinner, is a social faux pas; of course, in the days of the thumb wheel and the track ball, repetitive stress injuries were common enough. Thumb work allows the CrackBerry addict to slide downward under the table toward the feet. Under the table there are more seductive games of contact between feet, calves, thighs, and knees in play. Even here, the connotations are not entirely propitious as the out-of-view remains suspect; it is a cultural site of cheating. With the exception of the fetishist, our eyes are closed to the toe-work of seduction. What could be more ludicrous than a keyboard angled for the big toes? Yet this is the Toe Mouse's genius—to affront and enliven our senses in a barefooted computing in which the prospect of the big toe leads to a hands-free, postthumb tomorrow.

The elevation of the big toe by way of the digital from the squalor of the shoe, a nasty python boot like Frank Zappa's "Stinkfoot," is unstable. The Toe Mouse is a new species in a land of desktop mice that erases "the inscriptions of the boundaries between mainstream and specialist technology" (Goggin and Newell 2006, 164–165), at once enabling and disabling, deterritorializing and reterritorializing. The big toe remains on a collision course with smartness. It remains under the desk: a floor-top unit.

Knee-Jerk

Yet it wasn't always this way, even in the annals of computing history. Information philosopher Luciano Floridi has remarked somewhat dryly that "Douglas Engelbart once told me that, when he was refining his most famous invention, the mouse, he even experimented with placing it under the desk, to be operated with one's leg, in order to leave the user's hands free" (Floridi 2010, 11). It is instructive to review Engelbart's own papers from the late 1960s in order to regain in all of its vividness under the table experimentation. As I discussed earlier, the linkages between casino hacks and big toes are well grounded. Innovation from below in this respect is condensed around a hidden toe trigger in a hacking operation. And this is seductive, or at least I am claiming it is so, in the same sense as Bataille. As Denis Hollier (1989, 78) points out, Bataille's focus on the big toe in its singularity is a condensation of all of humanity and what makes the toe seductive is precisely the effect of this concentration.

Engelbart's papers display another series of productive tensions about activities below the tabletop. It is widely known that the original experiments to select the most effective device for moving a "bug" (cursor) around a CRT screen had only a few contenders: a light pen, joystick, or knee-control device (a vertical bar). Effectiveness, efficiency, and the avoidance of awkwardness and fatigue (a major concern with toe-triggers) are discussed by Engelbart and his coauthors. The tabletop mouse won out and in its original incarnation was made of wood, with two rotating wheels on the bottom and several functional buttons on top. However, the story of its selection is a bit murkier.

A knee-controlled "bug-positioning device" was not fully developed during the crucial period of testing and is referred to as "preliminary." From the outset, then, it occupied a marginal position. According to English, Engelbart, and Berman (1967, 7), "it consists of two potentiometers and associated linkages plus a knee lever. The linkage is spring-loaded to the right and gravity-loaded downward." The knee-bar is mounted underneath the table or desk and is illustrated by an unattributed photograph of a bare right knee at work on the bar. The bug shifts edge to edge by the side-to-side movement of the knee, and from the top to the bottom of the screen by the up-and-down movement of the knee, with the assistance of a rocking motion of the ball of the foot. Unfortunately, the knee-control device was not ready for full testing with experienced device users, but in check tests it performed less accurately (especially with regard to vertical movement) and more slowly (and unsmoothly) than other devices, especially the mouse. The findings include positive assessments of the knee-control device as well: it requires "no access time" (unlike the movement of the hand from the keyboard and back) even though this gain was not included in the final assessment. The key conclusion is twofold:

> Although the knee control was only primitively developed at the time it was tested, it ranked high in both speed and accuracy, and seems very promising. It offers the major advantage that it leaves both hands free to work at the keyboard. [...] The fact that a no-hands bug-control device can allow both hands to

remain on the keyboard is an important factor in its consideration. Even if its selection speed and resolution could not be developed to match that of a good hand-controlled device, what we are learning about the importance of smooth coordination between the different primitive operations would make it a strong candidate. (English, Engelbart, and Berman 1967, 14)

The first conclusion that the device involves no-hands is a freedom that humankind possesses more than the species (*Homo sapiens sapiens*), arranged hierarchically below or before it (in taxonomic rankings). But, like the big toe, hardware developers see promise ("a strong candidate") but refuse to follow through on it; in Bataillean terms, they fail to see what is really *meaningful* (Hollier 1989, 86). They fail to grasp what is below and under the tabletop. Still, they flirt with knees and big toes in quite Bataillean ways, since they tarry below and under that which designates an exemplary place of innovation and experimentation—a place that has a strange cultural lineage in the duck-and-cover rituals of the Cold War: tawdry scandals of sex under the desk, or storage cavities and sites of voyeuristic and fetishistic interest. What remains under the table is quite literal—if not completely realized and appreciated—in the technopoetic imaginary. It can, and should be, occasionally—even furtively—glimpsed. But probably not photographed, except for scientific purposes, only if phallocratic intent can be stifled. This is a kind of thing that stirs up trouble as up-skirt photographers know well, although such creepshots have only recently become criminalized in the United States and the United Kingdom, whereas voyeuristic imagery, including cell phone stills and video, almost exclusively shot by men targeting women, have been subjected to privacy protection and sexual consent laws elsewhere.

Conclusion: Below Innovation

Why persist in the use of the term *innovation* for this glorious downward thrust? First of all, innovation from and to below is not a metaphor. On the contrary, I have extracted from the history of computing exemplary moments of discovery involving big toes, feet, and knees, against the tyranny of hands. I have identified a place, under the table, as a site of experimentation, and I have heavily and with a certain delight valorized its unofficial ways and entanglements. My goal in persisting with the use of innovation is to regain it from the current deployment of the term as a governmental strategy linked to research funding priorities and global economic positioning. I am resisting the economic misappropriation of innovation linked to tax exemptions and other stimuli for public–private partnerships in education and industry, for the sake of a big toe computing that has not forgotten—or indeed neglected—the many innovations from below in this field. Whereas *innovation* is often used to promote incommensurable ends like transparency and surveillance, control of piracy, and better copyright protection, I dress it in the clothes of Bataille's brand of surrealism (augmented by photographic enlargements of male and female big toes by Jacques André Boiffard) to emphasize the perverse and singular. Even if *innovation* and its cousin *excellence* restrict institutional autonomy by flattening differences and erasing distinctions (among parts of and between institutions like universities), I persist in my poetic vision of an unannointed place that affords creation and augments intellection and action without parroting *excellence*. To the *innovative* production of highly qualified personnel, I counterpoise a well-grounded apprenticeship in the perverse as a way of heightening action and insight, beginning with the big toe, one of the human body's best button pushers.

The exercise of imagining body interfaces with computing, by means of the lower legs and feet as a kind of apprenticeship in unknowing, may be wrapped in the rigor of anatomy and cultural references; system considerations of capturing input and managing output; and semaphoric descriptions of interactions (Velloso et al. 2015). A new dictionary of big toe computing is a possibility.

In order to get such an apprenticeship off the ground, it would be necessary to unravel an entire tradition of metaphysical media studies that wrapped itself around fingers. From Marshall McLuhan's (1964) scanning fingers as tactile viewership in the age of the cathode ray tube, to Byung-Chul Han's (2017) digital finger as a counting device that deteriorates the link between handi-craft and thinking, there is no place for feet and big toes. Breaking the link between all-thumbs and awkwardness is a good start, in order to hang one's head a little lower in the direction of a foot-craft, of sorts, that releases the big toes from their bondage. Although the foot may never properly write, it can click, and in so doing throw off the decay of alleged and overhyped technological atrophy.

References

Barrera, Salvador, Piperakis Romanos, Suguru Saito, Hiroki Takahashi, and Masayuki Nakajima. 2004. WARAJI: Foot-Driven Navigation Interfaces for Virtual Reality Applications. *PCM/Lecture Notes in Computer Science* 3333: 1–7. https://doi.org/10.1007/978-3-540-30543-9_1.

Bass, Thomas A. 2000 [1985]. *The Eudaemonic Pie*. Lincoln, NE: Authors' Guild Backinprint.com Edition.

Bataille, Georges. 1995. Big Toe. In *Encyclopaedia Acephalica*, 87–93. London: Atlas Press.

Beaumont, Matthew. 2015. In the Beginning Was the Big Toe: Bataille, Base Materialism, Bipedalism. *Textual Practice* 29 (5): 869–883. https://doi.org/10.1080/0950236X.2014.987689.

Christie, Mike. 2016. Is the Hoverboard Cool? *New York Times*, January 10. https://nyti.ms/1OU2pbH.

English, William K., Douglas C. Engelbart, and Melvyn L. Berman. 1967. Display-Selection Techniques for Text Manipulation. *IEEE Transactions on Human Factors in Electronics* 8 (1): 5–15. https://doi.org/10.1109/THFE.1967.232994.

Floridi, Luciano. 2010. *Information: A Very Short Introduction*. Oxford: Oxford University Press.

Genosko, Gary. 2005. (Im)possible Exchanges: The Arts of Counter-surveillance. In *Canadian Cultural Poesis: Essays on Canadian Culture*, edited by G. Sherbert, A. Gérin, and S. Petty, 31–50. Waterloo, ON: Wilfird Laurier Press.

Goggin, Gerard, and Christopher Newell. 2006. Disabling Cell Phones. In *The Cell Phone Reader*, edited by Anandam Kavoori and Noah Arceneaux, 155–172. New York: Peter Lang.

Han, Byung-Chul. 2017. *In the Swarm: Digital Prospects*. Cambridge, MA: MIT Press.

Hollier, Denis. 1989. *Against Architecture: The Writings of Georges Bataille*. Cambridge, MA: MIT Press.

Leroi-Gourhan, André. 1993 [1964]. *Gesture and Speech*. Translated by Anna B. Berger. Cambridge, MA: MIT Press.

Mann, Steve, and Hal Niedzviecki. 2001. *Cyborg: Digital Destiny and Human Possibility in The Age of the Wearable Computer*. Toronto: Doubleday.

McLuhan, Marshall. 1964. *Understanding Media*. New York: McGraw-Hill.

McQueen, Rod. 2010. *BlackBerry: The Inside Story of Research in Motion*. Toronto: Key Porter.

Schlesinger, Henry. 2010. *The Battery: How Portable Power Sparked a Technological Revolution*. New York: HarperCollins and Smithsonian Books.

Sweeny, Alastair. 2009. *BlackBerry Planet: The Story of Research in Motion and the Little Device That Took the World by Storm*. Toronto: John Wiley & Sons.

Tanaka, Noriko, M. Nakao, T. Sato, K. Minato, M. Yoshida, and K. Kouketsu. 2007. The Kinematic Characteristics of a Big Toe and a New Input Device—Toe Mouse. *IFMBE Proceedings* 14 (6): 3778–3781. https://doi.org/10.1007/978-3-540-36841-0_956.

Velloso, Eduardo, Dominik Schmidt, Jason Alexander, Hans Gellersen, and Andreas Bulling. 2015. The Feet in Human–Computer Interaction: A Survey of Foot-Based Interaction. *ACM Computing Surveys* 48 (2): Article 21. https://doi.org/10.1145/2816455.

8   Doing Time in the Home-Space: Ankle Monitors, Script Analysis, and Anticipatory Methodology

Suneel Jethani

Machines and devices are obviously composite, heterogeneous, and physically localised. Although they point to an end, a use for which they have been conceived, they also form part of a long chain of people, products, tools, machines, money, and so forth. Even the study of the technical content of devices does not produce a focused picture because there is always a hazy context or background with fuzzy boundaries.

—Madeleine Akrich (1992, 205)

Introduction

Not all computing is embodied by choice and not all embodiments of technology can be anticipated. The generic notion of "electronic monitoring" gained currency after the passage of the US Correctional Reform Act in 1984. Shortly after passage of the act, an electronic bracelet was used to monitor compliance with house arrest after a New Mexico State district judge, Jack Love, having been inspired by cattle-tracking technology and a device featured in a Spider Man comic, commissioned the design of a telemetric system that could be used to confine an individual to their home. When the home (and its occupant) are technologized in this way, it is transformed into a place of deviation from socially governed norms and personal expectations of what a home means to an individual. The experience of home while under house arrest is made more complex, given that, most of the time, people who are incarcerated in their own homes are required to pay mortgages, rents, utilities, and bills in addition to the costs of administering and maintaining the electronic monitoring technology.

In *Do Artefacts Have Politics?* (1980), Langdon Winner argued that critical understandings of technology could be established not only through examinations of how useful a certain type of technology could be, but also through the ways that they may bring about the embodiment and internalization of external forms of power that are embedded into them during their design and development. With the rapid increase in the use of wearable technologies in everyday settings we should be seeing users "weigh[ing] in on future design and configuration" of the products that they use in the context of their homes and lives (Feenberg 2002, 17), but this is something that is unlikely to occur in the case of house arrest bracelets.

Many other wearable monitoring devices are now quite common, and they are envisioned through a number of sociotechnical histories. They range from the use of barcoded wristbands to denote admittance to an entertainment venue or event or to identify hospital patients through to sophisticated sensor-enabled fitness-tracking devices. Thus, the proliferation of sensor-enabled and data-driven technology that can be worn on the body has complicated the analysis of technological embodiment and surveillance that is commonly predicated on Michel Foucault's panopticon model presented in *Discipline and Punish* (1977).

Within the field of science and technology studies (STS), the idea that technical artifacts are imbued with a power relation between designers and users has been explored from several different perspectives (Winner 1980; Pinch and Bijker 1984; Ihde 1979; Arnold 2003; Verbeek 2006). In recent years, there has been an increased exploration of the intersection between design studies and methodological approaches developed in STS. However, the direct transfer of methods between the domains of human-centric "theory" and "design" can be challenging. As I have argued elsewhere, studies into embodied technology can sometimes be limited due to "slippages" occurring when different disciplines are used concurrently to study a particular class of technology (Jethani 2015, 35).

In this chapter, I extend this line of thinking by looking at how wearable electronic monitoring technologies used in house arrest are lived and coped with. I argue that as precursors to the wearable devices that are commonly available today, manufactured for the consumer market, house arrest bracelets have much to teach us about the politics and futures of contemporary wearable technology.

Designing technology *for embodiment* can be a particularly fraught practice that requires broad thinking, the rationalization of competing actor interests, cost-based design compromises, and several other trade-offs (Sullivan 2017, 1–8). As we have seen in this book, the design of embodied technology involves the combination of wearability, location tracking, the incorporation of sensors, and a range of ergonomic factors, in order to create something that a user can *live* with. When features like tamper proofing are incorporated in designs of embodied computing technology, as they are in electronic monitoring systems, the technology absorbs a range of underlying sociotechnical histories, along with a range of semantic cues that are inherited from antecedents such as handcuffs, shackles, and hospital identification bracelets. The designer's perspective on these features matters, and it has a significant biopolitical impact on the ultimate users of the technology. Beyond this, the unclear framing of house arrest as being either a punitive or a rehabilitative technology might further confuse the design process.

In what follows, I argue that wearable electronic monitoring devices are conflicted technologies with an enormous potential for unintended effects of prisonizing the home and making deviant the usually benign and comfortable confines of the home-space. In this chapter, I want to suggest that this tension can be channelled productively into developing methodological techniques that might contribute to the critical analysis of embodied technology, addressing specifically the effects of their framing (Orlikowski and Gash 1994), de-scripting (Akrich 1992), and conflation with other products (Krippendorff 1989). I relate these ideas to critiques of data-driven technologies such as their tendency to: be used in countersurveillance (Mann et al. 2002); dehumanize (Pedersen 2005); conduct profiling based on biological and behavioral data (Noble and Roberts 2016; Brulé 2015); and be emergent forms of technically afforded surveillance at various stages in the formation of a networked society (Lyon 1994, 2001; Mann and Ferenbok 2013; Castells 2000), and I argue that these frames of reference are often overlooked by designers when they seek to better understand the scope and implications of electronic monitoring technology. Further, I want to suggest that a type of sociotechnical anticipation can be developed if the lateral flow of potentially humanizing and dehumanizing affordances between different types of embodied technology is foregrounded and the matter of harm-minization is engaged with as a design priority.

This type of thinking could form the basis of a methodology that can facilitate the exchange of critical literacies between researchers and designers. The chapter proceeds by first providing a brief tracing of the evolution of electronic monitoring technology before discussing the emplacement and embodiment of electronic monitoring technology in the domestic environment and broader life-world of individuals who are subjected to the conditions created by these devices. I end by considering the affordances of electronic monitoring technology and propose a methodological approach to studying wearable technology based on the incorporation of new, more intrusive technical features into existing technologies and anticipating how certain devices might evolve. In the next section, I trace the evolution of electronic monitoring technology.

The Evolution of Electronic Monitoring Technology

Throughout history, different forms of technology have been affixed to the body at the neck, wrist, or ankle for the purposes of restraint punishment, and the production of immobile states in the wearer. Unlike wristwatches or fitness tracking devices, electronic monitoring devices are designed so that they can be locked onto the body, and they often have some form of physical tamper proofing.

Wearable electronic monitoring for home confinement was first developed as a means to restrict an individual to a physical location or dwelling for punitive purposes (Lilly and Ball 1987). As an alternative to imprisonment, house arrest—enabled by the use of electronic monitoring devices—is seemingly a more cost effective and lenient alternative to being housed in a correctional facility with other prisoners. The use of electronic monitoring technology is not limited to penology and is increasingly employed in monitoring political dissidents, protecting the children of high-profile individuals from kidnapping, remotely monitoring patients in health care, and even as sophisticated in-home baby monitors.

As early as 1965, radio frequency (RF) transmitters were being prototyped for monitoring prisoners. Early examples of this generation of the technology generally comprised a transmitter that could be worn on the body powered by battery packs attached at the waist on a belt. The wearer's location could be determined by an array of multidirectional antennas (Schwitzgebel and Schwitzgebel 1972). A decade later, single assigned radio frequencies were being experimented with in clinical settings, where telemetric monitoring systems with electrocardiogram sensors were being tested on ambulatory patients to remotely monitor body functions (Mandel et al. 1975; Depedro et al. 1975). Applications for this type of technology were limited because telemetric and telephonic technology of the 1970s was not capable of coupling location data and information on vital signs in a single transmission. By the 1980s, systems that assigned passive tags to moveable objects that could be interrogated by active but fixed transceivers in the immediate environment were being prototyped. Functional and scalable electronic monitoring systems did not arise until there had been sufficient advances in areas of database architecture, interface design, mobile telephony, and materials technology.

By the end of the 1980s, a research team led by James Hargrove developed a "wrist mounted vital functions monitor and emergency locator" (1989). The device could measure body temperature and pulse in real time and compared this data to preprogrammed upper and lower values that defined a normal range. If the data collected about the wearer's state fell outside these limits, then the device could send a radio signal alerting emergency services. Systems of this era relied on the same type of components used in emergency aircraft beacons and lacked the capacity to be manually activated by the wearer.

With the introduction of cellular telephones and the Global Positioning System (GPS), combined biometric and location data could be transmitted between devices that were attached to the body, cell phone towers, and remote computers. This enabled the wearer's location to be assigned to other data points relating to the wearer's physiological state or other mobility-based patterns of behavior. Since the late 1990s when the GPS was declared a dual use system accessible for civilian purposes, there has been a steady development of location-based and biometric electronic monitoring technology. For example, in 2015 Stephen Bonasera filed a patent for a technique entitled "life-space data collections from discrete areas" (2015; May et al. 1985, 182–185). Unlike previous techniques for life-space analysis, which relied on paper-based diary keeping to track personal mobility (May et al. 1985, 185), the system described in the patent by Bonasera and his team demonstrated the feasibility of using smartphones to more comprehensively gather and cross-reference information in order to determine aberrations from regular daily routines. Once a set of baseline patterns had been established any deviation would trigger an alert to a caregiver or prompt message being sent to the user.

Beyond the ability to be able to trigger some form of communication after the device detected an event, later iterations of electronic monitoring technology also become more intimate, sampling the skin directly. This was a significant development in the adoption of electronic monitoring technology, given that devices could now be equipped with continuous transdermal monitoring for the presence of alcohol or other illicit substances when sobriety and not using drugs might have been a condition of home incarceration. The Secured Continuous Remote Alcohol Monitor (SCRAM) was introduced into the market in the early 2000s (Hawthorne et al. 2005). Continuous monitoring was a solution to the issue of random testing methods being only partially effective. There are an estimated 483,000 persons who are using the device (Alessi et al 2017, 417). The SCRAM device detects the presence of alcohol vapor near the skin via an electrochemical sensor. It has two circumvention detection sensors that monitor skin contact and temperature. The device collects samples every thirty minutes under standard operating conditions, and this becomes more frequent if alcohol is detected or if the device detects a tamper attempt. Date- and time-stamped data are uploaded to a central server via a USB connection or modem, though from the material available at the time of writing it is not clear how this transfer of data occurs.

Even from the early cumbersome and inefficient examples of electronic monitoring technology, it is not hard to imagine how attaching devices to the body that track location and mediate human physiology or behavior might bring about changes in behavior that positively impact health, work, education, and personal security. However, there are also "unanticipated and unfortunate" (Lilly and Ball 1987, 366) consequences associated with their use. For example, shackles and handcuffs are not routinely viewed as everyday technologies, but they are antecedents to contemporary electronic monitoring devices. Because they are considered primarily as punitive devices, their ergonomics are rarely considered beyond the efficacy of their primary function: restraining the wearer.

Electronic monitoring technology establishes unique human-to-human, human-to-device, and data-to-human relations that work to simultaneously intensify and obscure the presence of technology on the body in addition to the exteriority of the act of being watched. Embedded within the *experience* of wearing an electronic monitoring device is a set of assumptions that have accumulated from antecedent technologies that predated them. These assumptions can mask some of the negative outcomes of house arrest. These assumptions also contribute to a rigidity in how such technology is applied, studied, and regulated.

This brief tracing of the evolution of electronic monitoring devices suggests that the translation of prototypes to market-ready systems is not exactly linear. Contemporary offender monitoring systems are typically a *lateral* combination of the features and use cases described above. To understand the impact of electronic monitoring devices is to also consider how the spatial, temporal, public, and private aspects of dwelling are arrayed and reconfigured when an electronic monitoring device is attached to a prisoner serving their sentence out in the community. In the next section, I consider the dimensional politics of electronic monitoring when emplaced within users' life-worlds (Schutz 1970).

Embodying and Living with House Arrest Bracelets

A manufacturer of electronic monitoring technology, Omnilink claim on their website that "house arrest programs have the potential to reduce jail and prison overcrowding," are "more cost effective than incarceration," and provide "greater social benefit" than serving a sentence in prison. Despite the fact that they act like tethers for human beings, electronic monitoring technology is embodied differently when the wearer is under home confinement and home incarceration. Maya Schenwar, a prominent writer engaged in humanitarian critiques of prison-related issues points out: in both instances, a visible ankle monitor acts "as a 'scarlet letter' [for] those permitted to go to work [because they have] a difficult time finding or holding jobs," which is a problem given "that gaining employment is a crucial step in community-based rehabilitation" (Schenwar 2014; Schenwar and Jan 2015).

When responding to the question "what is it like to be on house arrest?" posted on Quora, an online platform for crowdsourced questions and answers, a user with the moniker "John Wayne" makes this distinction between home incarceration and house arrest clear, describing each as:

Home confinement: I had a[n] 8pm curfew, ankle bracelet and a separate monitor that required a phone line. The ankle bracelet was about half the size of a pack of cigarettes. It required a battery which lasted 8 months or so. It did not have GPS or whatever else. If the monitor did not sense the bracelet within the proximity by 8pm it would send a[n] alarm to my [Prison Officer] PO. It required a phone line and $40 service fee to BI which is the company that monitors and provides the equipment. I only missed my curfew once and nothing happened. If I missed it again he threatened to lock me down for 24 hours. After the first month curfew was still 8pm but I was gradually able to request it be extended to 9–11 depending. I adjusted to it rather quickly and it wasn't too bad. Worse part was the stress of my PO randomly showing up. Whether I was doing anything wrong or not it was still stressful. Obviously you miss being able to enjoy night life, late night errands, etc.

Home incarceration: The biggest difference between home confinement and home incarceration is that under home incarceration you are locked down 24/7. On rare occasion I could leave for court, lawyer meetings and emergencies. Besides that, I couldn't go anywhere. No holidays, haircuts, groceries or whatever else. I wore a much larger bracelet which was probably about the size of 2 packs of cigarettes stacked one on top of the other. This bracelet had to be charged nightly. It was equipped with cell phone and GPS and did not require a phone line. It was also [two]-way. My PO could page me which would cause it to start beeping. I would press a button and it would play a pre-recorded message such as "call your officer now." My PO said that he would allow me to return to home confinement after 60 days but somehow he made excuses and it ended up being close to 100. Even when I was allowed to return to home confinement it was still much more limited. Basically work and a small amount of time allotted on weekends for whatever else. The first week was pretty easy. After that it was pretty rough for the first month. You eventually get used to it. Under home incarceration a phone line was not required but the monthly monitor fee was $100. (John Wayne 2016)

Among the perceived benefits of all this is the idea that house arrest is—according to proponents—a less coercive measure given that an individual *opts in to* wearing an electronic monitoring device as an *alternative* to serving time in prison. As a form of imprisonment, house arrest is rarely imposed as the sole available option by a judge or prosecutors. Moreover, it is thought that house arrest grants an individual the right to work and protects individual liberty and privacy compared to the communal nature of prison life and social conventions that displace an individual from the positive virtues of having a private home-space and access to a community and its resources. But house arrest programs also promote forms of public humiliation or stigma, when offenders are required to be placed on a publicly accessible register and are discriminated against by neighbors (Petty 2016) or when electronic monitoring devices are visible to others and it results in other forms of humiliation.

The cost of administering and maintaining electronic monitoring devices is normally covered by the user from their own funds, and faults or failures of the technology may result in inappropriate questions about tampering and user compliance. When undergoing home incarceration, prisoners face further, more basic, challenges that their counterparts in prison do not. Daily meal planning with nutritional and caloric management and structured outdoor exercise time are available for prisoners—albeit substandard in terms of quality of food and facilities (Kilgore 2014)—that are not available for those incarcerated at home, though features supporting better health and nutrition could be integrated into house arrest systems if one looks toward the consumer health and fitness-tracking technology market for inspiration.

Narrow and preexisting attitudes and expectations about prison rights are a driver of the technological developments being made in house arrest technology, and it is the assumptions made in this regard that forge new technical trajectories that lead to the incorporation of new features (Winston 1998, 2–3) into existing systems. For example, tamper proofing, sampling of biological material though the skin, the incorporation of biometric sensors, the integration of other types of stored data about users, and the use of algorithms to predict certain behavioral or physiological patterns in the user are all likely to be given greater priority than optimizing the technology to improve prisoner health and well-being. These functions will be given priority even though the concept of market responsiveness (Hurley and Hult 1998) dictates that technology innovators anticipate the needs of potential or ultimate users and understand problems through the requirements of intermediaries rather than those most affected by house arrest—the individuals wearing the device. Discursively constructing use contexts—a process that involves a selection of how a certain device's utility is conveyed—also results in acts of political violence and a *strategic* editing of how a technology's functionality is represented.

When an individual is placed under home incarceration or confinement, the home-space is transformed in many ways. To give this transformation ontological grounding in the relation between space, time and the body, one can consider the layers of meaning ascribed to the home-cum-prison that would not be apparent to the external observer. Two concepts in Foucault's analytical vocabulary are useful here. First, the notion of heterotopia is useful in understanding how home-spaces are simultaneously ordered and imperfect when they become spaces of incarceration. Second, his notion of "technologies of the self" shows us how we might understand the existential and psychological aspects of electronic monitoring.

Foucault first introduced the concept of heterotopia in *The Order of Things* (1970), where he contrasts them to the utopian delocalized and ideal places that are careful configurations of symbolism and discourse. The prison is a prime example of this delocalization and disorientation. Heterotopias, for Foucault, disturb this ideal. They are standardized spaces "running against the grain of [the spatial] language" (1970, xix) that is usually associated with the normal conventions under which punitive spaces function and how this is experienced by prisoners, correctional officers, visitors, and so on.

Although a cohesive account of heterotopias remained somewhat illusive in the Foucauldian *oeuvre* (Urbach 1988, 686), it is this conceptual openness that can help us understand how wearability, location awareness, telepresence, biological sampling, and tamper proofing impacts on the sanctity of home-spaces. If we apply the idea of heterotopia to spaces where someone is under house arrest and is being electronically monitored, then we might have an opportunity to shift the assessment of electronic monitoring systems away from design priorities, like their accuracy or robustness, and shift the focus toward their ergonomic, psychological, and biopolitical impacts on users.

For those being monitored in their own homes, the home-space juxtaposes several places. At the same time it becomes a space of respite, it is also transformed into a space of structured discipline and rehabilitation when one of its inhabitants is required to embody the logics and flows of a monitoring device. The home-cum-prison only fully functions in this regard when there is a break with normal experiences of time and daily routines. Wearing an electronic monitor alters not only the nature of the hours and days spent at home but also their relation to the past, present, and future as a function of *duration*. The use of in-home electronic monitoring is predicated on a system of opening and closing the home in ways that both isolate the occupant from certain people, social interactions, and mobilities and at the same time make the home-space penetrable to nonnegotiable entry, both physical and virtual, by law enforcement agents or their delegates.

Considering the above, Jacques Rancière's account of heterotopias, which differs from that of Foucault, might help to clarify the connection between spaces where location awareness is mediated by hidden omnipresent technologies and spaces of safety, comfort, and refuge. Regardless of the form that they might take, the carved-out spaces into which the technical presence of monitoring equipment is installed is done so via the intermediary of the wearer's actual body. This technologized body is sequestered to confinement and curfew, and the way that is negotiated by users as they try to go about their daily lives carries with it a unique individual subjectivity. When these subjectivities are accounted for in the design process as "user journeys," with the technology they are reduced to an "aesthetics is a reconfiguration of sensible experience" (Rancière, 2010), and when designers and researchers try to understand how concepts of space, time, and body are reconfigured when electronic monitoring devices are worn, they may do so through limited conceptual frameworks and ontologies.

Given that the purpose of electronic monitoring devices is to constrain their users while granting conditional personal mobility, an ontology of space and time is embedded into the logic of these devices, which suggests to designers that user compliance is something that should be understood through data capture and the continuity of information transmission. Because the home is also a space for the expression of private desires, difference from the outside world and a safe space creative experimentation, people under house arrest might develop unique workarounds so that they can act with some degree of strategic agency and noncompliance in terms of how they live with their monitoring device.

When the home-space is prisonized via the installation of technical objects that mediate the bodily positions and routines of the occupant, they become existential *and* material objects that imbue the spaces and times they become part of with a multivariate function. I also see this multivariate function in the analytical framework "technologies of the self" in Foucault's work, which proposed that forces supporting the objectives and patronage models of institutions progressively invade the production of human subjectivity. For Foucault, these are technologies of the mind rather than material objects, though I argue that electronic monitoring is an example of how physical objects can be configured and framed in the service of psychologically persuasive "technologies" because they are embodied (c.f. merely attached or worn).

Within this schema, such technologies are embodied through several interlinking modalities. The first is that of disclosure and cultivation. Under house arrest, a reformed self is cultivated through the constant disclosure of location and of personal movements and social interactions. The second is that self-examination and reflection is afforded by forced isolation, not in the carved out institutionalized space of the prison, but within the everydayness of familiar spaces—the home and the life-world. The third relates to mental discipline and the training of the body into the "memorisation of [these] deeds and their correspondence to rules" (Foucault 1988) that a user needs to learn to comply with (or subvert) the device's logic. The fourth is to remember and learn from past activity to transmit this knowledge across space and time (Foucault 1988) once the conditions imposed by the device are removed and the normal conventions of home life are, seemingly, restored.

The fact that "people will strive to develop competencies with new technical objects in order to feel comfortable in their presence" (Krippendorff 1989) is commonly assumed in the design of human-centered technology, and we should also assume that this would also include ways to interfere with the normal operations of the device. For example, a Reddit user going by the name "SureSheDid" posted the following during an Ask Me Anything session (AMA) about what it is like to be under house arrest:

> I was working for a computer repair shop at the time and the techs and I kind of dissected the thing, did a lot of research on it online, and did some experiments (under the guise of "I was at work so it doesn't count") and we determined that the damn thing wasn't even on. Turns out that the particular one I had [came] with a service with 2 monitoring options (agents can pull reports as needed or it is monitored for activity 24/7 and the agent is called anytime the person goes anywhere) We figured that the supervising agency had to pay for any time the bracelets were activated. Based on a combination of what we found out online, the lights on the bracelet when I was in various locations, and the reaction (or non-reaction) of my agent to my movements (like one time I stayed at work until [midnight] when I was supposed to leave at 5pm) we figured it wasn't even being monitored. We were right. From that point on I just did whatever I felt like.[1]

Considering this anecdote, compliance becomes difficult to design for in terms of human-centricity. Especially when compliance is tightly scripted into the device as a requirement of standard operation.

The idea of compliance in this sense conflates rules associated to the physical device itself, its software, a prisoner's sentence, and the law more generally. Errors in compliance "largely arise out of a mismatch [between] what a [device] can actually do and what it symbolises to [users] as being capable [or good at] doing" (Krippendorff 1989, 8). Two theories of compliance can be applied here to better understand its relationship to the individual approaches to, and resistances of, conditional agency during house arrest. These are *formal* and *substantive* compliance. Formal compliance refers to the minimal requirements required to meet the terms dictated by the device, the sentence, and the law. Substantive compliance refers to deep engagement with the terms of the sentence and deep engagement with the overall ethos of house arrest at the level of ideology (Robinson and McNeill 2008, 434). In a study of noncompliance and house arrest, Hucklesby found that technical issues with the ankle bracelets were often exploited to engage in noncompliant behavior without consequence by simply "blaming the equipment" (2009, 263).

Affordances and Scripts: Tamper proofing

In *Design Methods* (1992), John Chris Jones noted that "the designer must be able to predict the ultimate effects of their proposed design[s] as well as specifying the actions that are needed to bring these effects about." In designing electronic monitoring technology, compliance can overshadow other aspects of a design strategy that might result in the technology being more humane. A focus on compliance narrows the aesthetic, ergonomic, functional, and biopolitical possibilities of a design. Script analysis offers a way to ratify the mode of thought considered to be design intuition (Wendt 2015). It challenges the tendency for designers to address only the prefigured and normative aspects of a particular technology. The concept of script analysis (Akrich 1992; Latour 1992; Verbeek 2006, 361) holds that a technical artifact prescribes human actions through physical properties that are inscribed into the object during the processes of conception and design—for instance, a cup made of paper suggests disposability whereas one made of fine porcelain suggests fragility and value. Script analysis offers a way to document and understand a "designer's more or less informed presumptions, visions or predictions about the relations between a [technical object] and the human actors surrounding it" and potentially achieve this *outside* narrow definitions of user behavior that overlooks the fact that in certain contexts users will want to ignore, discard, and reject elements of the standard scenario of use for which a design has been optimized (Fallan 2008, 63).

At the heart of technical scripts, the concept of technical affordance is appropriated from the field of ecological psychology and attributed largely to the pioneering work of J. J. Gibson (1979). It is particularly suited to the study of embodied technology, given its emphasis on possible but not necessarily realized juxtapositions of bodies, the environment, artifacts, and knowledge systems. As one element of the different "actionable combinations" (Letiche and Lissack 2009, 62) that make up electronic monitoring systems, tamper proofing is predicated on assumptions about preexisting patterns that can be observed within an individual's home-space and lifeworld, and then, on newly acquired competencies that may be developed through living *with* the device.

Affordances are made sense of through the unspoken communication that occurs between designers and users of technologies. The flow of instructional or sense-making information is the result of a complex configuration of design choices made when problems, use cases, and prototypes for a technology are formulated collaboratively between actors who make certain assumptions about how ultimate usage occurs. When users are consulted in the design process or in ethnographic or observational research, the discovery of usage and coping strategies is likely to be partial, given the implications for users if their noncompliance is discovered.

As Gibson notes:

> The supposedly separate realms of the subjective and objective are actually only poles of attention. The dualism of observer and environment is unnecessary. The information for the perception of "here" is of the same kind as the information of the perception of "there," and a continuous layout of surfaces extends from one to the other. (1979, 116)

Affordances cannot simply be "built into" or "read out of" the hypothetical or staged and carefully configured observation of an emplaced technology (Fisher 2004, 26). These assignments of *an* affording capacity for a device are made meaningful not only by its materiality but also by semantically and experientially driven frames of reference that become attached to the physical embodiment of a given technical object. The experience of wearing a house arrest bracelet when considered as a sociotechnical script can be understood through "the symbolic qualities of man-made forms in the [cognitive and social] context of [how bracelets are used] and [the] application of this use to industrial design" (Krippendorff and Butter 1984, as cited in You and Chen 2001, 26). Moreover, the application of knowledge about how these symbolic qualities contribute to wearer compliance with various aspects of the device's design when subsequent designs are iterated.

The assumption made when developing tamper-proof wearable technology is that the device must meet certain standards to be difficult to remove and be able to signal when a removal attempt is made. One could argue then that the relationship between the material and semantic aspects of tamper proofing can be established on the shared presumption that an individual under house arrest will not entirely perceive house arrest through the full set of experiences of the technology, but instead focus on those intentionally designed to frustrate.

The efficacy of tamper proofing can be observed through the behaviors and attitudes (or documentation of these actions and attitudes) of someone who is under house arrest and wearing an ankle monitor. These interactions with the device may reflect aesthetic concerns or ergonomic frustrations, or both—for example, the device being visible or awkward looking when certain types of clothing are worn, or uncomfortable to wear while sleeping. The sociotechnical script comprises in equal parts the physically afforded cumbersome aspects of wearing the device, their experiential embodiment in the form of frustration and discomfort, and the extent to which a wearer develops tolerance or circumvention strategies.

Historical and commercial trends in the design of wearable offender-monitoring systems are a vital component in developing new analytical frameworks for critical research, which, in my view, are enhanced by work already going on in the field of media archaeology (Huhtamo and Parikka 2011). As I have argued elsewhere, "drawing on this media archaeological notion also gestures to the way that [technical devices] never operate outside the constraints imposed on them by the internal and external influences that existed at the time of their production" (Jethani and Leorke 2013, 492). Reframing electronic monitoring in this way is particularly important given that the issue of "product conflation" (Faraj and Azad 2012, 241) of electronic monitoring devices with antecedent technology tends to provide us with convenient labels to group technologies together based on similar features or the location worn on the body. Further, such labels often represent mature categories employed by industry—categories that ossify as the number of vendors and products in a category increase. As Faraj and Azad note:

> Each product class enshrines a shared worldview among its adherents in regard to what the ... product class is supposed to do and is good for. As a result, the product classes (market categories) are generally adopted by researchers as pointing to an important differentiation in the technology. However, ... this nominal difference is problematic for researchers who are concerned about a technology's materiality. (2012, 240–241)

Further, as Nagy and Neff note, in engaging with the concept of affordances that scholars and designers all "too often ... separate questions of the materiality of technology from discussions of social construction of human agency, rather than to engage with materiality with any scholarly seriousness" (2015, 2). These speculative yet material relations (constructed specifically for research) which exist up- and downstream of the present and observable reality we see today offer a way to move beyond framings of the utility, and benefit, of electronic systems that are based on neoliberal product semantics.

The key problem that needs to be pointed out with the types of frames established in the conveyance of product semantics is that when they are part of a conversation between designers and users (Norman 1999, 2008), strategic human agency is presented as being contingent on design choices and, in the case of electronic monitoring devices, this agency is a conditional and changeable state. Such a design strategy assumes that the material properties of a device, when communicated in the context of utility, play a role in the communication of how meaningful a technical object is and the things that people might achieve by using it. This scripting carries a different materiality into the final product, one not so concerned with the physical manipulation of an object or the movement of that object between use contexts, but rather with controlling what that object *could* mean in the minds of idealized users as one gives oneself over to the logic of the device.

Toward an Anticipatory Methodology

When technologists make *a priori* assumptions about the context in which the objects they design are used, they sharply define certain relations and downplay others. The assumption within the so-called "design thinking" (Buchanan 1992) approach is that through empathy building, observation, and ethnography, designers of products become authorities on the look, feel, and ideal use of technical objects by accumulating knowledge of different contexts of use. To address the biases arising out of narrow constructions of users and scenarios of use, including the nonstandard ways in which electronic monitoring devices are subverted, requires unprecedented collaboration in the areas of design and production.

The domain extension of the logics inscribed into electronic monitoring technology into other intimate areas of life means that established, emerging, or potential markets are treated as *outcomes of processes* that contribute to the diffusion of technical systems in which wearable data-garnering devices are already present. These processes are then, in turn, shaped by the interests of those who *need* to cater to a market and then, by extension, contribute to the shape that market takes as it forms and approaches maturity. Reflecting on this, Ruckenstein and Pantzar state:

> Techno-anthropological projects need to intervene here in order to ask whether this is a valid goal: in the long run, research with no promises of immediate financial productivity might be socially and economically more rewarding simply because it aims for a deeper understanding of long-term effects and trajectories, rather than simply taking for granted the current state of affairs. Consequently, reflexive and critical accounts of researchers' involvements with technology companies, including the developers and promoters of their wares, are of great interest for techno-anthropological research, because they can illuminate the commercial, political, and ethical underpinnings of research endeavours and promote down-to-earth perspectives on how technology companies—in the course of affecting and shaping people's daily lives and futures—interpret, design, and aim to produce those lives. (2015, 14)

Patents can be a particularly useful resource through which the evolution of a class of technology can be studied outside the confines of semantically constructed frames of reference. They reveal connections between funding bodies, research institutions, industry, and markets, bringing them into sharp focus. Patents are based on the idea that the inventor knows what a technology is for. The appropriation of technology designed for the criminal justice market might seldom yield radical innovation in the form of spin-offs because their logics and architectures do not necessarily cater to other marginal markets and niches that are not necessarily profitable if those developing the technology have never dealt in these markets before.

The tendency within electronic monitoring technology might be for incremental innovation through existing parallel lineages of technical affordance, which are assumed to be related or relevant during the process of design research.

As an object to use in research, the patent document is "open" for such analysis. The basic anatomy of a patent document has within it certain conventions that situate it in a set of predefined, though relatively subjective, relations to other patents via what is termed a citation to "prior art." The references to this prior art are defined by both the inventor and the patent examiner, forming a common ground through a set of USPC codes (Callaert et al. 2006). It is not only traces of innovation that we see reflected in patents, but it is also a certain factor of relatedness present in differing degrees both at the level of the device and then also at the level of the documents themselves, through the coding and analysis of the prior art citations with affordance flow and transfer as a hermeneutic priority. Such hermeneutics might then be used as a gateway to discovering not only material relatedness between objects as linked according to intellectual property assignments but also in a more open and exploratory fashion, which could in turn exert influence over the regulation and governance of electronic monitoring systems as they become more intensive and sophisticated. However, within this general field of openness, the document itself cannot be forsaken for the context in which it was produced (Prior 2003, 26).

In analyzing patents, we should be asking questions about the functions served by the objects under study—who has put it forward? Who is utilizing it and under what circumstances? Where and how has it come into being? How does discourse circulate within it? How do they create self-reflexive systems? (Renzi 2008, 73) By incorporating the above-mentioned objects into design research, designers and developers achieve a type of provenance that allows others examining the technology to report on: who it is that has authored the documentation being used to make design decisions; the extent that the documentation reflects or structures the relationship between the author and user of the documents being examined; the way the documentation features in everyday use-contexts of the technology; and the extent to which this material acts back onto the institutions or individuals who are engaged in the labor of producing and maintaining this documentation (Prior 2003, 93) in raw and curated formats so that it may remain analytically relevant.

Such analyses of wearable technology seek to discover material that already exists about certain devices and use cases across defined domains and product classes. It is necessary to complement rather than replace theories of technological and social determinism when it comes to the question of the political stakes that accompany the mainstreaming of self-tracking technology. The challenge of developing a critical understanding of self-tracking technology is how the social dimension of the technology, which naturally changes over time, is reasserted against material understandings of the technology. As I have suggested elsewhere with Dale Leorke, a "media archaeological notion gestures to the way that [technology and their associated cultural practices] never operate outside the constraints imposed on them by the internal and external influences that existed at the time of their production" (Jethani and Leorke 2013, 9).

Anticipation as a methodological approach seeks to extrapolate from a known understanding of things, a deeper understanding of hidden surfaces, relationships, and interdependencies. In anticipating the sociomaterial evolution of electronic monitoring, we may be able to consider some of the iatrogenic outcomes of technical developments in house arrest systems so that trade-offs can be ethically and pragmatically assessed relative to an uncritical acceptance of tighter mechanisms of compliance and control, as simply a matter of "human contingency" (Akrich 1992, 205) in design brief. What anticipation offers is a more nimble discourse that extends the "finite vocabulary" (Krippendorff 1989, 10) attached to house arrest as a scenario of use for electronic monitoring systems. As Krippendorff argues:

> Only when designers [and researchers] are able to see themselves as part of the larger system of meaning, an ecology that guides the creation and use of artefacts, changes in the material world including their own understanding of it, can designers assume responsibilities for their own ecological interventions, which ultimately are interventions into ... practices of living (1989, 31).

To these ends, the FABRIC of Digital Life archive, an initiative funded by the Social Sciences and Humanities Research Council of Canada and managed by researchers at the Ontario Tech University, catalogues various examples of embodied computing, has developed a valuable online archive of such documents and it is a model for a platform through which such discourse could occur.[2] In an article describing the project, Iliadis and Pedersen (2018) state:

FABRIC is an online digital archive for storing media related to embodied technologies—things like patents, news releases, instructional videos, and art. The archive allows users to track, catalogue, and view artefacts related to human-computer interaction platforms, designs, and ideas, including images, videos, texts, websites, and data sets that document emerging trends. Curated sub-collections are hosted on the archive that relate to a variety of themes, including ethics, surveillance, and vulnerable populations.

The archive itself is structured by an ontology for devices, which consists of categories such as: a HCI platform that categorizes a device as carry-able, wearable, or implantable; the location on the body where the technology is attached or implanted; the discourse type, that is, if the document is describing an invention or if it is a response to a certain invention or development in the field; the persuasive type, which refers to if the document is academic, marketing material, artistic, and so on; and labels for the organizations or individuals who might be involved in producing or be mentioned in the documents. So, returning to the notion of anticipation, if we are to think about the materials amassed in the design, production, and research process, archives such as FABRIC prove valuable and point to a responsibility on the part of actors involved in the production, administration, and analysis of wearable technology to "donate" material to publicly available and open access repositories.

To think seriously about documentation and paratextual research materials also points to new underexplored areas of wearable technology for future empirical investigation. For example, within agile software production environments, documentation is an integral part of the production process and analyses of this material might produce knowledge about how certain decisions are made, which makes self-tracking technology potentially iatrogenic, less efficacious, or marginalizing—anticipating the possibilities of the technology and what people do with it.

Conclusion

The approach I have outlined in this chapter is not one that seeks to study social impacts through just talking to or observing people; rather I want to focus on processes that *mediate* the body—how they are designed, how well they function relative to the technical capacities available, and how true to form they are. This produces a type of materialism where the objects of critique themselves are ontologically coherent in the social context of their use, and the "technological frame" for relations around a technology not necessarily understood through current conventions of use but also in a way that can guide future developments (Bijker 1995, 123). It is here where disciplinary vocabularies might be a help rather than a hindrance. The work of management consultants, for instance, frames human–technology relations in a way that is action-oriented and makes possible future ontological configurations; we can either write these things off as "technocratic jargon" or we can use them to form the basis of a *pragmatic* ontology into which certain speculative designs can be projected and alternatives explored.

This type of speculative modeling ascribes a materiality that could link different ontological configurations of the same set of relations based on the difference between enunciation (the production of data) and utterance (what that data says), the assumptions of the discipline in which the analysis is occurring, and the objectives of the system under examination. This helps us grasp the material traces of dynamic processes and see change over time; speculate on the rationale of decisions and identify mechanisms of marginalization; and overall access an emerging dimensional politics flowing though this class of technology. To access the deeper confines and intimacies of the everyday lives of electronically monitored persons, especially given that we know little about how individuals adjust after serving their sentence, requires a two-fold examination of the past and afterlives of such technologies.

Notes

1. trappedinahouse (alias). 2010. I'm On House Arrest AMAA. Reddit, July 31. https://www.reddit.com/r/IAmA/comments/cw0a0/im_on_house_arrest_amaa/.

2. https://fabricofdigitallife.com/.

References

Akrich, Madeleine. 1992. The De-scription of Technical Objects. In *Shaping Technology/Building Society: Studies in Sociotechnical Change*, edited by Weibe E. Bijker and John Law, 205–224. Cambridge, MA: MIT Press.

Alessi, Sheila M., Nancy P. Barnett, and Nancy M. Petry. 2017. Experiences with SCRAMx Alcohol Monitoring Technology in 100 Alcohol Treatment Outpatients.

Drug and Alcohol Dependence 178 (September 1): 417–424. https://doi.org/10.1016/j.drugalcdep.2017.05.031.

Arnold, Michael. 2003. On the Phenomenology of Technology: The "Janus-Faces" of Mobile Phones. *Information and Organization* 13 (4): 231–256. https://doi.org/10.1016/S1471-7727(03)00013-7.

Bijker, Wiebe E. 1995. *Of Bicycles, Bakelites, and Bulbs: Toward a Theory of Sociotechnical Change.* Cambridge, MA: MIT Press.

Bonasera, Stephen J., A. Katrin Schenk, and Evan H. Goulding. 2015. Lifespace Data Collection from Discrete Areas. US Patent 9,106,718, issued August 11. https://patents.google.com/patent/US9106718B2.

Brulé, David Allen. 2015. Wearable RFID Storage Devices. US Patent Application 14/408,740, filed June 25, 2015. https://patents.google.com/patent/US20150178532A1.

Buchanan, Richard. 1992. Wicked Problems in Design Thinking. *Design Issues* 8 (2): 5–21. https://doi.org/10.2307/1511637.

Callaert, Julie, Bart Van Looy, Arnold Verbeek, Koenraad Debackere, and Bart Thijs. 2006. Traces of Prior Art: An Analysis of Non-patent References Found in Patent Documents. *Scientometrics* 69 (1): 3–20. https://doi.org/10.1007/s11192-006-0135-8.

Castells, Manuel. 2000. *The Rise of the Network Society.* Oxford: Blackwell.

Depedro, Donald, and Robert Cannon. 1975. Electrocardiographic Telemetry and Telephone Transmission Link System. US Patent 3,882,277, issued May 6. https://patents.google.com/patent/US3882277.

Fallan, Kjetil. 2008. De-scribing Design: Appropriating Script Analysis to Design History. *Design Issues* 24 (4): 61–75. https://doi.org/10.1162/desi.2008.24.4.61.

Faraj, Samer, and Bijan Azad. 2012. The Materiality of Technology: An Affordance Perspective. In *Materiality and Organizing Social Interaction in a Technological World*, edited by Paul M. Leonardi, 237–258. Oxford: Oxford University Press.

Feenberg, Andrew. 2002. *Transforming Technology: A Critical Theory Revisited.* Oxford: Oxford University Press.

Fisher, Tom H. 2004. What We Touch, Touches Us: Materials, Affects, and Affordances. *Design Issues* 20 (4): 20–31. https://doi.org/10.1162/0747936042312066.

Foucault, Michel. 1970. *The Order of Things: An Archaeology of the Human Sciences.* New York: Vintage Books.

Foucault, Michel. 1977. *Discipline and Punish.* New York: Pantheon.

Foucault, Michel. 1988. Technologies of the Self. In *Technologies of the Self: A Seminar with Michel Foucault*, edited by Luther H. Martin, Huck Gutman, and Patrick H. Hutton, 16–49. London: Tavistock Publications.

Gibson, J. J. 1979. *The Ecological Approach to Visual Perception.* Boston: Houghton Mifflin.

Hargrove, James L., Lloyd D. Lillie, and Arthur T. Whittaker. 1989. Wrist-mounted Vital Functions Monitor and Emergency Locator. US Patent 4,819,860, issued April 11. https://patents.google.com/patent/US4819860A.

Hawthorne, Jeffrey, Michael Iiams, Glenn Tubb, Richard Stoll, and Gary Shoffner. 2005. Bio-information Sensor Monitoring System and Method. US Patent Application 11/104,810, filed August 11. https://patents.google.com/patent/US20050177615A1.

Hucklesby, Anthea. 2009. Understanding Offenders' Compliance: A Case Study of Electronically Monitored Curfew Orders. *Journal of Law and Society* 36 (2): 248–271. https://doi.org/10.1111/j.1467-6478.2009.00465.x.

Huhtamo, Erkki, and Jussi Parikka, eds. 2011. *Media Archaeology: Approaches, Applications, and Implications.* Berkeley: University of California Press.

Hurley, Robert F., and G. Tomas M. Hult. 1998. Innovation, Market Orientation, and Organizational Learning: An Integration and Empirical Examination. *Journal of Marketing* 62 (3): 42–54. https://doi.org/10.1177%2F002224299806200303.

Ihde, Don. 1979. *Technics and Praxis.* Dordrecht, The Netherlands: Reidel.

Iliadis, Andrew, and Isabel Pedersen. 2016. Reverse the Perspective: It's Time to Track the Development of Embodied Technologies and Their Creators. *Decimal: Digital Culture and Media Lab* (blog), December 21. https://www.decimallab.ca/uncategorized/reverse-the-perspective-its-time-to-track-the-development-of-embodied-technologies-and-their-creators/.

Jethani, Suneel. 2015. Mediating the Body: Technology, Politics and Epistemologies of Self. *Communication, Politics & Culture* 47 (3): 34–43. http://mams.rmit.edu.au/hb3lesdtmp9fz.pdf.

Jethani, Suneel, and Dale Leorke. 2013. Ideology, Obsolescence and Preservation in Digital Mapping and Locative Art. *International Communication Gazette* 75 (5–6): 484–501. https://doi.org/10.1177%2F1748048513491904.

John Wayne (alias). 2016. Answer to question "What Is It Like to Live Under House Arrest?" Quora, March 16. https://www.quora.com/What-is-it-like-to-live-under-house-arrest/answer/John-Wayne-170.

Jones, John Chris. 1992. *Design Methods.* New York: John Wiley & Sons.

Kilgore, James. 2014. The Grey Area of Electronic Monitoring in the USA. *Criminal Justice Matters* 95 (1): 18–19. https://doi.org/10.1080/09627251.2014.902201.

Krippendorff, Klaus. 1989. Product Semantics: A Triangulation and Four Design Theories. Paper presented at the 2nd Conference on Product Semantics, Helsinki, Finland, May 16–19. http://repository.upenn.edu/asc_papers/254.

Krippendorff, Klaus, and Reinhart Butter. 1984. Product Semantics Exploring the Symbolic Qualities of Form. *Innovation* 3 (2): 4–9. http://repository.upenn.edu/asc_papers/40.

Latour, Bruno. 1992. Where Are the Missing Masses? The Sociology of a Few Mundane Artifacts. In *Shaping Technology/Building Society: Studies in Sociotechnical Change*, edited by John Law and Wiebe E. Bijker, 225–258. Cambridge, MA: MIT Press.

Letiche, Hugo, and Michael Lissack. 2009. Making Room for Affordances. *Emergence: Complexity and Organization* 11 (3): 61–72. https://journal.emergentpublications.com/article/making-room-for-affordances/.

Lilly, Robert J. and Richard A. Ball. 1987. A Brief History of Home Confinement and House Arrest. *Northern Kentucky Law Review* 13 (3): 343–374. https://heinonline.org/HOL/P?h=hein.journals/nkenlr13&i=351.

Lyon, David. 1994. *The Electronic Eye: The Rise of Surveillance Society*. Minneapolis: University of Minnesota Press.

Lyon, David. 2001. *Surveillance Society: Monitoring Everyday Life*. Buckingham, UK: Open University Press.

Mandel, Louis, Algernon M. Ong, and Paul Singer. 1975. Ambulatory Patient Monitoring System. US Patent 3,898,984, issued August 12. https://patents.google.com/patent/US3898984A.

Mann, Steve, Jason Nolan, and Barry Wellman. 2002. Sousveillance: Inventing and Using Wearable Computing Devices for Data Collection in Surveillance Environments. *Surveillance and Society* 1(3): 331–355. https://doi.org/10.24908/ss.v1i3.3344.

Mann, Steve, and Joseph Ferenbok. 2013. New Media and the Power Politics of Sousveillance in a Surveillance-Dominated World. *Surveillance and Society* 11 (1–2): 18–34. https://doi.org/10.24908/ss.v11i1/2.4456.

May, David, U. S. L. Nayak, and Bernard Isaacs. 1985. The Life-Space Diary: A Measure of Mobility in Old People at Home. *International Rehabilitation Medicine* 7 (4): 182–186. https://doi.org/10.3109/03790798509165993.

Nagy, Peter, and Gina Neff. 2015. Imagined Affordance: Reconstructing a Keyword for Communication Theory. *Social Media + Society* 1 (2): 1–9. https://doi.org/10.1177%2F2056305115603385.

Norman, Donald A. 1999. Affordance, Conventions, and Design. *Interactions* 6 (3): 38–43. https://doi.org/10.1145/301153.301168.

Norman, Donald A. 2008. The Way I See It: Signifiers, Not Affordances. *Interactions* 15 (6): 18–19. https://doi.org/10.1145/1409040.1409044.

Noble, Safiya Umoja, and Sarah T. Roberts. 2016. Through Google-Colored Glass: Design, Emotion, Class, and Wearables as Commodity and Control. In *Emotions, Technology, and Design*, edited by Sharon Tettegah and Safiya Noble, 187–212. London: Academic Press.

Orlikowski, Wanda J., and Debra C. Gash. 1994. Technological Frames: Making Sense of Information Technology in Organizations. *ACM Transactions on Information Systems (TOIS)* 12 (2): 174–207. https://doi.org/10.1145/196734.196745.

Pedersen, Isabel. 2005. A Semiotics of Human Actions for Wearable Augmented Reality Interfaces. *Semiotica* 2005 (155): 183–200. https://doi.org/10.1515/semi.2005 .2005.155.1-4.183.

Petty, James. 2016. The London Spikes Controversy: Homelessness, Urban Securitisation and the Question of "Hostile Architecture." *International Journal for Crime, Justice and Social Democracy* 5 (1): 67–81. https://doi.org/10.5204/ijcjsd.v5i1.286.

Pinch, Trevor J., and Wiebe E. Bijker. 1984. The Social Construction of Facts and Artefacts: Or How the Sociology of Science and the Sociology of Technology Might Benefit Each Other. *Social Studies of Science* 14 (3): 399–441. https://doi.org/10 .1177%2F030631284014003004.

Prior, Lindsay. 2003. *Using Documents in Social Research*. Los Angeles: Sage.

Rancière, Jacques. 2010. The Aesthetic Heterotopia. *Philosophy Today* 54 (suppl.): 15–25. https://doi.org/10.5840/philtoday201054Supplement42.

Renzi, Alessandra. 2008. The Space of Tactical Media. In *Digital Media and Democracy: Tactics in Hard Times*, edited by Megan Boler, 71–100. Cambridge, MA: MIT Press.

Robinson, Gwen, and Fergus McNeill. 2008. Exploring the Dynamics of Compliance with Community Penalties. *Theoretical Criminology* 12 (4): 431–449. https:// doi.org/10.1177%2F1362480608097151.

Ruckenstein, Minna, and Mika Pantzar. 2015. Datafied Life: Techno-anthropology as a Site for Exploration and Experimentation. *Techne: Research in Philosophy and Technology* 19 (2): 191–210. https://doi.org/10.5840/techne20159935.

Schenwar, Maya. 2014. *Locked Down, Locked Out: Why Prison Doesn't Work and How We Can Do Better*. San Francisco: Berrett-Koehler Publishers.

Schenwar, Maya, and Thu Jan. 2015. The Quiet Horrors of House Arrest, Electronic Monitoring, and Other Alternative Forms of Incarceration. *Mother Jones*, January 22. https://www.motherjones.com/politics/2015/01/house-arrest-surveillance-state -prisons/.

Schutz, Alfred. 1970. Some Structures of the Life-World. In *Collected Papers III*, edited by I. Schutz, 116–132. Dordrecht, The Netherlands: Springer.

Schwitzgebel, Robert L., and Ralph K. Schwitzgebel. 1972. *Psychotechnology: Electronic Control of Mind and Behavior*. New York: Holt, Rinehart, and Winston

Sullivan, Scott. 2017. *Designing for Wearables: Effective UX for Current and Future Devices*. Beijing: O'Reilly.

Urbach, Henry. 1988. Writing Architectural Heterotopia. *Journal of Architecture* 3 (4): 347–354. https://doi.org/10.1080/136023698374125.

Verbeek, Peter-Paul. 2006. Materializing Morality: Design Ethics and Technological Mediation. *Science, Technology, and Human Values* 31 (3): 361–380. https://doi.org/10.1177%2F0162243905285847.

Winner, Langdon. 1980. Do Artifacts Have Politics? *Daedalus* 109 (1): 121–136. https://www.jstor.org/stable/20024652.

Winston, Brian. 1998. *Media Technology and Society: A History: From the Telegraph to the Internet*. London: Routledge.

You, Hsiao-Chen, and Kuohsiang Chen. 2007. Applications of Affordance and Semantics in Product Design. *Design Studies* 28 (1): 23–38. https://doi.org/10.1016/j.destud.2006.07.002.

9   Click-Click-Gimme-Gimme: Pleasures and Perils of the "Opt In" World of Fashion Tech

Elizabeth Wissinger

Introduction

From smart fibers and tattoos, biosensing devices and implants, networked jewelry or an LED encrusted dress, there are many kinds of technologies that can be deemed "wearable." Wearable technology is by definition technology worn on the body, such as smart watches, activity trackers, internet- and communication-enabled jewelry or clothing, and e-textiles, the kind of "*embodied computing* technologies" that sit on the skin, referred to in this book's introduction. Wearables' functionality ranges from simple phone call and text alerts, to sensing emotional states or physical stress. Blinking, vibrating, hardening, extending, shocking—wearables' interactivity networks and connects bodies, and reveals their inner workings. Wearables' functions generally range from eminently practical—like tracking heart rate or counting steps—to utterly fantastical, as when, for instance, a dress responds to biometric indicators of interest or attraction by gradually becoming more transparent (Wipprecht 2011).[1]

The years 2014, 2015, and 2016 were each declared "the year of wearable technology" (Spence 2013; Gibbs 2014; Ingham 2015). Some even predicted the market would "double" by 2021 (Lamkin 2017), while for others, the blush was off the rose, leaving them to ask whether wearables would *ever* have their "iPhone moment" (Sullivan 2016). Despite the groundswell abating a bit, the production of new garments and gadgets continues apace (Wearable Team 2017), with some industry insiders expressing cautious optimism saying "We're finally past the honeymoon stage in wearables. We have a better handle on the future as it really stands and not as, four years ago, it was going to be" (Pan 2018). That being said, the reportedly "best" wearable at C.E.S. 2019 was just another version of the smartwatch (Hartmans 2019). The vision of seamless personal technology is a powerful one, whose promise has drawn venture capital funds, given rise to crowds of "know thyself" through numbers self-tracking enthusiasts, inspired designers to put chips into everything from t-shirts to "it" bags, and has employers and marketers salivating at the prospect of ever more precise, granular data on consumers' and workers' habits, preferences, attention, and moods.

Tracking personal information to achieve wellness or health has been the focus of much debate (Lupton 2016; Nafus 2016; Neff and Nafus 2016). Less attention is being paid, however, to how contemporary pressures of the #nofilter selfie society glamourizes and normalizes giving up one's data. Presenting oneself as fashionable is a way to be seen, and is key to mattering in the Instagram-fueled universe of clicks, likes, and followers (Wissinger 2015). The impetus for self-branding and constant connectedness in fashion tech culture creates strong incentives for users to share biometric and personal data in exchange for convenience and cool.

In keeping with this volume's stated goal of situating these kinds of technologies "within social, ethical, and political frameworks," this chapter employs the concept of "glamour labor" (Wissinger 2015)—the work of self-branding and control to become as attractive, exciting, and engaging in person as one's highly curated and edited online self—to argue that wearable technologies designed for fashionable body optimization and intimate consumer-oriented personalization lie on a continuum with previous tendencies of the internet and social media to harness and meter human energy for profit in return for the perceived benefits of "cool." This tendency is decidedly pronounced in the realm of fashion tech. Fashion tech refers to a range of practices that include online shopping, miniature RFID (Radio Frequency Identification) chips in products (Halzack 2016), beacon technologies that personalize shopping and other customer experience (Kline 2016), AI-informed customer service and clothing design (Snow 2017), electronically connected or responsive clothing (Peirce 2017),[2] and wearables that seek to be both functional and fashionable (Allison 2018).[3] In the fashion tech domain, cheery chat-bots and personalization protocols facilitate data mining under the guise of offering consumers what they want (while generally accepted in the areas of the field I researched, there is some concern regarding how consumers perceive these issues, as evidenced by this recent "creepy or cool" survey) (RichRelevance 2017). In these transactions, users engage in a cost–benefit calculus, putting up with potentially creepy levels of data gathering in exchange for the convenience of personalization, and the access to "cool" events, services, and feedback (Wissinger 2018).[4]

In the "creepy or cool" trade off, users unwittingly choose to opt into data gathering and sharing, actively giving away their Personally Identifiable Information (P.I.I. in industry lingo) to get the goods. As the following discussion will illustrate, designers I spoke to in the field of fashion tech tend to exacerbate this tendency by pushing responsibility for data protection onto consumers. When discussing data vulnerability, the majority of my respondents emphasized that users *choose* or "opt in" to giving up P.I.I. as part of interacting with their product. In other words, these producers consistently cited the fact that in the creepy versus convenience or cool calculus, the perks tend to win, and this choice figured prominently in their treatment of customer data.

The respondents' assumption that it is users' responsibility to protect themselves is of particular concern, given the newly invasive tech/body interfaces made possible by biotech-enabled wearables now on the horizon. The dry 1s and 0s of geolocation or shopping preference will soon be upstaged by new and juicy biometrics, such as heart beat, galvanic skin response, tears, and sweat composition (Mandavilli 2019; Fellman 2016; Pedersen and Ellison 2017; Sawh 2016; Sullivan 2014). Measuring everything from emotional responses, energy levels, and pinpointed details of stress, diet, and environment, these new data metrics are valuable not only to those seeking to maximize optimum performance, but also to governments, employers, and marketers. As prototypes are being advanced that read this newly invasive and individualized data, it is logical and increasingly possible to move to even more specifically pinpointed biometrics, such as, for example, tracking microbial traces left behind by a finger swipe (Vanin 2015).

Outlining the scope of attitudes toward data protection displayed by practitioners in the fashion tech field, this chapter provides a look into the design culture in which these coming biometric technologies are being introduced. I contend that the attitudes I encountered in the field of fashion tech reveal a relatively uncritical affinity for the move toward biometric identifiers. The coming wave of biotech wearables will blur the already fuzzy line between health data (e.g., pulse rate, sweat composition, eye movement, activity levels) and consumer engagement or predictive data (e.g., pulse rate, sweat composition, etc.). While the need to protect sensitive health data is fairly clear, how and when to keep consumer data anonymous is not well regulated, and is subject to ongoing debate.

In the age of the Fitbit, strapping technology onto your body to track and monitor yourself is not only doable, some find it desirable. Biosensing wearables meld together passive and active data collection, often offering round-the-clock and personal self-surveillance, knowledge, and control. These benefits are a mixed bag, however. Scholars grappling with the datafied body's interactions with wearables and portables point out that the choice of how—and to whom—that data is communicated can be quite murky. For some, choosing to track and share data blurs lines "between control and self-control, governance and self-governance"; consequently, interaction with self-tracking technologies can be conceived as a "nudge" to action that both "presupposes and pushes against freedom; it assumes a choosing subject, but one who is constitutionally ill equipped to make rational, healthy choices" (Schüll 2016). The arguable relief of ceding control to this "nudge" may go some way toward explaining why users seek to render the body more manageable through datafication, despite the fact that the "datafied" body is also more susceptible both to surveillance and to compromise by hacking. Further, opting in to gain self-knowledge can also open the door to third parties, complicating how privacy is managed (Crawford, Lingel, and Karppi 2015; Nissenbaum 2010; Nissenbaum and Patterson 2016). Some have gone so far as to claim that giving up data is a form of free labor, with the lion's share of benefits going to corporations, not users (Lupton 2016). Others have found evidence of the need for resistance and pushback via struggles over data ownership, and have called for more equitable participation in data gathering and interpretation (Nafus and Sherman 2014; Neff and Nafus 2016).

The tension between users' desires to expose themselves to technological tracking and the perceived benefits becomes particularly acute when fashion is concerned. Yet the literature in fashion studies, with a few exceptions, has tended to ignore the data question, skewing instead toward an uncritical cataloguing of practitioners' use of, and predictions for, new technologies, rather than examining the larger data and privacy consequences of their widespread penetration into the fabric of everyday lives (McCann and Bryson 2009; Quinn 2002). One notable exception is Susan Elizabeth Ryan's *Garments of Paradise: Wearable Discourse in the Digital Age*, a critical treatment of the historical and cultural context of wearable tech *as fashion* (Ryan 2014). Another is the cogent and timely conceptualization of this domain as "embodied technology." Embodied technologies "augment the body's phenomenological interaction with the world and depend on an agent's body to transmit energy and information" (Pedersen and Iliadis, this volume, and Pedersen 2013).[5] This line of thought usefully facilitates a critical analysis of fashion tech on a continuum from online shopping to implanted microchips.

As communication and digital sociology scholars have discussed at length, part of the issue at hand with regard to fashion, wearable, or portable tech is the complexity of determining what, exactly, privacy and data protection provided by a device looks like. Is protection the device's job, it is up to the user, or does responsibility lie somewhere in between? A cultural fondness for the idea that technology is neutral, that is, just a tool, complicates the notion of data protection or privacy in tracking, portable, and wearable devices. This idea threads through debates in communication scholarship and related circles regarding technological affordances, where the debate about this concept's meaning and use is widespread and ongoing (for a sampling of the issues at hand, see Bucher and Helmond 2018; Davis and Chouinard 2016; Evans et al. 2017; Nagy and Neff 2015). The rough idea that "affordances are the dynamic link between subjects and objects within sociotechnical systems," taken on by communication scholars Davis and colleagues, belies, as they argue, the complexity involved in determining whether or not a device can "afford" privacy to the user. As communication scholars Evans and colleagues have observed, "Privacy varies significantly depending on the technical features of a given medium, the knowledge and skills of a user to employ those features, and the individual's attitudes toward restricting access to some or all content" (Evans et al. 2017, 44). They go on to point out, "a desire for privacy is far from universal. Many users instead try to share content with as large an audience as possible, to achieve information diffusion" (2017, 44) as in social media, for example. The idea that users are increasingly willing to give up data protection in exchange for other "goods," such as convenience or cool, further muddies the waters.

Grappling with privacy as affordance, outcome, or something in between brings up the intricate relationship between designer and user. While it is users who opt into data sharing, how data will be shared is deeply affected by designers. Talking to wearable computing designers allows investigation of what sociologist and engineer Madeleine Akrich has called the "geography of responsibilities" built into devices by designers' decisions about "what should be delegated to whom or what," which potentially "naturalize ... moral judgments" (Akrich 1992) about the competences of users assumed by the object's design. In this sense, assumptions about user competency, or even about who or what a user *is*, become what Luciano Floridi has referred to as "constraining affordances," which "allow or invite certain constructs" and "resist or impede some others ... depending on the interaction with, and the nature of, the information system that processes them" (Floridi 2013). Similarly, when researchers Bucher and Helmond consider the material aspects of devices, for example, "power is placed in the hands of designers who have the power to enable and constrain certain action possibilities through their design choices" (2018, 6). From this angle, the notion that users "opt in" to data collection with any kind of comprehensive knowledge of what that means for the vulnerability of their data becomes politically contentious.

Many of the fashion and tech professionals I interviewed seemed relatively unaware of these politics, however. For those that were aware, the path to the best course of action on this issue was unclear. While they deeply felt the importance of their design choices, they expressed a wide range of attitudes about where the responsibility for protecting consumer data should fall. Some blamed the victim, saying they should know better than to carelessly engage in what I, and others, have called the click-click-gimme-gimme[6] culture of convenience and personalization. Others felt a keen responsibility for protecting consumer data and described the solutions they've worked on. Those that found themselves somewhere in between cited a range of reasons, pointing variously to assurances of standard anonymization, consumers' ability to choose whether to "opt in," the idea that the benefits far outweigh the costs to users for giving up their data, and the idea that users generally *want* to be recognized by technology.

As wearable technologies move in the direction of increasingly invasive and sensitive data collection via enhanced biometrics, it is imperative to ask: How well informed is the design community of issues surrounding data protection? What are the prevalent attitudes toward data gathering in wearable and fashion technology's current design culture? Is human data protection perceived as an obstacle or as a problem that can be solved within various fashion tech settings? To address these questions, as an ethnographer of embodied computing, I sought to uncover attitudes and behaviors that reveal patterns of underlying assumptions that have informed design in order to get at the kinds of politics at play in these assumptions.

This chapter draws from personal interviews with fashion and tech designers in New York and California, coupled with participant observation at numerous fashion tech summits, tech conferences, trade shows, and meet-ups. It engages with data from twenty-five interviews, which include conversations with fashion and tech designers, biofabrication professionals, and IP/patent attorneys working in the field of wearables and biotech.[7] Field notes comprise observations of the aWear conference about wearable tech in education at Stanford University in California; in New York City, the Decoded Fashion summit meeting of fashion and tech designers; BioFabricate, the annual gathering of synthetic biology researchers and designers; events at fashion tech accelerators BF+DA and Eyebeam; and numerous meet-ups, which took place at the Samsung Accelerator, Microsoft Research headquarters, Third Wave Fashion, and Kickstarter headquarters, among others, over the course of several years, from 2014 to the present.

The following provides a snapshot of data protection practices surrounding wearables currently on the market. The norms my respondents described reveal a culture where high-level user data protection is the exception, not the rule. These findings present a cautionary tale that does not bode well for consumers in the face of potentially invasive and powerful devices. The attitudes conveyed here predict a transition that demands interrogation, in an effort to push the industry away from proceeding with business as usual. The way practitioners and respondents spoke about the norms in the field of fashion tech predicts a transition that needs to be checked, interrogated, or signposted in some way as a warning to designers and future adopters of wearable biotechnologies. Without critique and correction of values in the field, the industry will proceed with business as usual, and users will be the losers in the transition to wearable biotech.

It's Cool, So Why Not?

At the meet-ups and professional gatherings I attended, as well as in design decisions reported by my respondents, I found varying levels of concern about users' personal data. Frequently, my questions about personal data protections were brushed aside with assurances about industry protocols that ensure anonymization.[8] The coming trends for using identifying markers such one's physical biometrics of blood, swear, and tears, or information parsed from DNA, did not concern many of my respondents. This attitude was only somewhat surprising, as the designers I interviewed work with wearable tech that does not depend on scanning biological materials for signals or information in order to function. Their comments about data protection protocols uncovered telling attitudes, however. They paint a picture of the design culture that comprises the space where new biotechnical wearables will develop, and therefore provide key insights into possibilities both positive and negative that these developments will afford.

Wearable tech pushes the envelopes of tracking and optimization, amplifying how technologically enmeshed bodies are metered, nudged, cajoled, protected, and connected. Why would anyone want to reveal their inner workings to technology so intimately? Because, as per many of the professionals I spoke to, it's *cool*.

A tech designer I met at a fashion tech summit in New York City typified this attitude.[9] Discussing sensors that could be embedded in clothing and other portable products, he was clearly excited about how great the results could be:

> If you go into retail space, a sensor can tell that you have that lipstick in your purse. It can offer similar products to you. Or you could register your product to your account, and then have a tie between the user and the products. That can work like remarketing opportunities, in-store personalization. Someone can walk up to you, and be like, "Hey, Betsy! I'm Jennifer. I know that you've bought these products before. Do you wanna check out this other stuff, which is really cool?"

He described this push technology as an advantage, something that consumers would want, where getting into concerts for free or other perks were things consumers would "earn ... by actually, physically doing stuff." The way he saw it, the idea of getting something cool in exchange seemed more than enough justification for giving up data; this view also resonates implicitly with the neoliberal assumption that customers want to "earn" special status in their constant striving to be the coolest or the best.

He deflected my concerns about data vulnerability in this scenario, claiming that basic industry standards are adequate protection for this type of consumer, saying,

> There are standards—yeah, depending on the industry. Obviously, banking compared to me wanting socks, you know? [Banks], they would either have custom terms, and custom systems, whereas, if I'm running a sock store, I'd probably be doing it on Squarespace, or Shopify. That platform has an—all-encompassing privacy setting, and—infrastructure, basically.

I heard this line often—data is adequately protected by the boilerplate settings in popular platforms, because information about someone buying socks is far less vulnerable to exploitation than one's bank account number.

It makes sense that designers in this area would convince themselves that data vulnerability isn't an issue, because ramping up data security for customers just isn't good business. In this designer's line of work, more draconian measure would hinder interactions with the "highly engaged" consumer who will want the kinds of benefits that being tracked can afford. When the "product is attached to the person," embedded in a jacket, for instance,

> you can give this exclusivity to people who use that product. ... If you rock out with your whatever product has the RFID in there, you could get into a concert for free. Something like that. Basically, all you have to do is be sensed in the space, and you get in free.

In this scenario, the consumer would be carrying or wearing devices that render him or her visible to the tracking internet of things (IoT)–enabled environments. This dream of seamless technology was described at the fashion tech summit where we first met, as a way to "dimensionalize the wearer's life" by giving the product a "unique digital signature used to unlock experiences in the real world."

The attitudes expressed here are consonant with those of many of the fashion tech professionals I met in the field. I encountered this designer at the DFNY Summit (Decoded Fashion New York), an exclusive, hot ticket event for design, fashion, and tech professionals. There, panelists talked about how best to help users get access to the information and personalization they "want and need." A smattering of both bricks and mortar and online fashion professionals got visibly excited about the possibility for this chip technology in clothing and consumer products. Onstage, they animatedly discussed how to "drive brand experience" to "reach and inspire" a new generation of shoppers, with one panelist exclaiming, "in the future everything will be scannable!" Warming to the subject, another predicted, "every physical thing is going to come to life, including the beers we drink and the clothes we wear," with another chiming in several times that everything will have "digital superpowers." These professionals were looking forward to the prospect of products that will "talk" to their environments, like the lipstick my respondent mentioned, eliciting interactions with store staff such as the one in which "Jennifer" tried to sell me on items complementary to the purchase I'd recently made, broadcasting its presence from my bag.

Not everyone was completely on board with this future "inspired by Toy Story," however. In a relatively rare display of critical awareness, another panelist wondered if, as "more and more adopt the technology," competitors attempting to outdo one another could get caught in "a sticky wicket between innovation and invasion." Despite the "sticky wicket" problem, however, the general consensus seemed to be that innovation was key, with invasiveness a necessary cost of business. As the panel wrapped up, another reminded the audience that "it is up to the user how much they want to share back." Yet her next statement immediately vitiated this nod toward nominal data security: she joked, "I have apps I tell things I don't tell my own mother!"

In the same manner, a fashion house executive speaking at Haute Tech, another private gathering of fashion tech professionals, justified his company's potentially "creepy" data gathering by saying his customers want what they get in exchange for giving up data:

> Immediate satisfaction is what our customer wants. Customization and personal styling are also what she wants. Data collection is the only way to accomplish this, but when we talk about data collection, it gets a little creepy.

In their RFID-enabled smart store, smart garments track customer behavior via interacting with a smart dressing room that maps in-store traffic patterns to assess whether try-ons result in purchases. Apparently, their 18–30-year-old customers love it. They can get a different size "without leaving the dressing room half naked," order drinks, or change to more flattering or occasion-specific lighting. For this target customer, these conveniences more than offset what the fashion executive called the "creep factor." Besides, he reasoned, knowing that "50 blue dresses went into the dressing room is not P.I.I."

In the intensified practice of biometric data gathering afforded by new technologies, however, there's a slippery slope between innocuous shopping data and P.I.I. As a software designer who had worked for several start-ups observed, once passive beacon technology combines with facial recognition and wearables, noting how long one stood in front of a display could ramp up to knowing the galvanic skin response and heartbeat associated with looking at particular items. He pointed out how stores already track "dwell time" as an important factor in consumer data collection:

> You walk in and look at everything and you walk by some things and some things you spend five seconds or fewer; some things you spend thirty seconds in front of or two minutes. So that dwell time is a really important indicator.

Although he observed that "there's nothing particularly sci-fi about that," combining facial recognition with biometrics could significantly change the kinds of information that is gathered:

> So, I mean … you can imagine combining biometrics [portables and wearables] and then saying "You stood in front of this display in this store and you got excited or not." I mean I think what's going to—the biometrics that we're talking about now, like perspiration might be [a factor], if you can know how reliably we can infer certain physiological states or intentions or things like that based on that data.

There are several things going on here. The observation speaks to the concern that our blood, sweat, and tears could soon provide saleable units of data in a retailer's dream of seamless technologies radically personalized to our desires—conscious or not. It also describes exactly where the industry hopes to be going. In his investigation, *The Aisles Have Eyes*, communication scholar Joseph Turow found practices such as "dwell time" already pervade the retail field and are poised to become far more invasive. At one conference, he reported, a professional confidently predicted that "by 2028, half of Americans (and by 2054, nearly all Americans) will carry in their bodies device implants that communicate with retailers as they walk down the aisles and inspect items" (Turow 2017). The notion that intentions can be inferred from physiological states is already a given, uncritically assumed to be fact, even though this relation is still being debated.

A wearables commentator and start-up entrepreneur I saw speak at an informal fashion tech meet-up group thought this level of invasiveness shouldn't really bother people, however. He told me in a subsequent interview that concerns about retail data collection stem mostly from people's fears of technology. He explained:

> We've always leaked data; it's just that we've never had the device or the means to catalog it or capture it or crunch it. The paths that we go through department stores has always been tracked on cameras for decades, but it's only now that there's the means to do it so that that data is, which has always been out there and available, it's just no longer anonymous.

People don't like facial recognition technology just because it "feels weird" as he put it, but

> for thousands of years, merchants have used their brains to facially recognize their customers. Yeah. It's not so much that we don't want to be recognized; in fact, we generally like to be recognized.

Once again, he assumes the customer wants to give up information in exchange for personalization, and he sees nothing creepy about what it takes to gain access to the "cool" perks of fashion tech. What he doesn't see, or is less interested in, is the importance of reciprocity. When a store clerk recognizes your face, you know they are looking at you, engaging with you, and the recognition is voluntary. When you are browsing a store minding your own business, and the lipstick in your purse triggers the product you are looking at to address you by name, there is something else going on.

Overall, for these professionals in the field, user data protection in the fashion tech realm isn't seen as much of an issue because consumers *want* access, personalization, and information about cool products. What's more, they actually *like* to be recognized. The majority in this group rationalized away possibly problematic industry practices around data protection, pointing to the necessity of sharing data to get relevant results, the nominal adequacy of industry protocols in place, and users' willingness to "opt in" to data gathering. From their perspective, the "cool" quotient outweighs any data issues or possible compromise. The user is choosing to enter the store, wear the jacket, buy the RFID-enabled lipstick, or don a wearable, in order to "earn" a perk, for which they have to give up some data. By opting in, users consent to devices sensing their presence, tracking their movements, and with the biometrics wearables may soon afford, registering their personal reactions in real time, whether they are conscious of them or not.

The User Gave Consent, So Why Not?

Not everyone I spoke to thought the benefits clearly outweighed concerns consumers could have about data sharing, however. In the area of fashion tech specifically focused on wearables, for instance, producers and designers seemed more aware of and careful about data protection. Nonetheless, even as they acknowledged a need to protect consumer data, they diminished their responsibility for doing so, since, after all, costumers can choose whether or not to "opt in" to data collection when they engage with the product. In their view, giving the customer a choice whether or not to expose themselves, absolves designers from having to protect them.

Interestingly, this smaller subset of respondents in the sample was comprised predominantly of women.[10] A designer of connected/smart jewelry I interviewed in a Soho café, was very clear about the lengths her company goes to protect their users:

> That was a huge thing we were thinking about as designers. There's no GPS information, and there's no—we don't have any user data on our servers. So we don't have any personal identifying information. So the signal's—so my bot can recognize your bot, but it's all encrypted and then it's all, it's not stored, so it has information about your bot when we're in the same proximity, but it doesn't store it.

These protections came at some cost, however. While these protocols were very important to her company and its customers, she admitted that they made it difficult to produce and maintain the kind of community that makes up the bread and butter of many wearable products that track personal information. To make up for this, her company provided a website where wearers could "opt in" and share with others on the site.

Similarly, a wearable fitness bracelet marketer was at pains in her phone interview to explain how the data in her product was very well protected both between users, and within the company, saying:

So, it's—yeah, even within the company. It's very few people who have the keys to really know me as a user, I've walked this many steps, or my weight is X. That's just not information that we as a company internally pass around lightly. So, the data is very secure and protected even inside the company.

She attributed this aspect of her product to the company culture in which she worked. Significantly, however, she placed the bulk of responsibility for protecting data that *is* shared while using the product on users, who might find it hard to resist giving up increasingly personal data in the face of attractive perks, putting users in a tough spot. While the interface is "totally opt in," inputs make the app "smarter" and work better. Thus, while the user can remain as anonymous as they want to and withhold that information ...

> when they do share that data with us, the smarter our algorithm can be in the future at providing them advice and insights and recommendations based on who they are.

Her statement raises the question: In the face of such smart advice and useful insights, who would want to choose anonymity? Is it really a choice at all?

Some designers I encountered felt strongly that there are readily available ways to protect users from the temptations to give it all up in the name of cool, and these respondents had trouble understanding why more people weren't using them. In a co-working space, replete with fresh flowers, trendy furnishings, and flattering lighting, a data scientist who has consulted for several high-end fashion houses talked with me about various ways to take data protection seriously, while still affording the kinds of customization and convenience coveted by fashion tech customers. She discussed her firsthand experience with groundbreaking innovations in wearable fibers, including the Zac Posen coded dress that made a splash in 2015, and Chromat's highly innovative and breathlessly reported-on Spring Summer 2016 collection, in which wired sports bras and body-conscious dresses gave haptic feedback by means of glowing and pulsating lights. In her experience, the problems encountered by designers stem from the messiness surrounding data privacy and vulnerability. She explained:

> I think it's messy—companies that are going to survive the longest are going to have really good algorithms, and not really good data, depending on how

regulations come down, what laws get put into place, what people start feeling comfortable about, how many more hacks happen, because right now people are pretty open and willing, as long as they feel like they are getting something back.

Problems are going to happen (see the outrage about Facebook's deal with Cambridge Analytica to sell personal information that prompted the #deletefacebook campaign in 2018). She thinks there are clear solutions to these sorts of problems and was interested to explain, at length, that when data science is used properly, it can protect the consumer by not caring who they are, by taking only part of their profile to use when needed, instead of assembling a comprehensive data picture of a person's habits and preferences. She laid it out as follows:

> Your algorithm's going to be the answer. It's not going to be like, "I have all the data." Unless you have all of it, unless you have all the tracking you could ever need, you're going to need to have really good algorithms, that don't care who *you* are, but just care what context you're in right now, and don't link it to all your other profiles.

At the same time, she talked about the "dream" of advertising tech—to know who you are in all instances in which you might engage with the product, akin to the situation described at this chapter's outset. This dream entails a frictionless or seamless interface that removes the need for a customer to register or log in, while still recognizing the customer, so that

> it "knows it's me" ... across devices, if I'm looking at my computer and then I go on my phone, they'll still know it's me, even if I'm blocking my IP address. You know what I mean? ... That's what ad tech really wants, to be able to definitively say my AI knows it's the same person based on their behaviors.

While she conceded this "dream" seems to be the rule of thumb right now, she tempered this scenario by describing the "other side," where technologies are coming out with what she called "differential privacy" where "the rule is" if the

> individual's inclusion in the data significantly changes the output of the algorithm, then you can't use it, it's not differentially private, like a mathematical fact. So, you add random noise, into the data, and you get "good enough" results.

In this scenario, she claims that individuals can worry less about whether their specific data is traceable, because the type of profiling that gathers as much data as possible about a particular person is not allowed by that system. The "theory's there," she explained, but "people are only starting to figure out how to implement it." If it were to be adopted, this technology would break a decades-old mold of consumer tracking, where knowing everything about the costumer is considered essential to predicting future behaviors. The time might be coming, however, when consumers are becoming aware enough of the problems to push for differential privacy, especially when it comes to the deep engagements with tracking personal data wearable biotechs will allow.

"If You Break Consumer Trust, You're Toast." So Why?

Why aren't the fashion tech designers I spoke to more careful about designing data protection protocols that can protect users while still giving them what they want? Why aren't they more careful about data protection when engaging with data gathering in order to offer consumers convenience and cool? After all, respecting customers' trust is paramount to doing good business. As a former employee of a large search engine, discussing privacy and wearables, bluntly put it:

> My experience in this space, though, is that it is incredibly important—data privacy is incredibly important to the companies because they know. You break that trust with the customer and you're toast, right? So, all it really takes is the first person to get the app and it's targeted to them about something that they were talking about, and I've watched numerous people go into Def Con 1 over it and just get upset about everything.

Here the problem not only lies in the lack of knowledge on the part of consumers. It also lies in the lack of consistent legislation governing how producers provide data protection, which this group of respondents consistently brought up.

According to an intellectual property lawyer who lectures on privacy issues for wearables, it is a no-brainer that people ignore creepiness and go for cool, because, as she explained it, they don't realize what is really going on:

> I think that when someone gets new technology, and you are about to stick it on your arm ... and it asks if you agree to the terms of this device, of course *I* read it because I'm a lawyer, but most people probably sit there and say, well what's the cost/benefit? Do I really care if this device knows where I've been all day? No!

> Because it's gonna give me more useful information than do harm to me. But, having said that, you know, if you don't realize that you are putting on something that has your data that could potentially be given to somebody else, you may not even understand or know what the ramifications are.

She emphasized that since privacy protections are in flux, it is up to the individual manufacturers to pay attention to how the field develops. In her experience, however, there are many start-ups that have not thought much about privacy. She cited a case in which a company

> had their prototype in pretty good shape, and probably could start to go out and think about marketing it at some of the conventions that they want to market it at, and they have not thought much about privacy, and I know they will come to me, before they get to the end user stage, [explain the product,] and say "we need some kind of privacy policy in place related to this piece of tech." And I will go back to my rolodex and I will get a list of the privacy attorneys in New York, and say these are the people you should be talking to.

She emphasized the importance for producers to know what laws are out there, and what they can and cannot do. From her perspective, it is the individual company's responsibility to be sensitive to these issues, as the consumer either doesn't care, or doesn't know they should.

Another I.P. lawyer joked in a phone interview, "maybe our leaking data should be protected as intellectual property!" She may not be too far off the mark. It may seem a stretch now to think about wearable tech as a norm rather than a novelty but, as costs continue to drop and capabilities increase, wearable tech is poised to become more prevalent as it merges with biotech. The majority of producers in my sample saw the tracked, geolocated, and sensed body as unproblematic because they believe that the perceived benefits of sharing data outweigh the risks to data protection this sharing entails. They saw no problem with the idea of consumers choosing to supply data about themselves in order to enjoy relevant results in their human–machine interactions. They passed the buck with respect to responsibility for data protection by pointing to the fact that users opt in, ignoring their own crucial role in creating a technology that does not afford a realistic option to opt out, in fact designing the desire to opt in directly into the technology so that choosing to opt out seems a ridiculous option that no one would consider.

Conclusion

The normalization and implementation of wearable tech and biotech are crucially in need of analysis and critique, to help guide them away from the kinds of tendencies illustrated here that rely on using the attraction of being "cool" to gloss over practices that are damaging to consumer data protection and to self-determination more generally. Many of the coming biometric identifier technologies, which promise ultra-personalized convenience and cool seamless interfaces, are so new that there are few legal precedents in place to deal with the invasiveness they portend. Your most personal identifying characteristic, for instance—your DNA—enjoys few legal protections once it leaves your body (Casebriefs 1990). In the face of dim public awareness of this fact, artists alarmed by this scenario have been doing work whose shock value aims at jolting viewers into new awareness, using DNA collected from the subway, or left in discarded chewing gum or in stray hairs, to reconstruct life like models of facial features created from such artifacts (Dewey-Hagborg, 2017). Another biofabrication artist/activist has grown a leather coat from human DNA collected from a hairbrush, only half joking that it represented the ultimate in made-to-order, completely personalized, haute couture (Gorjanc 2018). New developments in increasingly invasive forms of biometrics and personalization are poised to grant unprecedented levels of access to currently unprotected human data, bringing the data question into sharp relief within a culture that tends to minimize the importance of data-sharing issues.

As Donna Haraway and others have famously asked, what new forms of value are created by mixing the clean rationality of technology with the messy, unruly materiality of the body in the form of the cyborg (Haraway 1990)?[11] Cutting-edge developments in biotech have newly invigorated this construct. New developments in biofuel cells, biosensing devices, and synthetic biology are uncovering vast, untapped bodily potentials for energy and materials production. Who has the right to exploit this kind of biological energy? Who wins and who loses when these new developments become more commonplace?

There is no doubt this future is coming. After his cancer diagnosis, Steve Jobs envisioned the dawn of a new era: "The biggest innovations of the twenty-first century will be the intersection of biology and technology. A new era is beginning, just like the digital one when I was [my son's] age"

(Isaacson 2011). Some have called this the Fourth Industrial Revolution (Schwab 2017), coming after the first three, in which we have moved from mechanical to electrical to digital to biological forms of production. A recent meeting of the World Economic Forum in Davos, Switzerland included not only discussions of the brain–machine interface, a common subject when it comes to wearables, but also presentations on the microbiomes of humans, animals, and soil, 3-D bioprinting, and synthetic food. If these topics are any indication, the futuristic possibilities this chapter describes are right around the corner, and investigating issues regarding bodies and data raised by wearable tech, and its new entanglements with biotech, is crucial to equitably shaping advances in wearable, social, and biological technology that are radically altering relations between bodies, technology, value, and ownership.

Notes

1. Categorization can be confusing, as these functionalities often overlap. A dress that displays twitter alerts is both a connected object and a form of computational fashion. A ring that alerts you to incoming calls that also notifies you of elevated heartbeat or stress levels combines biosensing, fashion, and networked connectivity.

2. Levi's recent foray into Jacquard technology is only one of many examples.

3. While some still maintain that the term fashionable wearable is an oxymoron, this article describes some of the many examples of connected jewelry and otherwise style-conscious devices on the market.

4. This chapter expands on and provides evidence for an argument referenced in a comment I made on wearable technology in the CITAMS Special Issue of the journal *Information, Communication, and Society* cited here.

5. Pedersen's analysis is of particular use with regard to the tensions involved in wearable technology's tendency toward both humanizing and dehumanizing.

6. Pace Clay Shirky, in a group email exchange.

7. The interview respondent pool breaks down as follows: two corporate in-house academics at large technology companies, six fashion tech designer/founders, three fashion designers, six software and/or hardware tech engineers, two wearable tech marketers, two wearable tech fashion artists, two synthetic biologists, and two IP attorneys working in biotech. The interviews were hand coded for themes pertaining to incidences of the terms "data," "privacy," "protection," "sharing," "coding," "identification," "programming," and "algorithm(s)."

8. "Anonymization" removes all identifying markers from data that could trace it back to a particular person, in an attempt to disaggregate identifying markers in the data from individuals that produced it. These efforts do not remove metadata, however, or prevent the possibility of identification by associating data points across various information pools.

9. Quote is from an in-person interview a few weeks after the event.

10. The relationship between femme-identified subjectivity and attraction to strong data protection emerging from this data is a subject that merits further research.

11. She also was famous for her prescient concern about biotech, outlined most prominently in *Modest_Witness@Second_Millenium.Female_Man_Meets_Oncomouse: Feminism and Technoscience* (New York: Routledge, 1997).

References

Akrich, Madeline. 1992. The De-scription of Technical Objects. In *Shaping Technology/Building Society: Studies in Sociotechnical Change*, edited by Wiebe Bijker and John Law, 205–224. Cambridge, MA: MIT Press.

Allison, Conor. 2018. Semi-precious: The Best Smart Jewelry. *Wareable*, October 16. https://www.wareable.com/fashion/semi-precious-the-best-smart-jewelry-582.

Bucher, Taina, and Anne Helmond. 2018. The Affordances of Social Media Platforms. In *The SAGE Handbook of Social Media*, edited by Jean Burgess, Alice Marwick, and Thomas Poell. London: Sage. https://doi.org/10.4135/9781473984066.n14.

Casebriefs. 1990. *Moore v. Regents of the University of California.* https://www.casebriefs.com/blog/law/property/property-law-keyed-to-cribbet/non-traditional-objects-and-classifications-of-property/moore-v-regents-of-the-university-of-california-2/.

Crawford, Kate, Jessa Lingel, and Tero Karppi. 2015. Our Metrics, Ourselves: A Hundred Years of Self-Tracking from the Weight Scale to the Wrist Wearable Device. *European Journal of Cultural Studies* 18 (4–5): 479–496. https://doi.org/10.1177%2F1367549415584857.

Davis, Jenny L., and James B. Chouinard. 2016. Theorizing Affordances: From Request to Refuse. *Bulletin of Science, Technology & Society* 36 (4): 241–248. https://doi.org/10.1177%2F0270467617714944.

Dewey-Hagborg, Heather. 2017. Hacking Biopolitics. *e-flux*, February 13. https://conversations.e-flux.com/t/heather-dewey-hagborg-hacking-biopolitics/6045/.

Evans, Sandra K., Katy E. Pearce, Jessica Vitak, and Jeffrey W. Treem. 2017. Explicating Affordances: A Conceptual Framework for Understanding Affordances in

Communication Research. *Journal of Computer-Mediated Communication* 22 (1): 35–52. https://doi.org/10.1111/jcc4.12180.

Fellman, Megan. 2016. Researchers Develop Soft, Microfluidic "Lab on the Skin" for Sweat Analysis. McCormick School of Engineering News, November 23. http://www.mccormick.northwestern.edu/news/articles/2016/11/researchers-develop-soft-microfluidic-lab-on-the-skin-for-sweat-analysis.html.

Floridi, Luciano. 2013. *The Philosophy of Information.* Reprint edition. Oxford: Oxford University Press.

Gibbs, S. 2014. 2015 Gears Up to Be the Year of Wearable Tech. *Guardian*, December 25. https://www.theguardian.com/technology/2014/dec/25/apple-watch-spring-launch-wearable-technology.

Gorjanc, Tina. 2018. PureHuman. https://www.arte.tv/fr/videos/071498-009-A/fashion-geek-9-10/.

Halzack, Sarah. 2016. The Tiny Chip That Could Power Big Changes in How You Shop, *Washington Post*, January 20. https://www.washingtonpost.com/news/business/wp/2016/01/20/the-tiny-chip-that-could-power-big-changes-in-how-you-shop/.

Haraway, Donna. 1990. *Simians, Cyborgs, and Women: The Reinvention of Nature.* New York: Routledge.

Hartmans, Andrew. 2019. Best Wearable We Saw at CES 2019. *Business Insider*, January 12. https://www.businessinsider.com/ces-2019-best-wearable-withings-move-ecg-2018-12.

Ingham, Lucy. 2015. 2016 Will Be the Year of Wearable Technology. *Factor*, November 2. factor-tech.com/wearable-technology/20578-2016-will-be-the-year-of-wearable-technology/.

Isaacson, Walter. 2011. *Steve Jobs.* New York: Simon and Schuster.

Kline, Kenny. 2016. How Bluetooth Beacons Will Transform Retail in 2016. *Huffington Post*, January 15. https://www.huffingtonpost.com/kenny-kline/how-bluetooth-beacons-wil_b_8982720.html.

Lamkin, Paul. 2017. Wearable Tech Market to Double by 2021. *Forbes*, June 22. https://www.forbes.com/sites/paullamkin/2017/06/22/wearable-tech-market-to-double-by-2021/.

Lupton, Deborah. 2016. *The Quantified Self.* Cambridge: Polity.

Mandavilli, Apoorva. 2019. Your Sweat Will See You Now. *New York Times*, January 18. https://nyti.ms/2HmRb2b.

McCann, Jane, and David Bryson, eds. 2009. *Smart Clothes and Wearable Technology.* Boca Raton, FL: Woodhead Publishing.

Nagy, Peter, and Gina Neff. 2015. Imagined Affordance: Reconstructing a Keyword for Communication Theory. *Social Media + Society* 1 (2): 2056305115603385. https://doi.org/10.1177%2F2056305115603385.

Nafus, Dawn, ed. 2016. *Quantified: Biosensing Technologies in Everyday Life.* Cambridge, MA: MIT Press.

Nafus, Dawn, and Jamie Sherman. 2014. This One Does Not Go Up to 11: The Quantified Self Movement as an Alternative Big Data Practice. *International Journal of Communication* 8:1784–1794. https://ijoc.org/index.php/ijoc/article/view/2170/1157/.

Neff, Gina, and Dawn Nafus. 2016. *Self-Tracking.* Cambridge, MA: MIT Press.

Nissenbaum, Helen. 2010. *Privacy in Context: Technology, Policy, and the Integrity of Social Life.* Stanford, CA: Stanford Law Books.

Nissenbaum, Helen, and Heather Patterson. 2016. Biosensing in Context: Health Privacy in a Connected World. In *Quanitified: Biosensing Technologies in Everyday Life,* edited by Dawn Nafus, 79–100. Cambridge, MA: MIT Press.

Pan, Angela. 2018. Wearables as a Fashion Statement. Quoted in 2018 Big Ideas. Wearable Tech, March 1. https://wearabletechnologysummit.com/2018-speaker-quotes/.

Pedersen, Isabel. 2013. *Ready to Wear: A Rhetoric of Wearable Computers and Reality-Shifting Media.* Anderson, SC: Parlor Press.

Pedersen, Isabel, and Kirsten Ellison. 2017. Hiding in Plain Sight: The Rhetoric of Bionic Contact Lenses in Mainstream Discourses. *International Journal of Cultural Studies* 20 (6): 669–683. https://doi.org/10.1177%2F1367877915625234.

Peirce, David. 2017. Google and Levi's Made a Jacket That Connects to the Internet. *Wired,* September 25. https://www.wired.com/story/i-wore-the-jean-jacket-of-the-future/.

Quinn, Bradley. 2002. *Techno Fashion.* London: Bloomsbury Academic.

RichRelevance. 2017. Creepy or Cool? 3rd Annual RichRelevance Study Finds Global Consumers Willing to Share Data in Return for Better Customer Experience. *RichRelevance,* June 27. https://www.richrelevance.com/blog/2017/06/27/creepy-cool-3rd-annual-richrelevance-study-finds-global-consumers-willing-share-data-return-better-customer-experience/.

Ryan, Susan Elizabeth. 2014. *Garments of Paradise: Wearable Discourse in the Digital Age.* Cambridge, MA: MIT Press.

Sawh, Michael. 2016. Sensors Explored: Galvanic Skin Response. *Wareable,* August 24. https://www.wareable.com/wearable-tech/what-does-galvanic-skin-response-measure.

Schüll, Natasha Dow. 2016. Data for Life: Wearable Technology and the Design of Self-care. *BioSocieties* 11 (3): 317–333. https://doi.org/10.1057/biosoc.2015.47.

Schwab, Klaus. 2017. *The Fourth Industrial Revolution*. New York: Crown Publishing Group.

Snow, Jackie. 2017. This AI Learns Your Fashion Sense and Invents Your Next Outfit. *MIT Technology Review*, November 16. https://www.technologyreview.com/s/609469/this-ai-learns-your-fashion-sense-and-invents-your-next-outfit/.

Spence, Ewan. 2013. 2014 Will Be the Year of Wearable Technology. *Forbes*, November 2. https://www.forbes.com/sites/ewanspence/2013/11/02/2014-will-be-the-year-of-wearable-technology/.

Sullivan, Mark. 2014. Bionym's Heartbeat Authentication May Be the Key to Smartwatch Mobile Payments. *VentureBeat*, November 3. https://venturebeat.com/2014/11/03/mastercard-and-bionym-will-test-wrist-based-mobile-payments-no-phone-required/.

Sullivan, Mark. 2016. Will Consumers Change Their Minds about Wearables in 2017? *Fast Company*, December 28. https://www.fastcompany.com/3066703/will-consumers-change-their-minds-about-wearables-in-2017.

Turow, Joseph. 2017. *The Aisles Have Eyes: How Retailers Track Your Shopping, Strip Your Privacy, and Define Your Power*. New Haven, CT: Yale University Press.

Vanin, Stefano. 2015. Bacteria on Shoes Could Help Forensic Teams Catch Suspects. *Guardian*, May 15. http://www.theguardian.com/science/blog/2015/may/15/bacteria-on-shoes-could-help-forensic-teams-catch-suspects.

Wareable Team. 2017. Fifty Wearable Tech Predictions for 2018. *Wareable*, December 15. https://www.wareable.com/wearable-tech/best-wearable-tech-2018-506.

Wipprecht, Anouk. 2011. Anouk Wipprecht on Intimacy 2.0. V2_Lab for the Unstable Media, October 18. http://v2.nl/lab/blog/anouk-wipprecht-on-intimacy.

Wissinger, Elizabeth. 2015. *This Year's Model: Fashion, Media, and the Making of Glamour*. New York: NYU Press.

Wissinger, Elizabeth. 2018. Blood, Sweat, and Tears: Navigating Creepy versus Cool in Wearable Biotech. *Information, Communication & Society* 21 (5): 779–785. https://doi.org/10.1080/1369118X.2018.1428657.

10 TechnoSupremacy and the Final Frontier: Other Minds

Maggie Orth

A New Authoritarianism

> **TechnoSupremacy, *n.*** An often subconsciously held classist ideology based upon the belief that those skilled in technical fields are superior to those with expertise in more subjective domains, such as arts, language, history, ethics, philosophy, and law. TechnoSupremacists also hold that all problems—whether generated by society or by the unintended consequences of their own inventions—are best solved through the creation of more technology. Alternative domains of thinking and action, domains that might provide contrary solutions or limit the creation of new wealth-generating technologies, such as ethics, law, and regulation, are considered luddite, anachronistic, or sentimental—and systematically disempowered. Thus, the solution to nursing shortages is not to embrace the proven importance of social contact in human health and then educate more people in empathy and care. Instead, it is to create robotic nurses.

In 2016 and 2017, the years of Donald Trump's candidacy and early presidency, we Americans were in a paradoxical place. Alarmed by the spectacle of Trump's burgeoning authoritarianism, we were deeply distracted from other crises facing our society, such as climate change. At the same time, we were still in the honeymoon period with our tech giants. Facebook had not been exposed for its role as propaganda machine in Trump's election, nor for its exploitation of our personal data; we still believed our social-media big brother to be a benevolent, delightful service, joyfully uniting kids in California with grandparents in Mumbai. At the time, most press about the shiny technology corporations who promised both social utopia and economic greatness remained Pollyanna-ish.

Within this moment—one of retained innocence regarding the dangers of our mesmerizing devices and social media, combined with fear of new fascist political voices—two actions by the TechnoSupremacist Elon Musk were characteristically hyped for their TechnoPromise while being overlooked for their authoritarian nature.

First Musk predicted—with typical TechnoSupremacist hubris—a future in which humans would need brain implants to compete with artificial intelligence (AI). Then, nine months later in March 2017, Musk quietly founded Neuralink, a brain implant company (Winkler 2017).

Like most TechnoSupremacists, Musk began his sales pitch for brain implants by constructing a hypothetical problem, a problem he described as inevitable and therefore desperately in need of a solution:

> If you assumed any rate of advancement in AI, we will be left behind by a lot, so even in the benign situation, if you have some, you have ultra-intelligent AI, we would be so far below them in intelligence, that it would be like a pet ... Like a cat.[1]

Ironically, Musk has personally—through his companies Tesla and SpaceX—done much to advance and profit from AI, the very technology he asserts threatens humanity. Yet at the time of the above statement, Musk's solution to his proposed AI threat did not include abstaining from developing AI (Reedy 2017). Nor did his solution involve ethical considerations, regulations, religious concerns, or democratically chosen options (Markoff 2015). Like a typical TechnoSupremacist, Musk simply proposed more technology:

> the solution that seems maybe the best one ... is to have an AI layer ... if you think of like, you've got your limbic system, your cortex, and then a digital layer, a sort of a third layer above the cortex, that could work symbiotically with you.

After tentatively making this modest proposal for brain implants, Musk then used his vast wealth to found Neuralink, a company dedicated to creating brain implants (Winkler 2017). And while Musk presented this investment as purely altruistic—an attempt to cure various brain diseases as well as save humanity from an AI dystopia (at least partially of his own making)—Musk's interest in brain implants is also highly personal, as Neuralink's success will undoubtedly increase Musk's wealth.

Since his 2016 brain-implant statement, Musk has become so alarmed by the monstrous potential of AI that he *has* called for its regulation (Gibbs 2017). Musk has not, however, divested from or called for increased regulation of brain implants, a highly invasive technology with the potential to radically alter our bodies and minds—indeed humanity itself.

And while Musk has not imprisoned or tortured anyone, his promotion of brain implants represents a new type of authoritarianism: TechnoSupremacy. This antidemocratic tyranny is driven not by Trump or the state, as George Orwell imagined in *1984*, but by today's spectacularly wealthy TechnoSupremacists, digital robber barons who believe that their vision for humankind—a vision that includes augmenting our minds with technology, potentially eliminating subjective reality and privacy of thought—is wisest and best.

Nor is Musk's undisclosed but undoubtedly large investment in Neuralink a mere tycoon's lark. Musk's money and statements are dangerous, self-fulfilling prophecies; they lend significant economic and intellectual momentum to ongoing efforts by governments, medical researchers, and entrepreneurs to advance brain implants, efforts whose scale nearly guarantees that one day brain implants will become a reality—with or without Musk's imagined malevolent AI threat.

The Value of Human Cognition

Although assessing Musk's prediction of dark AI is not my main goal, and others have done it far more completely,[2] AI's relation to the function of brain implants, as well as our valuing of human cognition, makes a brief discussion of Musk's prediction worthwhile here.

Already Musk's claim that AI will one day outthink humans has much to support it. IBM's Deep Blue and AlphaGO have beaten humans at chess and Go; and though these programs are not perfect, they predict a world where solutions to intractable, complex problems—such as highway design, climate change, or discovering routes of hidden spy planes—are found by, or in collaboration with, machines (Aldhous 2017).

At the same time, Musk could be wrong about AI's ability to outthink human beings (Dowd 2017). Perhaps human intelligence is so deeply linked to our senses and bodies that machines can never imitate it. In a study by cognitive scientist Paul Bach-y-Rita, live-video images were drawn tactilely on the backs of blind people with haptic interfaces (Bach-y-Rita 1984). "As long as the subject can control the movement of the camera, he can perceive (the image made by the camera as) the three-dimensional visual spatial world of which he is a part." This experiment suggests that bodily movement combined with our senses may be necessary to perceive and interpret the world; that without access to our human senses and bodies, machines might never outthink us. In an ironic reversal of Musk's prediction, machines might only acquire true intelligence when connected to human bodies and senses through brain implants.

But even if AI *does* succeed in outstripping human intelligence, Musk's prediction of AI's malicious threat is likely not quite right. For one thing is certain: the future always surprises. Already humans are learning new Go moves from AlphaGO, just as AlphaGo learned strategies from humans. Maybe our flexible minds do not need an implanted chip to learn from computers. Maybe AI will become our teachers, not our competitors. Or maybe, once connected to human minds via brain implants, instead of hatred for humans, machines will develop empathy.

Nor are the economic "winners and losers" of AI guaranteed to be who Musk predicts. If AI *does* become widespread, maybe it will be rendered nothing but a commodity; maybe then truly human modes of thinking, subjective forms of reasoning, drawn from art and humanities, will become more valuable.

For underlying Musk's hypothetical AI threat and potentially authoritarian brain-implant solution is the concept that not only *should* machines mimic human reasoning, but that ultimately human reasoning *should* mimic machines; that the human mind's greatest value is solving multivariable problems of engineering: an assumption that is classic TechnoSupremacy. But measuring human intelligence against machines ignores less quantifiable forms of human cognition: forms that are uniquely human; forms that rely on the subjective truths of psychology, language, and art; forms that interpret what it means to be born of a mother and father, to breathe and age, to rot and die.

And while today's researchers *are* exploring ways in which AI can participate in subjective domains—such as identifying beauty by looking at images humans have labeled beautiful—machines cannot yet redefine beauty, a skill still unique to human artists (IBM 2017). And although today's computers can mimic artistic styles such as impressionism (Mordvintsev et al. 2015), their stylistic inventions have yet to out-innovate human artists (IBM 2017). Perhaps humanity's appreciation of art has more to do with wonder at our own mastery, at our human ability to transcend our flaws and create something sensually astounding. In that case, computerized art may never be as highly valued as human art. Or perhaps, just as photography freed painters from realism, AI art will one day free humans from a certain sort of rote creativity.

But though Musk's prediction of AI's malevolent success may be incorrect, the adoption of brain implants is far more certain. For it is competition with ourselves—not machines—which will bring cyborg brains about. Once brain implants offer any perceived advantage, no matter how dubious, people will adopt these invasive devices to compete on tests, in the workplace, in life. People will believe the hype, the snake oil, the promise that brain implants will make us smarter, better problem solvers, able to remember every fact and name. And so, even if AI never outthinks us, it remains likely that one day humans will choose—or be compelled by social and economic forces—to have a brain implant.

And the arrival date for brain implants is closer than you think.

Brain Implants: A Not So Distant Future

Musk's original four-year timeline (Dunne 2017) for Neuralink's medical brain implants (which will treat brain injury and disease) may seem wildly optimistic, but between 2002 and 2012, 80,000 deep brain stimulation (DBS) devices were implanted in Parkinson's patients. By 2017, that number had nearly doubled to 150,000 (Strickland 2017). Currently in psychiatry, brain implants—complete with wires running through the skull, under the skin, behind the ear, and down the neck to a battery pack implanted in the chest—are already used to treat obsessive compulsive disorder (OCD) and depression (Giesen 2015). All of this suggests that Musk's goal, at least for medical devices, is not only attainable but already partially achieved (Pouratian et al. 2012). And although Musk's original eight- to ten-year trajectory for consumer implants is longer and less plausible, input and output—the essential components of any interactive computing device including brain implants—have existed for decades (Dunne 2017).

In 1983, William Dobells installed electrodes on the brain's surface and projected images onto the visual cortex, an early form of input. Today, electrodes implanted in brains of paraplegic individuals, a process conducted by companies like BrainGate,[3] read neural signals and use them to control artificial limbs, an example of output. Indeed anyone can download a DIY Instructables[4] video explaining the use of brain signals from external electrodes to control robotic arms—another form of output.

Of course, many technical challenges remain for brain implants, including the creation of biocompatible electrodes that deter gliois, a barrier that forms between the brain and today's platinum iridium electrodes. But medical researchers, such as Oxford University's Hagen Bailey,[5] are creating artificial nerves and electrically conductive biomaterials that could be adapted for brain implants. Low-power, wireless neural communication is also being developed at places like Jan Rabaey's Wireless Research Center at UC Berkeley.[6]

Thus, the necessary technologies for interactive brain implants—input and output, as well as physical interface—are well underway.[7]

Government regulation is also unlikely to slow the progress of consumer brain implants. For though early brain-implant research has been medical—meaning it falls under FDA regulation and medicine's ethical guidelines, and consequently has preceded slowly—no similar restrictions on US consumer devices exist. Nor do restrictions exist in China, where researchers are already forging ahead with another technology that threatens to alter humanity—CRISPR. And as we have seen with companies like Uber and Facebook, many TechnoSupremacists are willing to bulldoze regulations for profit. Indeed, it is unclear what can be done to stop today's Techno-Supremacists from imposing their visions on society—visions that include brain implants—especially within the frame of today's capitalism.

Our Fiercest Helicopter Parent: Capitalism

TechnoSupremacy, *n*. (continued): Society's deep belief in TechnoSupremacism is underpinned by the vast economic power of today's technology elite: a power rooted in the economic exclusive granted by the utility patent, the US military–industrial complex, entrenched laissez-faire capitalism and neoliberalism, and the dominance of BusinessThink in today's universities—that is, the reduction of all value in society to a quarterly return on investment. TechnoSupremacism also refers to the ecosystem of venture capitalists, billionaire entrepreneurs, inventors, corporations, universities, and researchers who maintain the economic and cultural authority of technology.

Whereas some describe capitalism as a fierce filter, a mimicker of biological evolution that promotes only the fittest ideas and products, I perceive capitalism as a tenacious, overprotective father—a doting system that defends its children, no matter how troublesome, to the death. For while 80 percent of companies *do* fail in their first year, enterprises with the largest investments generally survive, and the larger the investment in any product, no matter how trivial or socially destabilizing, the more incentive there is to shepherd that product to success (Speights 2017). Companies like Uber can lose money for years, but still attract investment because of their unicorn potential—the promise of becoming a privately held start-up worth $1 billion. And as more investors join a company, the incentive to salvage that enterprise also increases, because if the company fails, investors' money is lost. So more investors are brought in to cover losses, and more marketers are hired to sell products to wider audiences—no matter how hyped or unnecessary those products may be. Of course, start-ups can also be acquired by bigger corporations for vast sums based on their hypothetical value before they ever fail.

This incentive to helicopter-parent any product, business idea, or technology in which there is large investment is ultimately societal, because when any company fails there is a reduction in wealth and growth—and capitalism demands growth. In *Prosperity Without Growth* (2017), Tim Jackson articulates the difficulty of having an economy without growth. Without growth, the economy contracts and jobs are lost; and without a return on investment (growth), there is no incentive for investment; and without investment there is no way to create complex things that require large amounts of capital. Things like vaccines, hospitals, rockets, housing developments, video cameras, microprocessors, computers, iPhones, AI, and now brain implants, could not exist without vast capital investment and economic growth.

This is why Musk's financing of Neuralink matters so much. Musk's actions are part of a broad investment in brain implants, an investment our economy and society will be reluctant to discard.

For Musk is not acting alone. On July 10, 2017, the US government announced it would be awarding $65 million in DARPA grants for bidirectional brain implants that can read a soldier's thoughts and vision and, unsurprisingly, send them commands (Hatmaker 2017). These forces—the paternalism of capitalism, the dreams and wealth of TechnoSuprema-cists, the TechnoOptimism of researchers seeking cures and social utopias, as well as governments seeking perfect soldiers—will ultimately lead to consumer brain implants. And the most surprising part of it all?

People want brain implants!

Today's Transhumanists

In a 2015 marketing survey by Vrge, 25 percent of Americans wanted a chip implanted in their brain (Zecher 2015). In Pew's 2016 survey, 36 percent of Americans were somewhat enthusiastic about brain implants (Funk et al. 2016). Those studies are why I began this research. *Who are these people?* I wondered. Why would anyone want to be connected to the internet 24/7? Aren't they afraid of something invading their minds, of corporate control, of losing their sovereign thoughts and identity?

On the extreme edge of those who want brain implants are today's transhumanists—a growing movement whose members have little squea-mishness or reverence for the sanctity of body and mind; but who instead long to become cyborgs. Transhumanists want to radically modify their bodies and minds through technology, whether it be chemicals, hormones, electronics, prosthetics, or gene manipulation like CRISPR.[8] They imagine a world where "furries,"[9] people who identify with animals, can become part animal. They call the body a *meat sack*, referencing William Gibson's *Neuromancer* (1984), whose protagonist Case declared: "The body is meat." They long to escape their humanity by replacing every morsel of biodegradable flesh with technology. They want to download the contents of their minds, escape their mortal bodies, and live forever.[10]

To achieve these goals, transhumanists already independently teach and perform self-surgery, implanting magnets in fingertips to sense magnetic fields, inserting light-up circuit boards under skin in their arms, and chips in their palms to log into their computers. But this DIY cyborgism and the trivial functionality it affords is not enough to achieve their visions. Today's transhumanists also demand the *legal right* to technologically transform their bodies and mind with whatever technology is available. Transhumanists want doctors to exceed their current ethical charge of curing illness and restoring health, and instead improve the body with technology, just as is done with cosmetic surgery. Transhumanists also demand cognitive liberty (Barfield and Williams 2017), the right to improve their thoughts and minds through any technology, including brain implants.

And so there is already a market for consumer brain implants; and once some people choose them, everyone will need one to compete. Of course, some will argue that having a brain implant will still be a choice—that everyone is free *not* to have brain implant. However, this assertion ignores the social and economic imperative of successful consumer technology: no one can participate actively in modern society without a smartphone or computer. People without these computing devices simply cannot compete in the job market or in any industry, even creative ones. How will any future human compete without what will certainly be marketed as an indispensable brain implant?

And in a world where people must pay for these devices, any illusion of meritocracy will vanish. If you cannot afford the latest greatest brain implant, you will simply become obsolete.

But if, as I have argued, brain implants are inevitable—even desired—if we are already too late to save our fragile, imperfect humanity, perhaps we should be asking another question. Perhaps we should be asking:

What will brain implants do?

Beyond Output

TechnoSpeak, *n.*   A euphemistic, hyperbolic, and circular jargon, which is widely used in technology research and industry and has two primary functions. First, through TechnoHyperbole, TechnoSpeak renders all benefits of new technology, no matter how incremental or dubious, as earth shattering. Second, through TechnoEuphemism and TechnoOptimism, TechnoSpeak masks and ignores any negative social, ethical, or environmental side effects that new technologies may possess.

In his June 2016 interview, Musk provided a euphemistic answer to the function of his proposed brain implants (abridged):

Musk: So the fundamental limitation is input/output. We're already a cyborg [...] You have a digital version of yourself online, in [...] your emails and social media [...] you have basically super powers [...] with your computer and your phone [...] you have more power than the President of the United States had twenty years ago. You can answer any question; you can video conference with anyone [...] send a message to millions of people instantly [...] But [...] your output level is so low, particularly on your phone [...] two thumbs sort of just tapping away [...] Our input level is much better because we have a high-bandwidth, visual interface to the brain [...] Our eyes take in a lot of data. So effectively merging in a symbiotic way with digital intelligence revolves around eliminating the IO (input/output) constraint. So it would be some sort of direct cortical interface.

Interlocutor: But doesn't that imply surgical insertion ...

Musk: Not necessarily. You could go through the veins and arteries because that provides a complete roadway to all your neurons [...] It gets macabre, but ...

In *1984*, Orwell imagined an authoritarian state, Oceania, that suppressed the thoughts, minds, and emotions of individuals though direct manipulation of language. Orwell's state publicized its intention in the "Principles of Newspeak," which can be found in *1984*'s appendix. In the above quote, Musk demonstrates mastery of what I call TechnoSpeak. He softens the reality of hypothetical brain implants both physically and functionally. He admits his technology "gets macabre" while minimizing the current need for bloody surgery and proposing a theoretically less-invasive technology (Strickland 2017) that reaches neurons through veins, rather than hacking through brain and skull.

To be fair, some technical solutions for Musk's less-invasive proposal are in the research phase (Strickland 2017). Neurologist Thomas Oxley's "sten-trode" is designed to replace problematic electrodes that contact brain tissue. Inserted through a vein and into a tiny blood vessel that feeds neurons, the stentrode cannot read neurons directly, but it will potentially sense and decode other signals. Harvard professor Charles Lieber and postdoc Gousong Hong are creating a foldable electronic mesh that will be inserted into the brain and then opened; and Berkeley professor Michel Maharbiz is developing a neural dust that will potentially be scattered through the nervous system where it will read signals.

But even brain researcher Oxley does not expect results from these sorts of devices anytime soon (Strickland 2017), implying that, for Musk to reach his timeline, he will likely have to rely on surgical implantation. Moreover, these devices, no matter how small, would still spread the materials of technology, metals, and toxins throughout our bodies and brains. The potential negative physical consequences of these sci-fi devices, including the clogging of arteries and the spread of brain disease, are, as is usual in TechnoSupremacy, ignored (Strickland 2017).

But even if the health impacts of his imagined surgery-free implants are overcome, Musk makes other euphemistic claims that are far more dangerous. Despite his earlier assertion that brain implants will merely increase human intelligence—a feat that would require *input* into our minds—Musk then claims that a benign increase in speed of *output* is his only goal—a goal that may, for many people, seem a small, comfortable leap.

Many people can easily imagine a neural display, like that of our smartphones, projected onto our visual cortexes (for the moment, let's forget that this display is a form of input). We can then imagine our minds controlling a pointer and choosing letters or words to output our thoughts. Such an interaction feels familiar, like sitting at our computer; and indeed, researchers have already demonstrated that people with brain implants can control a pointer on an external computer screen to play pong.[11] To many, this activity sounds familiar, similar to typing. But manipulating a pointer or keyboard with our minds would barely outpace typing. To dramatically increase our brain's output speed, Musk must do something more invasive than speeding up typing: Musk must read our thoughts—a feat also well underway.

Researchers at Carnegie Mellon University are already mapping a path to such mind reading (Wang and Just 2017). Using MRI images of brain activity taken during speech, they create models that predict what subjects will say based on live MRI images of the same subject's brain waves. This is a significant step toward reading human thoughts articulated by language. Thus, brain implants that could mimic an MRI—Musk's greatest challenge as it requires imaging millions of neurons—could potentially read human thoughts and increase our mind's output speed.

But what Musk also omits from his modest proposal for faster output of human thought is that any electrode that can read our thoughts can also send us thoughts. For the great trick of antennas, and indeed many devices that receive electrical signals, is that they can also transmit signals. Thus, the same piezo sensor that creates a small voltage when physically bent will move infinitesimally when receiving a voltage. Marconi's antennas and electronics encoded signals, broadcast them across the Atlantic, and then received and decoded them. In brain implants for psychiatric patients, this bidirectional potential is called *closed loop*.[12] In closed loop, the same brain implant could both stimulate the brain (input) and read the brain (output). For psychiatrists, this means the same device could simultaneously treat and evaluate mental illness. For consumers, this means that no matter what brain-implant marketing says, any electrode implanted in our brains will have bidirectional potential; it will be capable of both reading our minds *and* sending us messages, messages that may be indistinguishable from our thoughts.

Since Musk's statement in 2016, his initial coyness over the bidirection-alilty of his proposed brain implants has vanished. Musk now imagines brain implants that will allow "consensual communication" (Dunne 2017). In this scenario, human minds will be able to speak with one another, implying both reading thoughts—and implanting them.

Future brain implants, Musk's or not, will likely combine the function of many current brain implants—much like today's smartphones combine many formerly separate electronic devices. Already, existing but separate brain implants can—or claim to—treat depression, aid in athletic performance (Farr 2016), augment lost vision, control seizures from Parkinson's, allow patients to control prostheses, and provide sexual stimulation so satisfying that some patients will press a button until their finger bleeds (Newitz 2009). Today's brain implants also allow cellphones to control roaches,[13] much as one would manipulate a remote-control car—or potentially a soldier. In the future, a single brain implant will likely be able to—or claim to—modulate our emotions, cure brain diseases and other illnesses, save our memories, send us data, make us smarter, and—because it is bidirectional—whisper sweet nothings in our ears.

And in a world where maximizing profit is an imperative, reaching into and manipulating consumers' minds will be both irresistible—and unpreventable.

The Myth of Neutral Software Devices

Technologists, transhumanists, and those who espouse cognitive freedom will argue that brain implants, like glasses or any other tool, will be *neutral*—that any political or social agenda that their technology may possess will not be *intrinsic* to the device. They will say that brain implants can be used safely, without threat to the privacy of our thoughts. Using this neutrality argument, brain implants will be marketed as devices that merely aid human health and strengthen mental capacity, devices that do not reflect any agenda of their makers. But this agreement ignores the fact that in capitalism, the agenda of any complex technological device is necessarily economic.

In capitalism, every product that requires investment must recoup that investment or there will be a reduction in wealth, and because today's complex technology always demands vast capital investment, no technology can be produced free of a long-term economic agenda. In general, corporations also have a legal fiduciary duty to maximize shareholder value.[14] So despite claims of life-saving medical benefits and increased intelligence, there can be little doubt that brain implants, which will require massive economic investment, will be designed to earn money.

Constitutional scholar Marc J. Blitz argues that brain implants, even if they are products of corporations, will be like journals (2010). They will, he asserts, extend our mind's ability to think and remember and thus promote freedom of thought. But this argument ignores what brain implants have that analog tools like journals do not: an element that transforms ordinary objects whose purposes are reflected in their physical design into devices with indirect and invisible functions. Brain implants have software.

A hammer is an analog tool, physically designed to whack or pry. If sensors and software are added however, it can sense heart rate and heat through its handle, or its impact might trigger a musical note on our smartphones. Indeed, today's smartphones are perfect examples of software objects; our phones are email readers, compasses, cameras, calorie counters, step measurers, heart rate sensors, GPS devices, music players, cash registers, maps—none of which is reflected in their physical design. Through software, our phones can also be usurped and transformed into hostile government spies (Ahmed and Perlroth 2017). Undeniably, these same possibilities will exist within our brain implants.

To date, privacy problems in our phones and computers appear intractable. Governments have failed to protect our personal data from hackers—our social security numbers, private love-texts, credit card numbers, and journalistic sources cannot be protected from nefarious actors. Indeed, the virtual part of Pedersen and Iliadis's *embodied self*—data about our bodies' movements, what we search on Google, where we buy dinner, and who we vacation with—is regularly exploited and sold without our knowledge.

Imagining a future where the reading of our thoughts and the valuable marketing data they contain is regulated seems at best naïve. If already we cannot protect the information in our email accounts, how will brain implants be firewalled to keep out unwanted voices, commercial or otherwise. The fight to control truth through media, a fight that is currently being waged on Facebook and Twitter by Russia, rightwing media, and political operatives will not stop once we have brain implants, no matter what those who promote the security of brain implants will claim. Social media and the internet were created by a utopian desire for a democratic media where all voices are heard. But these technologies also inadvertently gave hateful voices—the voices of racism, authoritarianism, and paranoia—a place to thrive. Brain implants will easily transport these angry voices of anarchy directly into our minds.

In response to these fears, Blitz argues that unwanted messages from brain implants can be overcome legally. Our government, he asserts, cannot compel speech; it cannot force citizens to say what it wants. That same right, the right *not* to speak, also extends to the right *not* to think something, he writes. But while this argument may in the long term provide some legal protection from unwanted implanted thoughts, courts have also supported the right to develop our minds with tools (Blitz 2010). Thus, working through the legality of freedom for vs. protection from brain implants will take time. Given the pace of technology development, courts will likely be too late to defend our minds from messages sent by consumer brain implants.

And even if our courts or government do eventually regulate brain implants, how will they assess a brain implant's actual function? How will we as users know if and when our brain implants speak? As subjects of these devices, how we will ascertain the origin of the thoughts in our minds? How will we even know if our ever-present brain implant has been turned off?

For brain implants do need to speak overtly or through words to control our thoughts—or our actions. Brain implants can control us subliminally.

Intentional Behavioral Control

TechnoOptimism, *n.* Typically, TechnoSupremacists believe that the invention of new technology, which they describe as progress, is always for good. Negative side effects of technology—such as environmental degradation, job losses, or societal destabilization—are seen as mere unavoidable externalities. Like most humans, TechnoSupremacists may also simply tend toward optimism; they may be incapable of imagining negative outcomes. TechnoOptimism also refers to the social pressure within in the technology field, where those who express or explore negative outcomes of technology are dismissed and/or shamed. Finally, TechnoOptimism plays a significant role in the successful funding of technology research and industry.

Our minds are not just repositories of articulated thoughts. They are places that control, through our autonomic nervous system, unconscious actions like walking. Our minds are places where emotions, fear and anger, take over; places where unspoken feelings and repressed desires lurk. Already, Vagus nerve stimulators can be used to affect the autonomic nervous system (Howland 2014). Over time, brain implants may also be able to decode the unconscious parts of our minds and speak to us unconsciously as well; and so subjective separation from the software made by the manufacturers of these devices or from others who want to send us surreptitious messages or secretly control our behavior, may be impossible.

As described by Pedersen and Iliadis in the introduction to this book, the embodied self is not merely a compilation of data about human subjects stored and analyzed remotely. It is also a self whose behavior is manipulated by that data. Today's tech giants and other less-identifiable organizations use the constant presence of our phones combined with such data to manipulate us into buying goods, into believing political messages and agendas. And the potential of our personal data to control our behavior intentionally transcends mere marketing and politics.

In her masterwork, *The Age of Surveillance Capitalism*, Shoshana Zuboff clearly documents the intention of technology researchers to use our private data to change our personal and psychological behavior. Zuboff names three strategies that tech researchers are actively using to modify human behavior with data: tuning, herding and conditioning. According to one researcher, the goal of these behavioral strategies is no longer to simply influence buying habits, but to "override what you are doing and put you on a path you did not choose" (Zuboff 2019).

Unsurprisingly, these potential behavioral changes are described by researchers with typical TechnoOptimism. "When people use our app, we can capture their-to-day decisions. Then we develop 'treatments' or 'data pellets' that select good behaviors. We can test how actionable cues are for them, and how profitable certain behaviors are for us," says one researcher (Zuboff 2019). As is typical in TechnoSupremacy, the intended and stated goals of technology researchers are always positive: helping people overcome negative habits, such as lack of exercise and overeating, while of course being profitable for corporations.

In such a world, software- and data-driven behavior changes would ideally be consensual, as in psychotherapy. Subjects of behavioral-change software might legally agree to be changed; they might give permission to healthcare professionals to enact such software. On other hand, given how Facebook already manipulates our behavior without consent, it is easy to imagine how TechnoSupremacists might use "supposedly" positive behavioral-change software in brain implants without our permission. And of course, our incarceration system, schools, or healthcare system will all be tempted, for supposedly positive social purposes, to use brain implants to control their subjects—us—human beings.

And although the potential use of brain implants to intentionally control behavior is frightening, purposeful control by some invisible force is not the only threat of brain implants.

TechnoSupremacy's Grand Behavioral Experiment: The Unintentional Shaping of Human Minds

> **TechnoSpeak, *n*. (continued):** Unlike Orwell's Newspeak, the intention of TechnoSpeak is not articulated or necessarily consciously employed by TechnoSupremacists. Many of them would not recognize themselves as participating in any classist structure or form of authoritarianism, or as purposefully manipulating people through language or the promotion of technology.

Already the effect of our portable devices, their software, and the data they store about us exceeds the behavioral changes intentionally desired by the tech corporations who make them. Because while our devices *do* actively use psychological strategies to keep us playing games, watching YouTube, hooked on our screens (Adar 2015), they also have unintended behavioral consequences, such as keeping us off our feet (Fennell et al. 2019). And while companies like Facebook brazenly admit to intentionally activating our dopamine receptors with "likes" (Parkin 2018), these processes also create unintended behavioral consequences (Brueck 2018). They cause depression, sleep problems, and distraction. In a recent conversation, a therapist friend described our relationships with our devices "as running a great behavioral experiment." The unintentional affects on our children are also frightening. Many recent studies relate increased screen time to increased ADHD symptoms (Ra and Stone 2018) as well as the anxiety epidemic in today's youth (Schroeder 2017). Perhaps most disturbingly, these affects on mood and behavior have the potential to span generations (Schroeder 2017).

And if our phones and their addictive software can cause such unplanned radical behavior changes, imagine the unintended psychological consequences of brain implants, devices that will trigger our pleasure centers, control our bodies, and perhaps most significantly, connect us to other minds.

The End of Subjective Separation

When I was four, I would lie in bed playing vision tricks with patterns on my plaster ceiling. If I changed my focus between the dark lines and blank spaces between, the background and foreground would shift; if I did it quick enough, the solid surface began to appear fluid, blending into the emptiness between me and the ceiling. It felt as though the edge of my mind—of me—was dissolving into the room. I would ruminate over my painful separation from my father and mother, aware I could never know what was inside their minds—never truly know them. Even then, I suspected their words did not reflect their true thoughts or feelings. But mostly, I feared my aloneness, my subjective separation from the world and others, because I knew it meant my existence was finite, bounded by my body. Our family still attended Catholic church on Sundays then, and at night I would contemplate the possibility of *living in eternity with the Father*—the possibility of my continued consciousness after death. My awareness, I reasoned, had not existed before I was born; and so I doubted that it could exist without my body; and I could never make sense of eternal life. To me, my subjective separation from the world and others meant death was final.

Humanity's subjective separation from others has many benefits. We can omit or soften unspoken truths and keep dark secrets. We are free, in monogamous relationships, to lust after someone at work and then secretly meet in a hotel room, or to dream of sex with that same someone and say nothing to our partner. Subjective separation means, with discretion, our private desires or scathing thoughts will never hurt those we love. It could be argued that all of fiction and much of philosophy is based on our inability to know the other.

Our subjective aloneness also seems entwined with intelligence itself. According to Dr. Rebecca Khul of the University of Washington, some language skills in infants develop only in social relationship with their mothers who are cognitively separate (Kuhl 2011). Psychology's theory of mind posits that intelligence in groups develops as each person tries to decode the meaning and intention of the other (Woolley et al. 2010). And if intelligence is the puzzle of who is hidden behind the other's eyes, what will it mean for human intelligence when we *can* see behind the other's eyes? Will our intelligence diminish when we no longer worry about the dangerous and ambiguous intentions of other human beings? Will our intelligence diminish with brain implants?

Or will seeing into the minds of others simply confirm that we are truly social organisms, not so different from ants; that our ideas and inventions arise not from the genius of individuals but from a stew of culture and people around the world? Perhaps the 36 percent of Americans who want brain implants are merely a reflection of the death of Western liberal individualism, a recognition that humans are not such rugged individuals, that humans need each other to survive. Or perhaps the 36 percent subconsciously recognize that already, through the internet, humans are part of a hive mind.

And how will we experience those other minds? Certainly, one can imagine hearing another's articulated thoughts or seeing them written on a neural display. In his 2002 novel *Feed*, M. T. Anderson creates a nightmare world of constant consumer messages and manipulation caused by widespread brain implants. Within that world, he presciently imagines bidirectional communication between teenagers much like a chat, where they can send each other dialogue silently. And just as in dialogue, meaning and language are misunderstood. Users in Anderson's world can also turn off their connection to others, much as one would turn off the phone. But if brain implants can read our secret thoughts, how will we use language to disguise our subliminal selves from others?

Anderson's novel also predicts the ability of brain implants to read our feelings and share them. With bidirectional brain implants, perhaps our bodies, when receiving the thoughts and experiences of others, could become a biological display. Perhaps everything that someone else thinks and feels could be mapped onto another's body and mind. Perhaps we could become capable of true empathy—of knowing what it feels like, in every sense of the word, to be another human being.

Of course, others will then *know*—with an intimacy perhaps far deeper than sex—us. The exposed self, as posited by Pedersen and Iliadis, already makes public aspects of ourselves that were previously unseen, both to others and ourselves. When our minds and feelings are rendered transparent, what will it mean for shame, for interiority and self-contradictions, all essential parts of our humanity?

But perhaps that is the true miracle of these emerging devices. Not increased intelligence, but how these devices may lead to the better understanding of others, and ultimately ourselves.

So, what about me? What would I say if offered a brain implant? I know that brain implants can never be neutral tools. They will always serve the master of profit—the messages they insert in our minds will never be free of salesmanship. Nor can our minds be protected. And though I already receive hostile media through my phone and computer, I want no such direct messages in my mind. Yet I also admit that it is nostalgia I feel, nostalgia for the fragile and achingly beautiful experience of my biological life. It has been an honor to walk this warm protective earth, to live in the vast cold universe as nothing but aging flesh, to feel physical pain that only animals can feel, to seek meaning in life while trapped in my human perspective, to search for why I feel as I do, for the boundaries of myself, boundaries determined by my moving and sensing and electrical, chemical body.

So, what would I choose, if offered a brain implant? Would I fear the control of some capitalistic overlord, or would I overlook it and elect to explore the thoughts of another—a friend, an enemy, maybe even an ape or whale? Would I open the lid of my mind, risk the angry voices that lurk in these devices, to better know myself?

You bet. In a heartbeat, I would.

Epilogue: Short- vs. Long-Term Reward

When I first reached the above point in my essay, that answer came immediately, like a pleasurable shock of pain. My editors have encouraged me to rethink those words, and indeed I have tried, but they stick there, like letters carved in stone. Yes, they were an instinctual reversal, the kind that is quite satisfying in writing. How nice it is for the reader *and* the writer, to be led to a surprising outcome—a twist at the end of the story. But upon deeper reflection, I believe those words were more than mere artistic instinct. I believe, in the end, those words were true.

If the technology were right, if it offered true insight into other minds, especially experiencing the final frontier of unknowable minds such as those of animals, I would choose a brain implant.

Which means I'm still human. I would still choose the novelty of new technologies and the expanded short-term sensual experience they promise me *as an individual*, while ignoring the long-term external dangers they create, including environmental collapse and the transformation and possible destruction of humanity.

For all of us, especially our TechnoSupremacists, this is the challenge of our time. Can we look beyond our immediate short-term pleasures and value our future world, a future world that needs more than gadgets to survive?

Humanity and our brilliant TechnoSupremacists have yet to answer that question.

Appendix:

Nominalizables, n. A type of TechnoSpeak that uses adjectives, such as implantable, as nouns. Like nominalizations, which turn verbs into nouns (for example illustration, failure, investigation), Nominalizables eliminate actors (subjects) from sentences and obscure responsible parties (Hitchings 2013).

By defining technology in terms of some novel quality it may possess (stretchable) or innovative means of deployment (implantable), Nominalizables appeal to our human desire for novelty while rendering the function of their technology nebulous. This obscuring of a technology's function is often self-serving, as many of these devices have purposes that are at best hypothetical. The suffix "able" is also misleading. It implies that Nominalizable technology has some meaningful ability, while in fact the technology's capabilities are unstated.

Syntactically, Nominalizables are twice removed from the original verb, such as wear, stretch, implant.

Examples include: Implantables, Edibles, Wearables, Weavables, Stretchables, Droneables, Immersibles, Ingestibles, Injectables, Nearables, Earables, Extendables, Tattooables, Friendables, and finally *Thinkables*.

Notes

1. Transcribed from video of interview with Musk, Code Conference, June 2016, https://youtu.be/wsixsRI-Sz4.

2. Peter Stone, Rodney Brooks, Erik Brynjolfsson, Ryan Calo, Oren Etzioni, Greg Hager, Julia Hirschberg, Shivaram Kalyanakrishnan, Ece Kamar, Sarit Kraus, Kevin Leyton-Brown, David Parkes, William Press, AnnaLee Saxenian, Julie Shah, Milind Tambe, and Astro Teller, "Artificial Intelligence and Life in 2030," One Hundred Year Study on Artificial Intelligence (AI100): Report of the 2015–2016 Study Panel, Stanford University, Stanford, CA, September 6, 2016, https://ai100.stanford.edu/2016-report.

3. "About BrainGate," BrainGate website, December 4, 2015, https://www.braingate.org/about-braingate/.

4. LeelaKrishna, "Mind Controlled Robotic Arm," *Instructables*, May 5, 2015, http://www.instructables.com/id/Mind-Controlled-Robotic-Arm/.

5. Hagan Bayley, "Bayley Group," University of Oxford Department of Chemistry, http://bayley.chem.ox.ac.uk/.

6. UC Berkeley Wireless Research Center, http://bwrc.eecs.berkeley.edu/.

7. For incredibly comprehensive explanation of brain implants and Musk's vision, see Tim Urban, "Neuralink and the Brain's Magical Future (G-Rated Version)," *Wait but Why*, April 20, 2017, http://waitbutwhy.com/2017/04/neuralink-cleanversion .html.

8. Paraphrased from interview with Ryan O'Shea, Grindhouse Wetware spokesperson, August 2016.

9. "Furry Fandom," Wikipedia, last updated August 10, 2019, https://en.wikipedia .org/wiki/Furry_fandom.

10. Paraphrased from interview with Ryan O'Shea, Grindhouse Wetware spokesperson, August 2016.

11. ITworld, "BrainGate Lets Your Brain Control the Computer," YouTube video uploaded March 14, 2008, 2:02, https://youtu.be/TJJPbpHoPWo.

12. "Closed-Loop DBS," UW BioRobotics Lab, May 2015, http://brl.ee.washington .edu/neural-engineering/closed-loop-dbs/.

13. Backyard Brains, "The RoboRoach: Control a Living Insect from Your Smartphone!" Kickstarter campaign launched June 10, 2013, https://www.kickstarter .com/projects/backyardbrains/the-roboroach-control-a-living-insect-from-your-sm.

14. Stephen Bainbridge, "Case Law on the Fiduciary Duty of Directors to Maximize the Wealth of Corporate Shareholders," ProfessorBainbridge.com (blog), May 5, 2012, https://www.professorbainbridge.com/professorbainbridgecom/2012/05/case -law-on-the-fiduciary-duty-of-directors-to-maximize-the-wealth-of-corporate -shareholders.html.

References

Adar, Dori. 2015. 7 Psychological Tactics Used in Games to Hook Users. doriador.com (blog), October 12. http://www.doriadar.com/2015/10/12/7-psychological-tactics -used-in-games-to-hook-users/.

Ahmed, Azam, and Nicole Perlroth. 2017. Using Texts as Lures, Government Spyware Targets Mexican Journalists and Their Families. *New York Times*, June 19. https://nyti.ms/2sFTAw6.

Aldhous, Peter. 2017. Here's How BuzzFeed News Trained a Computer to Search for Hidden Spy Planes. *BuzzFeed*, August 9. https://www.buzzfeednews.com/article/ peteraldhous/hidden-spy-planes.

Anderson, M. T. 2002. *Feed*. London: Walker Books.

Bach-y-Rita, Paul. 1984. The Relationship between Motor Processes and Cognition in Tactile Vision Substitution. In *Cognition and Motor Processes*, edited by W. Prinz and A. F. Sanders, 149–160. Berlin: Springer.

Barfield, Woodrow, and Alexander Williams. 2017. Law, Cyborgs, and Technologically Enhanced Brains. *Philosophies* 2 (1): 1–6. https://doi.org/10.3390/philosophies 2010006.

Blitz, Marc Jonathan. 2010. Freedom of Thought for the Extended Mind: Cognitive Enhancement and the Constitution. *Wisconsin Law Review* 2010 (4): 1049–1118. https://works.bepress.com/marc_jonathan_blitz/17/.

Brueck, Hillary. 2018. This Is What Your Smartphone Is Doing to Your Brain—and It Isn't Good. *Business Insider*, March 10. https://www.businessinsider.com/what -your-smartphone-is-doing-to-your-brain-and-it-isnt-good-2018-3.

Dowd, Maureen. 2017. Elon Musk's Billion-Dollar Crusade to Stop the A.I. Apocalypse. *Vanity Fair*, March 26. https://www.vanityfair.com/news/2017/03/elon-musk-billion -dollar-crusade-to-stop-ai-space-x.

Dunne, Daisy. 2017. Elon Musk Plans to Link Computers with Human Brains in Just Four Years to Create a New Language of "Consensual Telepathy." *Daily Mail Online*, April 21. https://www.dailymail.co.uk/sciencetech/article-4431314/Elon-Musk -mission-link-human-brains-computers-4-yrs-report.html.

Farr, Christina. 2016. A New Device Stimulates the Brain to Boost Athletic Performance. *Fast Company*, April 22. https://www.fastcompany.com/3058464/a-new -device-stimulates-the-brain-to-boost-athletic-performance.

Fennell, Curtis, Jacob E. Barkley, and Andrew Lepp. 2019. The Relationship between Cell Phone Use, Physical Activity, and Sedentary Behavior in Adults Aged 18–80. *Computers in Human Behavior* 90 (January): 53–59. https://doi.org/10.1016/j.chb .2018.08.044.

Funk, Cary, Brian Kennedy, and Elizabeth Sciupac. 2016. U.S. Public Wary of Biomedical Technologies to "Enhance" Human Abilities: 3. Public Opinion on the Future Use of Brain Implants. *Pew Research Center: Science & Society*, July 26. https://www .pewinternet.org/2016/07/26/public-opinion-on-the-future-use-of-brain-implants/.

Gibbs, Samuel. 2017. Elon Musk: Regulate AI to Combat "Existential Threat" Before It's Too Late. *Guardian*, July 17. https://www.theguardian.com/technology/2017/ jul/17/elon-musk-regulation-ai-combat-existential-threat-tesla-spacex-ceo.

Gibson, William. 1984. *Neuromancer*. New York: Ace Books.

Giesen, Jennifer. 2015. OCD Patient: Brain Implant Gave Me a Chance at Happiness. *Al Jazeera*, March 13. http://america.aljazeera.com/watch/shows/america-tonight/ articles/2015/3/13/ocd-patient-brain-implant-gave-me-a-chance-at-happiness.html.

Hatmaker, Taylor. 2017. DARPA Awards $65 Million to Develop the Perfect, Tiny Two-Way Brain–Computer Interface. *TechCrunch*, July 10. https://techcrunch.com/2017/07/10/darpa-nesd-grants-paradromics.

Hitchings, Henry. 2013. The Dark Side of Verbs-as-Nouns. *New York Times*, April 5. https://opinionator.blogs.nytimes.com/2013/04/05/the-dark-side-of-verbs-as-nouns/.

Howland, Robert H. 2014. Vagus Nerve Stimulation. *Current Behavioral Neuroscience Reports* 1 (2): 64–73. https://doi.org/10.1007/s40473-014-0010-5.

IBM. 2017. The Quest for AI Creativity. https://www.ibm.com/watson/advantage-reports/future-of-artificial-intelligence/ai-creativity.html.

Jackson, Tim. 2017. *Prosperity without Growth: Economics for a Finite Planet*. London: Routledge.

Kuhl, Patricia K. 2011. Social Mechanisms in Early Language Acquisition: Understanding Integrated Brain Systems Supporting Language. In *The Oxford Handbook of Social Neuroscience*, edited by Jean Decety and John T. Cacioppo. Oxford: Oxford University Press.

Markoff, John. 2015. Artificial-Intelligence Research Center Is Founded by Silicon Valley Investors. *New York Times*, December 11. https://nyti.ms/1Y35I4E.

Mordvintsev, Alexander, Christopher Olah, and Mike Tyka. 2015. Inceptionism: Going Deeper into Neural Networks. Google AI Blog, June 17. https://ai.googleblog.com/2015/06/inceptionism-going-deeper-into-neural.html.

Newitz, Annalee. 2009. The Curious Case of a Woman Addicted to Her Brain Implant. *io9*, November 11. https://io9.gizmodo.com/5402584/the-curious-case-of-a-woman-addicted-to-her-brain-implant.

Parkin, Simon. 2018. Has Dopamine Got Us Hooked on Tech? *Guardian*, March 4. https://www.theguardian.com/technology/2018/mar/04/has-dopamine-got-us-hooked-on-tech-facebook-apps-addiction.

Pouratian, Nader, Sandeep Thakkar, Won Kim, and Jeff M. Bronstein. 2012. Deep Brain Stimulation for the Treatment of Parkinson's Disease: Efficacy and Safety. *Degenerative Neurological and Neuromuscular Disease*, 2: 107–117. https://doi.org/10.2147/DNND.S25750.

Ra, Chaelin K., Junhan Cho, and Matthew D. Stone. 2018. Association of Digital Media Use with Subsequent Symptoms of Attention-Deficit/Hyperactivity Disorder among Adolescents. *JAMA* 320 (3): 255–263. https://doi.org/10.1001/jama.2018.8931.

Reedy, Christianna. 2017. Elon Musk Again Voiced Concern over the Risk of AI at a Tesla Earnings Call. *Futurism*, August 3. https://futurism.com/elon-musk-again-voiced-concern-over-the-risk-of-ai-at-a-tesla-earnings-call/.

Schroeder, James. 2017. More Bad News about Smartphones—When Will We Heed the Warnings? *Mad in America*, November 12. https://www.madinamerica.com/2017/11/bad-news-about-smartphones/.

Speights, Keith. 2017. What Percentage of Businesses Fail in Their First Year? *Motley Fool*, May 3. https://www.fool.com/careers/2017/05/03/what-percentage-of-businesses-fail-in-their-first.aspx.

Strickland, Eliza. 2017. 5 Neurological Experts Weigh In on Elon Musk's Mysterious "Neural Lace" Company. *IEEE Spectrum*, April 12. https://spectrum.ieee.org/the-human-os/biomedical/devices/5-neuroscience-experts-weigh-in-on-elon-musks-mysterious-neural-lace-company/.

Wang, Jing, Vladimir L. Cherkassky, and Marcel Adam Just. 2017. Predicting the Brain Activation Pattern Associated with the Propositional Content of a Sentence: Modeling Neural Representations of Events and States. *Human Brain Mapping* 38 (10): 4865–4881. https://doi.org/10.1002/hbm.23692.

Woolley, Anita Williams, Christopher F. Chabris, Alex Pentland, Nada Hashmi, and Thomas W. Malone. 2010. Evidence for a Collective Intelligence Factor in the Performance of Human Groups. *Science* 330 (6004): 686–688. https://doi.org/10.1126/science.1193147.

Winkler, Rolfe. 2017. Elon Musk launches Neuralink to connect brains with computers. *Wall Street Journal*, March 29. https://www.wsj.com/articles/elon-musk-launches-neuralink-to-connect-brains-with-computers-1490642652.

Zecher, Josh. 2015. Do You Have Internet on the Brain? *Vrge*, September 23. http://vrge.us/blog/2015/09/do-you-have-internet-on-the-brain/.

Zuboff, Shoshana. 2019. *The Age of Surveillance Capitalism*. New York: Hachette Book Group.

Contributors

Roba Abbas is a Lecturer in Operations and Digital Business in the School of Management, Operations and Marketing (SMOM) at the University of Wollongong, Australia, and is the Associate Editor for the *IEEE Technology and Society Magazine*. She is a multidisciplinary researcher who is interested in the adoption and application of sociotechnical and other organizational/systems theories to investigate the impact of emerging technologies on organizations and society.

Gary Genosko is Professor of Communication and Digital Media at Ontario Tech University in Oshawa, Ontario. His most recent book, with Kristy Marcellus, is *Back Issues: Periodicals and the Formation of Critical and Cultural Theory in Canada*.

Andrew Iliadis is an Assistant Professor at Temple University in the Department of Media Studies and Production (within the Lew Klein College of Media and Communication) and serves on the faculties of the Media and Communication Doctoral Program, Cultural Analytics Graduate Certificate Program, and Science Studies Network.

Suneel Jethani is a PhD candidate and lecturer in the School of Culture and Communication at the University of Melbourne. His theoretical and ethnographic research focuses on the intersections between data, bodies, design, and the politics of everyday life. Suneel has published work in *International Communication Gazette*, *Communication, Politics and Culture*, *M/C Journal* and *Persona Studies*.

Deborah Lupton is SHARP Professor and leader of the Vitalities Lab, University of New South Wales, Sydney, Australia. She is the author or coauthor of seventeen books, including *The Quantified Self* (2016) and *Data Selves* (2019).

Katina Michael is the Director for the Center of Engineering, Policy and Society at Arizona State University. She holds a joint professorial appointment in the School for the Future of Innovation in Society and the School of Computing, Informatics and Decision Systems Engineering. Katina is the founding editor-in-chief of the *IEEE Transactions on Technology and Society*.

M. G. Michael PhD (ACU), MA (Hons.) (MacqUni), MTheol (SydUni), BTheol (SCD), BA (SydUni) is an honorary Associate Professor in the School of Computing and

Information Technology at the University of Wollongong. He coined the term "überveillance" in 2006 to denote 24/7 embedded surveillance devices. His website can be found at http://www.mgmichael.com.

Marcel O'Gorman is a University Research Chair, Professor of English, and Founding Director of the Critical Media Lab (CML) at the University of Waterloo. O'Gorman has published widely about the impacts of technology on society, including his recent book *Necromedia*, his forthcoming book *Making Media Theory*, and articles in *Slate*, *The Atlantic*, and *The Globe and Mail*. He is also a digital artist with an international portfolio of exhibitions and performances.

Maggie Orth is a technology artist, former entrepreneur, and writer whose creative work explores our human and ethical relationship with technology. As an early practitioner in e-textiles and wearables, Orth earned a PhD at MIT's Media Lab and then founded International Fashion Machines (IFM), where she spent ten years writing patents, conducted research, and developed her own technology and design products, including the PomPom Dimmer. Her artworks include textiles that change color under computer control, fabric sensor and light pieces, and robotic public art. In order to more deeply explore our relationship with technology, Orth now writes both fiction and nonfiction.

Isabel Pedersen is Canada Research Chair in Digital Life, Media, and Culture, Associate Professor at Ontario Tech University, and Founding Director of Decimal Lab. She holds Associate membership at the Yeates School of Graduate Studies, Ryerson University. She is author *of Ready to Wear: A Rhetoric of Wearable Computers and Reality-Shifting Media*.

Christine Perakslis teaches at Johnson & Wales University, including courses in Operations Management and Contemporary Issues & Strategies. Prior to joining JWU's faculty, Perakslis held the post of Joint Chief Operating Officer of Champion Nationwide Services, Inc., which was the third largest general service contracting company in the meetings and conventions industry. In addition to teaching, she continues to work in a consulting capacity in various industries, which serves to broaden her industry-relevant teaching.

Kevin Warwick is Emeritus Professor at Reading and Coventry Universities. His research areas are artificial intelligence, biomedical systems, robotics, and cyborgs. Kevin is a Chartered Engineer and a Fellow of the IET who has published over six hundred research papers. His experiments into implant technology led to him being featured on the cover of the US magazine *Wired*. He achieved the world's first direct electronic communication between two human nervous systems, the basis for thought communication. He has been awarded higher doctorates (DSc) by Imperial College and the Czech Academy of Sciences. He received the IET Mountbatten Medal, the Ellison-Cliffe Medal from the Royal Society of Medicine, and was presented the Royal Institution Christmas Lectures.

Elizabeth Wissinger is a Professor of Liberal Studies at the Graduate School of the City University of New York (CUNY), where she teaches Fashion Studies, and a Professor of Sociology at the Borough of Manhattan Community College/CUNY. She has spoken about technology, fashion, and embodiment in the United States and internationally, and has published across a range of fields, including sociology, fashion studies, and communication. Her book, *This Year's Model: Fashion, Media, and the Making of Glamour* (2015), examines fashion models' "glamour labor." Her current research critically addresses the coming fusion of wearable and embodied technologies with biology, and examines this transition's gendered and bodily effects.

Index